My Theory of Evolution

Life with Meaning

Will Coakley

NEWMAN SPRINGS PUBLISHING
320 Broad Street
Red Bank, NJ 07701

First originally published by Newman Springs Publishing 2023

ISBN 979-8-88763-091-5 (Paperback)
ISBN 979-8-88763-092-2 (Digital)

Printed in the United States of America

I dedicate my book to my parents and sisters, who have been there throughout my good and bad moments. I also want to dedicate this book to all my close friends, who will always be there for me, and for my doctors, including my therapist, since they helped me for the past fourteen years.

Contents

Ten Percent Skills/Smarts 1
Twenty Percent Mind/Fun 31
Ten Percent Animals/Kids 56
Ten Percent Music...63
Twenty Percent Endless Connections/Signs 66
Ten Percent Intruding into the "Stars" of the World 97
20 Percent Concentrated Power of Will Coakley 224

Ten Percent Skills/Smarts

Ten percent skills/smarts can include reading books, textbooks, playing video games, working on business and business plans, athletes training for their games and playing in front of an audience, teaching in front of students at all different levels, listening to peoples conversations, and learning how to turn that into productivity into their own lives. When reading as an adult, you learn and relearn words that you might have forgotten as students, and you also learn concepts that are applicable within our lives. When I read books that register under different areas, I like to think about people that are suffering through certain brain malfunctions, diseases, etc., that, as a human race, we would like to think can be cured one day.

I was talking to my boy, Jeff, about possibly working again, after taking this prolonged time off. One idea he thought I would be good at was sports medicine. Sports medicine is a branch of medicine that deals with physical fitness and the treatment and prevention of injuries related to sports and exercise. The research I have done, it says that it is only since the late twentieth century that sports medicine has emerged as a distinct field of health care. Now how would I fit into this plan? Well, I can read and learn and interpret what it would take to make it in this field.

I was interested in this kind of work pretty much since I graduated high school, but it is never too late to live out your dreams. Maybe I can try to work on this part-time while I work on the business plans that would put me in place to become a millionaire. Sports medicine might be up my alley, and I could really make a big impact on the world by helping these athletes out.

I have been taking bowling seriously and am trying to get better each week. I've been going with my dad every Friday, and before that,

I was bowling with Jeff a lot. My best average so far has been around 157, and my next highest average was around 137. My mom's friend, Rida, has had a down year, but her average is 166. That is my number, so that is my doing. I answer people's prayers and requests at my house, and even though she is having a down year, I think it's crazy that her average is exactly 166.

I have been playing golf a lot at a par three course near my house, and on back-to-back weeks, I shot a 33 when the average score is a 27. That is plus 6. I know it's not great considering the pro, but it's a big improvement, and I am pretty confident that I can get my scores better with more practice. Tiger Woods won the last tournament because he was helping me out behind the scenes with my golf swing. I once said that if you fix me, then I will fix everything else, and I think that is starting to become true.

One of the reasons why I am alive right now is to break the curses that sports teams had before I was born. I did it with the Cubs, the Capitals, the Blues, the Eagles, and other teams. Now it was the Nationals' time. They ended up winning the final game of the World Series with a score of 6–2. I watched one of the games with my friend, Andy Lee, and I talked to my other friends, Ryan Bullock and Jeff Veltri. When the Astros went up in the series, 3–2, I was a little bit scared. I know the Astros just won in 2017, so it was the Nationals' time. They ended up winning the last two games, and to top it off, they won the last game with a high score of 6. This is a great accomplishment, but DC fans better not get too comfortable. Other teams now are in line to win, and everything will start to get more equalized in the world.

Part of things being equal was also the Giants winning as a wild card team in football and the Steelers winning as a wild card team. Now it was the Nationals' time to win as a wild card team. This is all I am going to say in this portion of my book. I will add my other thoughts to a different document because I have reached my goal of two hundred pages.

When I was bowling with my dad on Friday, June 21, I averaged a 466 series, which made it a series of 155. My dad stands for a

55, and I stand for 66, so everything is equal, and my games were all between 149 and 163 with the final score being a 155.

I have been thinking about quitting smoking for a long time now, and when I was in the car one day, I was thinking about Khalil and was driving to Allyn's. I was smoking a cigarette, and he had just crossed my mind. The next time I ran into him, he had quit smoking. I knew that was my doing because I was thinking about him and I was smoking a cigarette, and now he doesn't smoke anymore. I don't think that everyone has to quit smoking. It might be a fallacy, but maybe the world would be a better place if people did quit smoking. I'm not sure, but maybe.

I thought it was interesting that when I was looking at the NBA stats and back-to-back were Raymond Felton and Jose Calderon. They are both ex-Knicks point guards and however they calculated the stats on ESPN, they ended up back-to-back. Even though both of them aren't getting any playing time, I still think it's interesting.

In the below section, I had said that the Blues won their first championship in their fifty-second year. Well, I am all about connecting the dots and signs, and I am a numbers guy, so on the next Friday, I bowled a 152. This made perfect sense because I helped the Blues overcome this adversity and for my own life. I was able to bowl a series of three games that averaged out to a 152.

I am all about connecting the signs and symbols that can relate to each other. I believe fully that professional athletes get the positive things they deserve, mostly because of G-Eazy's song saying that "I put the good in the good life." Nevertheless, Julio Jones just received a nice contract for three years and 66 million. The ones and sixes stand for me, so this was him throwing this on me. Without certain people in this world, we would be doomed, and I am one of those people, so I am happy that he received this great contract.

There are two things I wanted to mention in this paragraph. It has to do with signs and connections, but I thought I would put it in this section. I was watching the Astros and Yankees game, and one of the best pitchers in the Major League, Gerrit Cole, was pitching for the Astros. He had the best ERA in baseball since a certain date, and that date was either August or the All-Star break. His ERA was exactly 1.66. As I said in this book, the 66s stand for me, and he stayed consistently at 1.66 throughout those few months. This was strictly my doing, and he will become a free agent this year and go to the team that wants him the most. It is crazy when you start to understand life and know why we are on the planet right now, the things you can figure out.

The second thing I wanted to mention was that Bradley Beal with get paid soon, and the figure that they came up with was $266 million. I know that is a lot of money, but I have people throw their backs on me sometimes throughout the day and at night a lot. I am not mad at the money amount because I know I'll be a millionaire or a billionaire one day, and these guys work hard and bring in a lot of fans all across the world, so with his contract of $266 million, he will deserve it, and it shows with his play on the field.

In a move that could rock the NCAA's business model, a new California law allows college athletes to earn money off their names. This was my doing, and when Hoodie Allen said no Avicii in his song, he meant it. This means that nobody should doubt my power, and everyone else's say in this world means anything when it comes to me taking over. Tim Tebow said this law shouldn't go into effect, but I thought that was a bad opinion, and I am helping out these college athletes by helping them make money. I don't think it's fair that professional athletes can make all the money in the world but college athletes can't.

To go along with my point above, this part is about hockey. The Maple Leaf's star forward got a $65 million extension. I am trying to make this life perfect for many of us, and this is just one example. I am sure that he got paid. Now all I ask in return is for him to help me out and get me out of this rut that I fell into by mistake. Thanks!

I was watching the scores of the Yankees and Red Sox game, and the final score ended up with 6–1 on this Friday night. Unfortunately, the Red Sox won the game 6–1, but I am still happy that the final score ended with a six because this just confirms that it was my doing with no one helping me. I wish that the Yankees won this game, but the Red Sox just outplayed them with the final score of 6–1.

4

When I was admitted to the hospital for paying the price of being alive, I ran into this one girl who was named JC. She said that the biggest thing she had to overcome was seeing her shadow and reflection in the mirror or on a chair in front of her. In one of Hollywood's songs, they said I was conquering everything. I knew it was a matter of time before this was going to happen to me. Nevertheless, it happened one day when they put this test on me, and I am not happy about it because it is really scary sometimes. Everyone you run into and talk to has something new to teach you, and this was something that she taught me. She also taught me that I have a lot of great qualities that a woman would love one day when I was losing all my self-esteem.

I am trying to be the person I used to be but am just more mature now. Anyway, I am conquering everything and am waiting for this cycle to end. I think it is soon and that karma is catching up. It is scary that I have to go through this thing that JC is going through. It is messed up, and when Jeff wanted to take credit alongside me, that was such crap. I have been through a hundred times worse things than he has been through.

I was talking to my therapist about mirrors and how they have impacted my life through comedy and scary scenes. Well, they came out with a TV series about how mirrors or shadows play with certain characters and how different scenarios play out. Shadow play was a way to put all the corrupt people in the world to their own ends, but it never quite worked out that way. Instead, I want them to help me achieve perfection, but it will be a way to end ISIS. I was losing my mind and looking at how different mirrors were reacting to the way I was reacting in front of them. It probably wasn't for the folks at home, but I was scared because I was getting older, but in my opinion, age is still just a number to me. Karma needs to catch up, and that will happen soon. I really want to watch those episodes to see how they interact with my life and to see how I can relate to those scenes.

I was watching the Yankee game on opening day, and they won the game 7–2. It takes two to connect the dots, and the other person is Ray, so the score was 6–2 for the longest time until Greg Bird hit a home run to make it 7–2. Since I have the magic in me, I was able to help the Yankees out through six runs and about eight innings then Ray supplied them with the seventh run. Tanaka played great, and the Yankees might be very good this year, but we'll see how this season plays out. It really depends on who dies throughout the year and which teams get cursed and how Mother Nature responds to these changes.

Even though I control Mother Nature sometimes, it is really unpredictable. I think it could be a rematch from the 2009 World Series with the Phillies when the Yankees defeated them. I am trying to do things right in this world, and the last ten World Series winners have a reason for it, so why couldn't it be the Yankees and Phillies this year? Anyway, the opening day is off to a good start, so let the good times continue!

On Sunday, I was paying attention to some of the games that had a winning score be 6. The first score I wanted to mention was that the Blue Jays beat the Red Sox 6–1. Nobody wants to see the Red Sox win again, so it was good to see that the Blue Jays over-came this adversity and won this game 6–1 against a Red Sox team that has been very dominant over the past several years. In B.O.B's song, he said that creation needs the devil as an advocate, I guess, so whenever scores end in 6–4, I know that it is because I am outdoing Jeff, and these scores are in favor of the winning squad. Nevertheless, the Marlins beat the Phillies 6–4, and I know that the Phillies really wanted to win this year, but they have lost, like, seven games in a row. This is great because I want to see Derek Jeter do good for the Marlins, and they swept the Phillies this past weekend on this Monday, June 24.

The next score I wanted to mention was that the Royals beat the twins, 6–1. The Twins have been playing really well this year, but the Royals were able to overcome that adversity and win this game 6–1. I love it because I have dealt with a lot of hate, and the athletes said they were going to put me into that exact same game, and I know that a lot of people don't show me the love that they should, so I just figured that I would kind of white knuckle this on my own, and I am proving my worth in this world. The next score I wanted to mention was that the Rangers beat the White Sox, 7–4. It takes two to connect the dots, and the Rangers were able to pull out a victory 7–4. The number 4 stands for Jeff, and when the games with the losing team ends in 4, then I know this is my doing. So these scores are great and just show what I can do for other people.

Furthermore, the next score I wanted to mention was that the Dodgers won against the Rockies, 6–3. They hit back-to-back-to-back home runs to make this score 6. I have proved my worth in this world and am doing a lot more for other people than words can describe. I am happy because I like the Dodgers, and they are playing great this year and won this game, 6–3. Lastly, the Sunday night game on June 23 was the Angels versus the Cardinals. The Angels won this game, 6–4, and this was great because Albert Pujols is going to retire soon, so he was able to win against his former team. As I mentioned in the previous notes that creation needs a devil as an advocate, so this score ended in 6–4.

It is crazy once you start to understand life, and if people haven't picked up on this, then I think you're not as smart, but not everyone has to understand, I just know life better than most people, so I get it. I put money on two teams this Sunday, and both scores were +144, and I won this bet. I thought this would put me in the right direction if I can one up Jeff and win this bet. I did, and we'll see what the benefits are in the future.

I put money on some games on Friday, June 28, and lost all of them. I have been doing pretty good with my bets and post them on Twitter every time I win. Anyway, I was looking at some games, and the first two games I wanted to mention were the Blue Jays beating Royals, 6–2, and the Braves beating the Mets, 6–2. The sports world is unpredictable, so we can never know who is going to win on a daily basis. On this particular day, the Blue Jays and the Braves won, 6–2, so the odds were in their favor.

I ended up losing my bets, which is bullshit, but I was happy that I was able to help them out and their fan bases. The next two scores I wanted to mention were the Marlins beating the Phillies, 6–2, and the Reds beat the Cubs, 6–3. The number 6 stands for me, and Ray is messing up, so the scores weren't really ending up in sevens anymore, and Hollywood wanted to put me back into that devilish game again, and so did the athletes, so I might not listen to that song that said that it takes two to connect the dots anymore.

These are four scores I wanted to mention so I want people to recognize in the future why the world is still spinning and how I got this far on my own with a little bit of people's help. There are actually two more scores I wanted to mention on this particular date. The White Sox beat the Twins, 6–4, and the Giants beat the Diamondbacks, 6–3. Nevertheless, there were six games that ended in 6 for the winning team. This is all I have to say about this subject for the time being, but I will add more to these sections at a later date.

In the above section, I mentioned the teams that I helped overcome adversity and win their games. Now I wanted to mention a different date in the year with similar results. The date is June 6, 2018. The first game was the Twins beating the Rangers, 7–4. It takes two to connect the dots, and Jeff is the person always on the wrong side of things, so the final score was the Twins (the favorite) beating the Rangers. Jeff stands for 4, and this is just how the game ended. He betrayed my trust by disrespecting me on the regular, so I really shouldn't feel sorry for him, and he used to play games with me all the time behind my back, so this is his payback. It is what it is, and I really don't want to talk to that kid anymore.

The next score I wanted to mention was the Nationals beating the Royals, 6–0. This was just a pure shutout by Max Scherzer. He is one of the best pitchers in baseball, and I shouldn't hold grudges against the Nationals team because there is somebody who roots for them who I thought was a good friend of mine. When the games start every day, you never know who is going to win these games unless you are using a cheat sheet and unless you are in Hollywood. Then I don't want people using these cheat sheets anymore.

The next score I wanted to mention was the Cubs beating the White Sox, 6–3. This was just pure 15 percent concentrated power of Will and overcoming adversity to help the Cubs win this game, 6–3, against the White Sox. The Cubs are a good team, and I haven't looked at the standings, but they just outperformed the White Sox on this day to win, 6–3. Additionally, the Mets beat the Phillies, 6–5, and the luck was just favored for the Mets to win this game with the final score of 6–5. My dad stands for 5, so this was just me outperforming my dad to help the Mets achieve victory in this game.

Allyn is a really good friend of mine, but he already had success with the Eagles winning the championship, so on this day, the Mets were able to play really well and win. The last score I wanted to mention on this day was the Mariners beating the Athletics, 6–3. Again, this was just the concentrated power of Will to help the Mariners score 6 runs to the Athletics' 3 runs and win this game. New teams win each year, and on any particular day, any team can beat any team. On this date, it was just the Mariners winning against the Athletics, 6–3.

The next score I wanted to mention was on the next day, July 7. I put money on the Orioles beating the Blue Jays, but the Blue Jays actually won this game, 6–1. As I mentioned in the previous section, you never know which way these scores are going to go, and in this particular game, the Blue Jays, who were the favorites, won by the score of 6–1. This sucked for me, but I bet the greedy fans of the Blue Jays were happy. If I never had bad things happen to me, whoever did that to me, I wouldn't be stressing so much about losing these games, but I need to get rich, and karma needs to catch up, and things need to start falling in line because nobody else can do the things I can do, and sometimes it gets really frustrating when things aren't going my way. I need to just be patient and let things develop a little bit more.

Hollywood started at the end, so I know I will be in good hands in the future. There is at least one more game I wanted to mention where I can relate to the final score on July 7, and this is the Red Sox and Tigers game. The final score was 6–3. The threes stand for Anna Kendrick, and I don't know why, but I feel like she is constantly helping me out. The Red Sox ended up victorious in this game, so the final was 6, which stands for me, and the 3 stands for Anna Kendrick. I am happy with this result because there are a lot of happy Boston fans. The next game that is worthy of mention is the Pirates versus Brewers game. The Pirates won this game, 6–5, and my dad stands for 5, and I don't think that most people can even realize the connections that are based on this system, but I don't really give a f——k.

The Pirates were victorious against the Brewers, and it seems like the teams that are destined to do good this year are doing good, and the teams that are meant to suffer this year are suffering. I believe that all things are created equal and should be equal, and I think that is part of the reason why NBA free agency was so crazy. The Warriors aren't going to be as dominant as they were in previous years, and maybe this will happen in baseball as well. Nobody wants to see the Red Sox win again for a while and probably not the Yankees either. Maybe we will have a new champion in baseball, but we'll see.

I developed a numbering scheme that is working, but I don't know how many people have seen a difference. It can help us dissect the universe and understand the meaning of life a little bit better. If the number 1 pops up, then that stands for me. So if the games are a one-run game in baseball or hockey or in other ways of life, then that is my doing. If the number 2 pops up, then that stands for my soul mate. Anything that relates to the number 2, then that's what that means. The number 3 stands for Anna Kendrick. I also figured out that with the naming scheme that Kendrick and Coakley kind of interrelate to each other, so if I ever make it to Hollywood, then maybe we could be a match.

The number 4 stands for Jeff, so anything and any number that relates to 4 is Jeff. The number 5 is my dad, so any numbering scheme that ends with the number 5 is my dad. The number 6 is again me; since the sky and the universe are mine, the numbers 6 and 1 are both mine. The number 7 is my cousin Ray. It takes two to connect the dots, so anything that ends in 7 is my cousin. The number 8 is Adam Seaman since he might be Jesus; the number 8 is him. He has been the worst friend out of all my friends, so I really don't know if I like when the number 8 comes up.

The number 9 is Anna, Jeff's fiancé. So the 49ers, the football team, would be a combination of Jeff and Anna. Anything that ends in 9 would be Anna's doing. The number 10 is Katy Perry. Since she makes all her music for me, she deserves to be on this list and is number 10.

Forming groups—I think it is always important to have a group surround you. Whether that is your group of friends, your family, your professional sports family, or your Hollywood family. I even think it's important for scientologists to be who they are and act exactly as they see to fit into their own society that they deem appropriate for a cause they thought was suitable within their own lives. Anyone who judges them should quiet down and let them do their own thing. They are not bothering any of us, so I do not see why it is such a big deal.

In terms of my own friends, I know I can count on them whenever I need someone to be there for me since they have been there for me since I came back into the world with vengeance. My world keeps on getting better each day, and I just hope the same for everyone else around the world.

I consider myself to be pretty selfless and always try to be there for people. In this section, I am going to give some examples of how I was there for people. First off, I want to talk about whenever people need me to help them move. I rarely have ever said no. Jeff and Anna needed me to help them move some dirt on their deck so they can grow out flowers and things of that nature, so I gave up half of a Sunday to help them out. Since Jeff is a great guy as well, he reimbursed me for my services that day. When Allyn needed a group of us to help him move about a year or two ago, I was there when he needed me to help him move. So I took four hours out of my day to help him move from Steph's mom's house to their new townhouse. Also, Kevin Pearson needed help to move out of his old townhouse one day, so he hit me up, and I helped him move and took two hours out of my day so that he could accomplish this. When it comes to athletes, I sort of work in the background whenever athletes get hurt and pretty much understand the healing process by now and reach out to these guys and try to get them back to playing as soon as possible.

Jussie Smollett got his charges dropped for sixteen felony counts, and one of them was lying about a hate crime. I believe in this life that everyone deserves a second chance, and he faced a lot of hate and disrespect from outsiders who like to form stupid idiotic opinions. This also goes with the saying that someone or a group of people put the bad in the best, and now we are all right. He is Black and openly gay, so he just needs to be a good citizen and not repeat the same mistakes that he did in the past. He is the actor in *Empire* who plays an important role in this series. Jeff disrespected him big-time, and so that's why he doesn't have any say in this world anymore because people are so hateful, and he doesn't deserve the right to judge Smollett for what he did.

People like to judge me but think about everything I have done for other people behind the scenes, and it is a disgrace that people are the way they are. We need to form peace, but unfortunately, there are certain pieces that don't belong.

The last Islamic State village had been captured, the US Allies say, ending a self-proclaimed caliphate that once was as big as Britain. The statelet controlled by the Islamic State has fallen after the remaining militants surrendered in the eastern Syrian village of Behrouz, according to the US-backed Syrian Democratic Forces. As defeat loomed in recent months, the group turned to sleeper cells, potentially opening a fresh chapter of insurgency across parts of Syria and Iraq. This was major progress in us defeating this Seven Nation Army and protecting the rights of the US citizens and making the world a safer place.

Everyone was saying that this war was going to go on forever, so I took matters into my own hands and listened to the "Past My Shades" song by B.O.B and "Fire Away" by David Guetta. I listened to this song twice on the flight to Boston to visit Shaker, and sixteen of them died. Every time "Past My Shades" would pop up on my playlist, I would hear that fourteen terrorists would die. It is what it is, but we need peace in this world, and nobody else can do this job in this world, so why not me? We need to bring the troops back home and end all of these stupid wars. I am so sick of people point-ing to the sky when you can rely on someone you can see every day (me). We need to see progress in this world, and part of the progress includes making sure the West wins this war.

I like to place bets on sporting events, but I lose more than I win. I've been noticing the games when the winning team scores 6 runs, and that is because of my doing, but when I put money on those games, I usually lose. I keep on wondering why that is hap-pening, and hopefully, in the future, it will change, but for the time being, I am losing those f——king games and I know these teams are winning these games because of me. For example, the Nationals lost to the Mets, 6–5, when I was rooting for the Nationals. I don't think the Nationals deserve to be a great team this year since they have just won a championship in hockey, but I would've loved to win this game.

In G-Eazy's song, "The Good Life," he said "you put the bad in the best and now we are all right." This hasn't been the case yet because my friends are still being very unreliable to me, my dad is still giving me the worst advice, and there are still a lot of injuries in sports. Anyways, I would love for the tide to turn and win these games that I put money on. I know the system is designed for the game makers to win the final round, but I am going to make an exception for myself because I have had it the hardest and am sick of these bullshit tests that are resulting in people suffering from it.

I saw that Chris Davis, the Baltimore Orioles player, was struggling with getting hits, so I made a few moves in my house to break him free from that streak, and now he had a two-hit game, then followed that up with a home run in another game. It is pretty cool what I can do for people, but the people who don't appreciate it can go f——k themselves. I want to live forever, but with people's personalities, it's kind of hard to keep up faith and make these plans everlasting. I don't know what the f——k it is, but I want to punish the people that keep on getting in my way every day.

I like to put money on sports games a lot because it makes the games more interesting to watch and it makes me keep busy and entertained. I often lose games because the games are fixed in the opposite direction. For instance, I put money on the Yankees beating the Twins, but instead, the Twins beat the Yankees, 7–3. It takes two to connect the dots, so the Twins were in favor to win this game, and it sucks because I put money on the Yankees. It was out of my control because it was up to fate for the Twins to win, 7–3. Maybe the "–" stands for zero, and it can help other people out that life in this zip code when the score is 7–3. Furthermore, maybe this means that other scores can determine the same outcomes. The zip codes of the final scores of baseball scores mean that people can be helped out in those specific zip codes.

I hate Mother Nature and fate sometimes when it's not catered in my direction, but that's just life sometimes. Cardi B released a song when Becka (my sister) first introduced me to her, and it was about the twins. I ended up winning that bet, and I can thank her for that. I am happy that I won a hundred bucks that I will be getting within the next week. It's just tough to know the names of the scores of these games before they happen unless you are living life with a cheat sheet. I am not. All I see is gray when I am in the zone. I am making these players play better, but I don't know how the games are going to go before I place bets before the games start.

As I have mentioned in the previous parts of my book, I love to place bets on games, and I hope that luck is turned my way so I can win these bets. Yesterday, on June 12, I put money on the Rays and the Indians. They both lost these games. The Rays lost, 6–2, and the Reds lost, 7–2. It sucks, but I was responsible for both of these teams winning these games. It takes two to connect the dots, and the other person is Ray. Therefore, the sixes stand for me, and the sevens stand for Ray. It sucks, but I was able to help out the A's and Reds, but it wasn't working in my favor. I'm sure they appreciate the help I am giving them, but still, I wish I were able to win these bets. Maybe sometime in the near future, I can help myself out as well. The game that I put money on last night was bullshit because the Pirates lost in extra innings, and it was because of people's stupid greed that made them win this bet.

I really need this money more than other people do, so I hope that people can help me out and do what I cannot do for the world and f——king please help me out. I can't do this on my own, and I need other people to come through for me.

Donald Trump got free from the charges that Russia interfered with in the election. He simply won because of Mac Miller's song, "Donald Trump," that I was listening to on repeat because if his opponent won, then things in this world would have remained the exact same when we were all looking for progress. Everyone has different opinions about different people in this world, but nobody has a bigger say than I do because I am who I am for a reason. I've had it the toughest, so I deserve the biggest payback than anyone else in this world. I am glad that we can finally put this to rest and move on with our lives instead of accusing someone who deserved to win something that never happened. He is a different president than anyone we have ever had before, and there are certain things he is doing great and others that he is not doing so well, but at least he is original and does things out of his heart instead of reading off a teleprompter and trying to impress everyone with fake bullshit like certain people that I probably shouldn't mention anymore.

If I look at the professional teams around the world, I think that coaches have a tough job to get all the players in sync and following the game plan flawlessly. It is also tough for captains to get all their players to play to their full potential and to have every player play within their given roles on their teams. You can look at classes as teams too. I am talking about the lower, middle, and upper classes. I did some experimenting on this on my own. To me, it seems like the upper class is killing it and are doing it the right way. I made a choice to live classless a long time ago, and honestly, there are so many flaws with the middle and lower classes. There are plenty of middle-class people that are not holding up their bargain in the world. They could do a lot better in certain things, like being friendlier to each other and giving money to the homeless.

When I used to play soccer when I was younger, I would look at our teams and be like "This should not be how teams should be." However, this was only with certain things, such as I was an outside midfielder on my soccer teams, and the inside midfielders would always give the ball to the forwards instead of spreading out the field and giving the outside midfielders a better opportunity to be more offensive instead of constantly going back on defense.

I even think that teams that work with production groups— whether that is TV shows, commercials, or movies—have many boundaries that they have to overcome. I was thinking about TV shows this week and was thinking about how the producers, cameramen, and actors have to all be on the same page in order for them to be as productive as possible and produce the best piece that they can. These are boundaries that must be overcome if people want to be successful in this world.

Neighbors helping neighbors. I saw on the news that neighbors were helping out a nearby school by making donations and helping the students get smarter. This has been a part of my plan for the last few years since I discovered Watsky's song. If we all come together as a part of a community, then I feel like we would all be happier together, and peace will be attained once we all become one. You can determine the concept of a neighbor in so many different ways, but those that we all reside with and those that we lean on are our neighbors.

Those with common belief systems and those that would stop at the beat of a drum to help you out in times of need are your neighbor. I would like to think of all of us as one big community, and we all have dreams and aspirations to become globally big. I am the leader of the rebellion, so people can trust me with all their hearts to be their blood. I am the primary reason why the balance is still being displayed in the real world and why everyone is still in full production mode every day. I want to see progress every day, week, and month. Whether that might be improvements on the gas stations, more small businesses opening up, the debt getting erased, better cuts on taxes, and a higher income earning for the middle class, these are a few things that need to be accomplished. Once we can all achieve our goals in the next four years, then we can form into one big happy family and appreciate each other's company.

When I have people throw their backs on me, I was thinking about Allyn and work for some reason. I texted Allyn on Saturday, March 9, and he had just gotten a promotion, so everything in my solution pit is real, and everything I have done for other people has been real, but it's a lonely life, and all the good things that I have done for other people have made me feel really isolated, but one day, it will change then I will be reunited with all my friends again.

Coincidences don't exist. I started thinking about this a few years back. I believe that every day that we are all still alive that coincidences exist even less, and the people that you are friends with and your family and your significant other are there for a reason and for a purpose. Even the random old friends and connections you used to have that you might see on the streets or in the bars are not coincidences. They are there for a reason, even if we cannot explain those reasons yet. Then there is definitely a reason behind it.

Correlation of events: this is a technique for making sense a large number of events and pinpointing the few events that are really important in that mass of information. I was thinking about this concept because it has been really applicable to my life. People tend to throw a lot of information at you at once, and it really depends on what they say and how they say it and how you translate this information to understand the meaning behind what the person is saying. For example, when you spend an extended period of time with friends and family, you take away from these people the most important information that they tell you. You might take away two or three things of the most important from any given meeting that you are with someone of interest to you.

Actions speak louder than words: if you say that actions speak louder than words, you mean that people's actions show their real attitudes, rather than what they say. This expression is sometimes used to advise a person to do something positive. There are several people in the world that just talk for the sake of talking, even if they do not make any sense with what they are saying. When people have evidence behind what they are saying and prove to other people that they mean it by their actions, then you can be like, "Wow, this person knows what they are doing."

I bring this section up because there are a lot of people in this world that think they are right too much of the time and don't agree with other people as much as they should, when in reality, they just sound stupid and should open up their minds to see the other person's perspective.

"What doesn't kill you makes you stronger." Kanye West and Kelly Clarkson both put this into songs, but these songs have really impacted me because I have been in a lot of near-death experiences, and through all of this, I have become a better person. Even things like cigarettes and dip make me feel stronger. When people go through adversity, it builds character and strength, and your insides start to feel like they are tougher, and people cannot really bring you down as much.

Procrastination is the avoidance of doing a task that needs to be accomplished. Sometimes procrastination takes place until the "last minute" before a deadline. Procrastination can take hold of any aspect of life—putting off cleaning a stove, repairing a leaky roof, seeing a doctor or dentist, submitting a job report or academic assignment, or broaching a stressful issue with a partner. I think that a lot of us are guilty of procrastination, and I wanted to add this to my book because I believe it has something to do with how humans have evolved, and I think our generation is guilty of procrastination in many areas of our lives.

When applying for jobs after not being at a company for the past six years, I have been procrastinating for a few months. Even though I landed a job, I still thought that this wasn't the right fit for me. When you get ready to do a task and you sit on your couch for thirty minutes to an hour, you are procrastinating because you think the task might be too hard to handle, which also has something to do with depression. I believe that once you can conquer these demons, life would be a lot simpler, and the possibilities are endless.

In my opinion, everyone procrastinates, at least a little bit. As mentioned above, when addressing issues with loved ones, you might procrastinate because you don't want to hurt their feelings or you are afraid that it might end up in a fight, and what we disagree upon might not be the best problem to have. It is great for people to see eye-to-eye when having a conversation. Sometimes I feel like I procrastinate every day. I try to stick to a game plan every day of things I need to accomplish, but in many cases, this doesn't seem to pan out the way I have envisioned. Procrastination can lead to people becoming lazy and not fulfilling their dreams to the fullest. I also wanted to bring this up because once people stop procrastinating, life becomes easier, and you can reach your full potential without any problems.

The Full Potential Theory—now, when I first starting coming up with this plan, I was on another level that was going to have some nasty parts to it. I ended up at the hospital with a mental disorder that is still not known exactly what is wrong with my brain. One theory involves that the globe is split into two different groups. One group is the sinners and the other group is the saints. Supergirl and

I would be monitoring the two groups. There are so many variations of this that could work, if this first method does not work. I think it's important to work in groups in some way sort of manner. I started making a list of a thousand people, mixed between superstars and people I know or used to know. This could be the basis for something even bigger when I can get this list to a functionable level and measure out everyone's talents to create even matchups in every sport and Hollywood performance, etc.

The Law of Averages means that the principle that supposes most future events are likely to balance any past deviation from a presumed average. You can notice this law a lot in baseball. For example, if Bryce Harper is having a terrific month in May, the law of averages suggests that his numbers will come back down to earth in June, and then maybe he'll start tearing up the baseball again in July. If a pitcher is pitching six great games in a row, the law of averages will suggest that he might struggle in his next two games. For myself, I averaged a 163 average one time when I went bowling with Jeff, and then the next time out, I averaged 125 through six games.

In this section, I also want to mention that I do not believe that 666 is the devil's code. I read online one day that if a god was born that he wouldn't age past the age of twenty-five. I bowled a 125 through six games, which is the epitome of the law of averages. Let's say that I am God, then the 125 would be because I wasn't supposed to age past the age of twenty-five, and the six games are because I have the code 666 in my phone number.

Mad Men—they came out with this script to describe the crazy people across the world that are strong, have common sense, and get very angry. Maybe some of these people are smart but mostly very angry and very aggressive. I thought of this when I was playing golf with this one guy who was getting very mad every time he hit a bad shot. It is definitely meant for the cool guys in my generation who get very competitive when playing sports or guys that just have a personality, not the people and the guys who don't have a personality and are just wasting my time. I never saw the show, but I will one day, but this is just the general consensus I got from this show.

One day, I was playing video games at home and thought to myself, "Hey, maybe if I keep winning games against the computer, then maybe it will help the Islanders' success." So I would sit at home in my season in the video game and destroy the computer to break the curse of the New York Islanders. About a week later, Matthew Perry appeared on ESPN, saying that he was the reason why the Los Angeles Kings had won two cups in the last twenty years because those were the years he was paying the most attention to hockey in Los Angeles. None of it happened by coincidence or by accident, and when I checked the standings halfway throughout this season, they were both in last place.

Within twenty games of me checking the standings, both teams started to play better and were actually making a push toward the playoffs. Neither team made the playoffs, but at least both the Kings and the Islanders received hope for the future during the 2016 regular season.

Another example is when I was playing the NBA game with Shaker. Video games are fake, and the team's games are real, but I felt that somehow, they were synced together, and the balance of the NBA teams was shown. Of course, this year, the balance is more spread out because teams like the Oklahoma City Thunder and Houston Rockets upgraded due to Houston picking up Chris Paul and the Thunder picking up Carmelo Anthony and Paul George. These moves will give the Golden State Warriors more struggles because the next two best teams in the NBA are now that much better with these additions.

Brandon Marshall wants to play two more years in the NFL before helping me change the mental health world. It's going to take science and faith to perfect this. At this point, I am pretty much, like, "I am going to accept all the help I can get." I have had visions of living in this perfect unified world for a long time, and I am available 24-7 for people's help. It doesn't matter if I am at home or if I am hanging out with friends. With all of the points I have laid out in this document, it should be simplified with our methods and techniques to make everyone happy. It is unfortunate that he been dealing with injury problems, but once he gets healthy, hopefully, he'll catch more passes.

I have seen a lot of celebrities that want to reach out to people that are dealing with mental illness problems, especially kids who are pretty much clueless on how you should survive with this illness forever. I saw on the *Today Show* that Lady Gaga was talking to some mental illness patients and giving her two cents. I think they all appreciated that all so much, and it probably gave them a better perspective on life. Emma Stone was another celebrity that gave children and adults a better perspective on mental illness. Hearing these two come out about it makes the world more unified, in my opinion, and helps people understand that it does not matter who you are, you can be infected with my different diseases and viruses.

Jay Cutler talked about how the NFL is a big community and how he feels like he is still a part of the team after he retired and joined the Fox NFL broadcast show. I have been self-observing the NFL and how they maximize their profits and keep a huge audience during the last few years. I use Jay Cutler because he is a player who fans kept on doubting, but because of his loyal supporters and his support system inside of the locker room and in his house, he was able to rise above the critics and play a great career, in my opinion. The NFL is only able to maintain high relations because of the players they recruit to be a part of their system, with most of the guys remaining on, low-key, and not getting into too much trouble. I also think that the guys that bend the rules make it big because people seem to like people that break rules, as long as it's not hurting anyone. For instance, I can see the whole touchdown celebration thing go back to its normal routes in the near future as Roger Goodell becomes more lenient. I say let the players do what they have to do to keep the fans entertained, whether it's using the ball as a prop or using the field goal post to throw down an alley-oop.

After I wrote this in my document, about two weeks later, on May 23, I saw a report on Bleacher Report that the rule changes have actually just been implemented, and Roger Goodell has become more lenient with the players on touchdowns. For the upcoming season, they are now allowed to celebrate in the group, they are allowed to do group demonstrations, and use the football as a prop after a touchdown. This is awesome. Things might actually be getting better!!

The NFL community is also a basis of what I would like the world to be. This includes all of us following rules and forming one as a union and even as a world. Furthermore, to erase all the extreme hate in this world but keep the friendly disrespectfulness. Peace cannot be attained if we are not civilized with each other. It doesn't matter what kind of religion you belong to or what your nationality is, because after all, we are all just human and we all want the same things in life. To be motivated and to excel and to become one is not only necessary but also instrumental to our development as one big community.

I helped Simona Halep beat Serena Williams to win her second title in as many years. I thought this was fair because Serena Williams has won so much, and Simona Halep is a baller who deserved to win this match.

During my free time, I was thinking about how we can get more people acclimated into the sports scene. I thought of a few ideas that we can create a league underneath the best athletes in the US in all sports. All these guys would get paid, but the salaries wouldn't be as high as the current athletes. I really think this idea could work. I mean, look at the MLS and WNBA. They do not really get the crowd support as the other sports but are still intact, and the players are doing what they love to do. This is definitely an idea worth exploring in the upcoming years. We could do it in so many variations and with different ideas and solutions in mind.

When I think of this, I also think about the movie *BASEketball*, when they created an entirely new game. This could also be a great way to get communities more involved with each other. We could create a three-on-three basketball tournament at the local courts and give prizes to teams that finish at different places. I really believe this could all happen. The people that *used* to run this world are f—king up, so now is our time to shine.

Niket was part of the marijuana experiment. So, when I was twenty-four years old, when I felt the whole world coming down on me, part of this started when I was smoking marijuana peacefully on St. Patrick's Day 2010. Allyn and Niket almost got busted for marijuana things, but thankfully, they got off. I didn't know what it was, but at the time, I thought it was the Russians kind of starting a World War III with America, and since I am whom I am, I was in the middle of it. If it wasn't for my survival instincts, I would've been dead a long time ago, but now I know how to survive, and not only that, but I also think I can figure out a long-term solution for marijuana as the marijuana industry keeps on blooming. Every day that passes, it comes across my mind a little bit more, and if I can fix myself with how marijuana affects my system, then this could reach global heights.

I think this whole situation turned into a positive when I was driving back from Roanoke with my parents approximately four years ago when I was twenty-seven years old. My dad had mentioned to me in the car that the Giants were playing at 4/20, that day and I had said that it sounds perfect to me. Then I looked to my mom and asked her, "How does that sound?"

And she looked me straight in the eyes and said, "Perfect."

Then I looked my dad straight in the eyes, and he said, "Perfect" as well. We all know that 4/20 is the day that potheads celebrate their smoking habit. I have no idea how this has happened, but if we can make weed legal in more states in the US, then I would assume that more people would be excited for the future.

The latest season of *Game of Thrones* started on 04/20, a landmark date for marijuana smokers, and maybe it is another important date in history for weed on 04/20/2017. I do not think it was a coincidence and could be crucial for marijuana to be legal in all fifty states. People might want to tune it to the fine details of the show this year. Adam and I are trying to make great strides in this area over the next few years. As long as we stick together as a team, we could really put a big dent into the marijuana industry with a lot of time and commitment into learning the ins and outs of the industry.

We are all very similar and different in so many ways. In ways that guys are similar, we all like to look at good-looking girls that we see, even when guys are in relationships. We have a rule: look but don't touch. We all want respect, most of us like football, we enjoy comedies and watching TV shows and movies. For girls, I think, in general, they want more say in the world, to get more recognition, to have equal rights, just as guys do. Everyone on this planet wants their goals and agendas to be met, regardless of what they are. We all are winners on the inside, and too many people care about how the world judges them. If we can all just be ourselves 24-7 without the weak people in the world calling them out for doing something, the world would be a better place.

Here is a way that we are different. Many people in this world root for underdogs and people that absolutely overcome adversities. Other people are bandwagon fans and only root for teams when they win the big title games. And there are other people who want to see the same teams win on repeat, no matter what other people are going through. My dad and I were having a discussion when we were like, "Underdogs are the teams and players to root for because they have much worse odds to overcome and more of an uphill battle."

Calm, cool, and collected. To be a professional athlete, when you're at work, when your around your kids, or if you are famous in Hollywood, it is important to remain calm, cool, and collected at any given point in time so that your haters can be quiet and not have a reason to question your motives. When you are in a job interview, when you are a waitress, or when you have guests over at your house, it is always important to remain calm, cool, and collected.

When you're in the batter's box, one thing you have to do is remain calm and make sure you can see the pitch coming and know what to do with it in the different counts and depending on whether you are a power hitter or a contact hitter. When you are playing in the NFL, you have to remain calm, cool, and collected when playing your positions at the optimal highest level. For instance, if you are a cornerback, you cannot just go out there and act you're the best player on the field. You have to play your position, cannot really step out of line, and make sure that you can beat the wide receiver in man-to-man and zone coverages. If you're a commentator or an analyst on ESPN, then you have to be cool and collected with goals in mind and make sure you relate to the general public in ways that they would like you to.

You have to talk about the points that are interesting and intriguing to keep them interested in the game. You cannot be too biased on your own teams and talk about the game in the same ways that you might've played the game or learn from your previous mistakes based on your past performances. In my opinion, this is a basic fundamental part of life that has to be executed for people to be successful.

Communication—when looking at how we have all revolutionized since the beginning of time, I like to think that communication is a big part of that. Based off all our belief systems in what we believe in or don't believe in, it all boils down to how this was communicated to us from the past. It could have been your parents, grandparents, friends, or any other historical person that relayed these messages to you. Communication is important with friends and family and with outsiders who you want as your allies. It is important with professionals, in the military, and in Hollywood.

If you and your friends and family are not on the same page and can equally agree on subjects, then you will be constantly fighting, and disagreements just lead us all to be off with each other. When coaches are teaching their students lessons on how to play sports, it is widely important on how we relay these messages to the future of the world. Personally, my life would be better if people around me would actually listen to me more often because I am actually a smart guy, and people have not given me enough credit until I started earning it because of my hard work. On the other hand, I have all these people I can rely on because of how well I have been able to communicate with them in the past. We can all work on this on a regular basis, and this is how we can become stronger and more unified.

How conversations should flow: from my experiences with people and what I've noticed from others who engage in conversations, there are some observations I wanted to add to this section. One of the first lessons of a conversation that I wanted to discuss is that they should be free of anxiety. If you are engaged in a conversation and feel like it is a burden or that you feel out of place, then the conversation probably is not as productive as they could be. Another thing about anxiety performances is that you are too worried about how others view you instead of getting your point across correctly. This is also problematic with a lot of people, and you should get in your comfy shoes before approaching a conversation with your friends or with strangers.

Another big problem is that the opposing party does not read your points that you try to say to others. This could be because you are trying to rush across your points to the other person instead of taking the time to say what is on your mind in an appropriate manner. To keep conversations flowing for a longer period of time, it is also important to listen to what the other person has to say and make good responses and not just one-word answers. You need to show the other person that you actually care and understand what the other person is going through. This is all I got for now, but I will add more at a later date.

Momentum—In sports, in business, in working out, and in other real life activities, momentum plays a big part in our society at different levels. In sports, the team with the biggest momentum swings in a game usually wins, but more importantly when those swings come at the most optimal times. In business, you and your partners or coworkers often feed off each other. If you want to stay ahead of the game, then you want to have more frequent positive momentum swings. If you want to stay in the game, then you want to make sure you are staying in competition with the big hitters in terms of momentum.

In terms of exercising, you want to make that momentum stick with you and never go away. Exercising without momentum, it will not last forever and probably make your fat ass sit on the couch a little more than you should. I just think that momentum is an instrumental aspect of life that people need to perfect over the long haul.

Intuition—I believe intuition is also important in terms of smarts and skills. When you can accurately guess something, then you are well off on being smarter than the people around you. I have gained a little bit more intuition throughout the years, and I don't judge people, but I am pretty good at picking up what people are good at and what people aren't good at. I have built inside of different people's minds intuition skills at the same time. I feel like every time my intuition gets better, the people around me and across the globe also feel a rise in their own intuition. Intuition can mean so many different things, but one of the ways that intuition has helped us as a community is leading toward a certain answer rather than another one or coming to a conclusion before others would have to reason to find that answer.

It is like a productive stream that flows across all of our brains and can carefully be established as a skill for the people that have passed certain tests that we were given since birth.

Purgatory. Right now, every living human is in this thing called purgatory. I learned this lesson from the TV show *Lost*. We are all given a life full of tests, and those that pass get to see the promised land. I figured that since I am the central point of this whole thing, I will decide who gets to be a part of this or not. I am the most welcoming human on this planet, so the tests that I have given to humans are not really that complicated or hard. They are basic tests that are not that demanding and just take a little bit of effort to exercise your free will.

I figured since I started handing out the tests, they are rewards each day, each week, each month, and every year. For me, the prize is the greatest in the upcoming full potential theory that should hit your theatres around 2020. That is one of my goals every day to plan for this and to knock out every obstacle that's in my way until that time.

I've also learned a lot from the books I've read. I read a book called *Outliers*, and the text that stuck to me the most was how athletes that make it to the pro leagues in sports have a much better competitive advantage because of the days and months of the year they are born in as opposed to others that are born in different days and months. I am sure this is also inclusive to people that are better at video games, smarter in school, and other aspects of life. I threw in another theory that people might be better at things because of their last name. Also, the first initial of their first name and first initial of their last name, which you see I pointed out in my book in another section.

In some of the books I've read, they use repetitive characters, even if the story line is completely different and different authors write the book. The types of books I read are a combination of fiction and nonfiction, but I can relate to the characters in the books, whether those sections and books are about me or about my life or about people that I've met in my town. I have learned a lot about the books that I have read.

27

In one book I read, I learned about the whole spaceman test and why it is important. It was a way for us humans to evolve in ways never seen before in human history. The spaceman means that I am immortal and our existence has something to do with my transgressions as The Killers and Justin Timberlake have put into songs. They have written a few songs that perfection is my direction, and Sum 41 put that into a song that was written around the year 2006. I still believe it, but I need people to believe in me, and I have to have a more clear memory and focus better, and this is why I haven't stopped working out for the past year and three or four months. This is just one example of things I have learned from a book.

I have also learned that rain and thunderstorms could come from our alien ancestries. They can originate from spirits and from unknown sources in this world. I created a rainstorm yesterday so that it would be great weather on Thursday and Friday. I know people are sick of the rain, but the environment needs it. Nevertheless, since things are right on cue for the first time in human history this year, if it rains, it is for a reason. Another thing I have learned from the books I've read is that the CIA are working on a solution for the human race that can increase our capacity for being alive. People have been on another level for a while, and as long as it is within reason, then this can be easily accomplished.

When I have read books based on true stories, I have understood the people's personalities and how they became famous. For example, Carly Lloyd really doesn't like fake people, and I can't say I blame her. I do not know why fake people exist, and I wish these types of people wouldn't exist anymore because in my opinion, these types of people bring nothing to the table and cause more conflict and are not a part of the solution. I read Maria Sharapova's book, and she worked her ass off to become one of the more famous tennis players in the world and one of the best tennis players in the world. I am going to work hard to max out at my potential and will do everything I can to achieve perfection. These two girls are people for the average human being to look up to.

I also learned about the dream team and a team that was put together to win the Olympics in 1992. He mentioned me in this book, actually, and said that he would like to say what the happy hypocrite would like to say about the fact the people call professional athletes immortal. I am a big believer that only one person should be called immortal (God) and the fact that people use the word *immortal* for athletes drives me crazy. Furthermore, there were different personality types that were mentioned in this book, and I think they were able to win because they understood each other and were able to straight dominate their opponents.

A lot of this was because of their talent and the coach that was able to hold their egos in check. People said, "What if the best players in today's game were to face off against the best players in the 1992 Olympics in their prime? Who would win?" I would probably lean toward the 1992 team because these guys were so good they would destroy their opponents, and they had better chemistry back then. These days, the players are softer, but they have more skill then players did back then. I think it would be a close matchup, and maybe the players of today's game would surprise us and win that title game.

In one of the books I read, the title was called *God Is Not Great*. I am bringing this up right now because there have been many signs that the apocalypse is happening right now. I don't want to worry, and I really don't want people to worry that the apocalypse is happening, so we should all pray that great things are coming and we should also erase all the hate in the world.

Surprisingly, video games can also help you get smarter, whether they are played on your phone or your computer or on your television. They can help you stay more alert, more social if you are playing around friends, and help with anxiety and stress. Also, it has also become a semi-competition on who is better or who is on the better board. I think when the full potential is at its highest form, people can play video games on their downtime. This is the type of society we are trying to build. It is up to people to hold up their end of the bargain.

Video games can also increase your smarts, such as sports games. You can get a better grasp of the game play of the real-life professional sports and understand the players and the roles each of these players have on the team. You can have a great time managing your players, drafting your players, and making trades, just as if you were the GM of the team. This can also increase your smarts, and you can make it competitive within your respective leagues that you are in.

The movie *Passengers* came out on Christmas 2016. It is about a boy and a girl who wake up early on a flight to take them away from home and into a new environment with an extended sleep to start a new life. Part of the reason why they came up with this idea was to work on all of our sleeping patterns to determine how we can all live forever as a community. I think this idea was brilliant, and Jennifer Lawrence and Chris Pratt were cast in it, both known to be in movies that have meaning to them. I am one of the reasons Chris Pratt has become who he is today, and part of that is because of his transformation, which happened around the same time as mine was starting to happen. His transformations led him to become the actor with the mindset and skills that he has today. I was watching a shitty Chris Pratt film about four years ago, when I was twenty-seven and my friend said that Chris Pratt was a C actor at best. Nowadays, people would consider him a first-rate actor at worst. I am sure if he could thank me in person, then he would.

Another great thing I have done has been for Dwayne Johnson. Although he had decent acting skills before his transformations, I turned him into a first-rate actor as well. When I saw his role in *Pain and Gain*, it really brought life to my insides, and I thought that he did one of the best performances I have ever seen. It didn't get great reviews, and the movie did not come close to winning an Oscar, but it was such an underrated movie. Furthermore, because of my comment out loud, he actually was voted sexiest man in Hollywood three years later, in 2016, and now he is a man on a mission to prove to the world how great of an actor and comedian he could be.

I also want to say here that this can become possible for so many other people in the world and for people in Hollywood. I will name more cases, but adversity only makes people stronger, and no matter how much you have to overcome, there is always a brighter side that can take a hold of you and keep you on the good side of the universe for a long time.

Twenty Percent Mind/Fun

Minds can be very complex and interesting. First you have to understand how each person works and their behavior instincts in different elements of life. I had the ability to dive into a thousand minds in the world, whether they be family, friends, athletes, actresses, actors, addicts, people with mental disorders, etc. and figured out the meaning behind all of it and performed different tasks throughout the day so that everybody would coincide with each other in manners never seen before in history. Every single human would become one once we can all get our minds focused in the right direction. One of the purposes of these exercises is to really value and understand the context behind one-on-one conversations with your support system and those that you count on for valued advice on an everyday, weekly, monthly, or yearly visits

One day, and I know it was all in my mind, I was literally in heaven. I was twenty-seven years old. I read on a website one day that a couple just experienced some tragic news of their parents' deaths, and before they died, they said that in heaven that a thousand years feels like one day, and one day feels like a thousand years. This is exactly what my day was like, and this trial experience was done in the safety of my home. I was with my mother and Chloe, the family dog, and it was easily one of the best days of my life. I believed then and still do to this day that it is part of the solution for the human race. It had to be experienced on me first and so that others would feel more comfortable to have this feeling and euphoria when the time is right.

Ever since this day, I have seen ups and downs with other people that always coincide with me, with euphoria. One day, it was around three o'clock on the day before I was about to see my therapist, and we had both broken free from the wrath of society and talked about it the next day in therapy about how I was happy doing chores around the house etc., and she was doing the exact same thing the day before we talked about it. I am hoping this part of the experiment is part of the solution for the human race.

Ninety-one percent of what we go through in life is mental, in my opinion. For example, the way we get up and take a shower and how we dress to impress people or to impress you is all mental. People love to impress people that are close to them and strangers that they might be meeting for the first time. When you go on a first date, the thoughts that are running through your head are mostly mental. When you place bets on sports games, this is a mental game. When you are trying to pick up on the trends and pick the teams you think will be winning each matchup or the over and under, this is also considered mental in my opinion. When you are at work and planning out your day and when it comes to job performances, I believe this is mental because people have a lot of insecurities and want to appear their best to get any advantage they can over another person. When engaging in conversations with other people and trying to understand how someone might react to what you are going to say, I would say this is mental as well.

Yogi Berra used to say that 90 percent of baseball is mental. Well, I'm saying that 91 percent of our life experiences are mental. These are just a few examples, but I will give more when it comes to my mind. Choosing the friends that you want to hang out with is also mental because you pick and choose your friends, and as you get older, you become wiser and also become pickier in choosing your friends.

I believe we can make baseball games shorter by having less foul balls on two strike counts. This will happen with a little bit of faith and fate. I think fans would appreciate it, and it will make the games more entertaining instead of the pitching count going up because of too many foul balls. This will also allow the pitchers to pitch further into the game and the managers to not pull the pitchers so early into the game.

I know that the CIA and people in the Pentagon have their theories that coincide with everything that I have been through, and

I have run into some of them on the streets and have driven past them in cars. I would have to meet up with them one day and discuss everything I have been accomplishing with everything they do for a living. This could be the best possible outcome for the American people and something that I think is inevitable to happen.

When I was twenty-four years old, I landed a job as an accountant for Comtek. It seemed like a great opportunity for my future at the time, working for a government contractor. Needless to say, I would become an enemy of the state within three months of working there. Let me just start by saying that I was targeting while minding my own business. What happened afterward and what led to me to be the person I am today is all because of *them*. For the time being, I am just going to mention that my coworker, Janice, and I would have a great time during the two or so years I was working there, and she was very nice to me the entire time. It is quite the opposite of what people have seen in the *Wanted*, where the kid wanted to kill his boss, Janice. Janice was working in the accounting department with me, and we would talk every day, and for the entire time I was there, she was the best support system I had. She has also maintained her role in society and is a part of the reason why I am writing this document. She would show me her kids rapping, and don't get me wrong, there were many other people I was close to at Comtek, but Janice had the same viewpoints on life as me, and we both hated our jobs equally, so we would consider ourselves outcasts from the rest of them.

I put a master plan together that started on Christmas of 2012 that no matter what everyone was going through, everything was going to be happening for a reason a little more every day until the world was perfectly fixed. Well, it is working, but it's not going to directly affect everyone every single day or every single time a life-changing event has occurred. It will affect me the most because I am the one who created this rule. The false belief that everything was happening for a reason before that was fiction. It is just to make sure the world as a whole is continually progressing.

Seven years in heaven—I believe this started happening when I was twenty-five years old, and hopefully it ends and we start to have a real solution for it when I turn thirty-two. Throughout this time, I have had so many memories, including that one day with Chloe and me where it seemed like a thousand years was one day and one day was a thousand years. I was on another level on and off for three years from when I was twenty-eight to thirty-one. When you are on that level that I am talking about, you feel like you are invincible, nothing can bring you down, and that you are saving the world (freeing the new world).

Once this picks up and picks up momentum, I feel like as a whole, we are happier. The "on another level" stuff originated from the *Limitless* movie and TV show, but I am the one who made it real in the real life. Even sometimes when I would eat food, I just had a different sensations toward it. The foods would be like salads and fruits, but the way they were going into my system just simply put me at peace with myself. Nevertheless, I figure if we can come up with pills, marijuana, or some other substance that can bring us all on these levels, we could all have a blast together.

Don't get me wrong, a lot of solutions within the system work for people, but if you can reach and go beyond the limits, people could be way happier and probably more like themselves.

Echosmith came out with a song called "Bright" that in a simple way explains what I have been trying to do. In her song, it says that you, the moon, and Neptune aligned to save me, and Jupiter conspired to get me. The whole premise of the song is to understand what my presence in this world could do for people and how she has benefitted in her career and in her private life. She was watching my highlights and knew it was me that was doing the majority of the work in this world and delegating my responsibilities according to the new plan for the world. It is a great written song that I still listen to on the regular.

I just had another experience with heaven on earth on May 7, 2017, when I was coming home from the movies with Gino and Becka. What I have noticed is that on the darkest and cloudiest of nights, there is always a spot in the sky that I think stands for hope. For whatever reason, that spot of the sky hit directly into my brain and mind, and I felt like I was light years ahead of my time again. It was kind of like when people used to feel heaven on earth way back in the day, which was my experience on this Sunday. I wish I could reach out to people sooner about this, but since I am not in the spotlight, it is kind of hard. However, because of the people that are corrupt in this world, it won't be too much of a problem letting people know somehow that I have attained these new heights again. I am blessed to be who I am because I am the vocal point to this whole revolution and cannot wait for it to reach more people.

Radiation poisoning—I think radiation poisoning affects all of us to some degree, and I believe it is a tiny source of our problems in the US. However, it really started to affect me one day when I was twenty-four years old, and I have sort of been recovering from this ever since then. I was under attack from other countries, the CIA, or some bullshit like that, so I was reading the signs in the sky that could follow me to the right path to figure out what the f—k was going on with my life when I felt everything was crashing down. I ended up going into an empty apartment room in Arlington, and in that room, I was being poisoned with radiation. I stayed in the room for two hours until a voice inside my head told me that I was allowed to leave now. I didn't put too much thought into it, except that I kind of thought it was cool that I was part of something bigger than me.

These people were somehow poisoning me with radiation that was flowing into the room through vents. Because of this experience, I am now actually more fit, more powerful, and I am starting to become a better version of my younger self. They say that radiation poisoning makes people go crazy and often can kill people instantly. Instead, on my end, I was just curious about it, so I would go home and read articles about it. I saw articles about what was going on overseas and how Russia also owns a lot of the radiation techniques that are applied to the world. This can also include the atmosphere we are living in, but as far as the US is concerned, I think we are all pretty good here. It was also how I was able to start fixing problems in the world and actually answered people's prayers in a timely manner. Maybe it was a part of the apocalypse that was brought to my attention way before it was brought to the general population's attention. Anyway, this was the path that I chose for myself, and I wouldn't change a thing about it. Everything happens for a reason, and the stars and sky obviously led me to that room for a reason.

The universe and the stars have a big part to play in the transformations and transgressions I have been through. Tinie Tempah put into a song that there was a message in the stars to the man talking about me and that it was something like a biblical thing. I didn't really understand it back then, but now I get it better. They came up with the *Star Wars* movies based off the problems I was able to solve just based off the messages from the stars. The universe is another equation in this progression. It's a huge universe that is owned by a godly character. That character would be me.

Kendrick Lamar put into a song that the stars are closer now, even though the human eye can't see it. Maybe they are closer than the millions of miles away that they were. This could be because it would be easy to circumnavigate the world and make it easier for humans to travel around the world. This could also be because plane flights could travel easier now and living will become easier.

One day, when I was losing my mind and was living in a lot of fear of the uncertainty of the world, I had run into my living room, where Chloe was lying down. She was either scared or wanted to be transported, so she disappeared. I was like "What the f—k is going on?" I was searching the entire house for her and then I saw her upstairs in my parents' room. Ever since that day, I saw my dog transport. I thought, *This is pretty damn cool*, but it was also a little bit scary at the same time.

The keys to staying more alert, awake, and active—I would say anywhere from six to eight hours of sleep a night is perfect. Grabbing a workout five days a week and mixing in cardio into that and eating healthy is essential. I think one of the things that "they say" that isn't actually accurate is that fact that you have to eat breakfast every day. I've stayed active every day without eating breakfast in half of those days. I do not think cheating is a bad thing either. Such as taking energy drinks, Adderall, or any other substance that is like these two is not a bad thing as long as you take them cautiously or under the right care. Trusting those around you is important and listening to only the good advice that you are given is instrumental to this. Having a great support group with these elements could put you in the best shape of your life.

Personally, I have my own formulas for staying alert, awake, and active during the day. I like to eat salads and fruits four or five days a week. I like to exercise six days a week. Three days for cardio and three days for lifting. My father had recently bought me a weight lifting machine that covers every body part, and I can do this three days a week while doing cardio the other three days. I drink water throughout the day, maybe like four glasses of water per day. I do not think we need eight glasses like "they say" we need. If you mix in bad eating habits as well, it is not the end of the world. You can still be healthy and not eat everything that is deemed healthy for you.

I know that this has already happened and that many people have participated in it before, but if we can somehow come with some ideas to create a worldwide beer pong tournament, this would be a great way to bring everyone together. I know for a fact that a lot of people love drinking beer, and many people love beer pong, so let's all get together and create a tournament together. I believe my group of friends and I can make this better than how it was done in the past. We can create groups, like celebrities, East Coast versus West Coast, people under the age of twenty-five versus twenty-five to thirty-five, and things of this nature. We can create fraternities versus fraternities and inter-fraternity friendly competitions. I also like the idea of maybe getting people together like we used to and playing sports against each other, every sport that we can think of, and we can create matches against each other. I am not just talking about the leagues that already exist but maybe create another league where we can have states versus states and regions versus regions, just like we had when we were growing up.

I always had a blast playing in competitions like this, and this would be a great way to live in ways that we used to without too many cares in the world. As different and equal units, we could all have trainers and physical fitness experts train us and have competitions every weekend. I mean, I know we all have fun watching professional athletes battle every day and every month and every year, but instead of just observing these athletes play, let's all get together and f——k around like we used to.

My cousin Ray once told me that humans are only allowed to be happy 4–6 percent of the time. So my theory in evolution says, why the f—k is that even the case? Who made up that rule? Ultimate goal: let's be happy as much as we can. F———k the old rule that allows you to be happy only a certain amount of the time, and let's aim for a higher goal in that ratio. I think with the right amounts of everything in our lives, we could be happy the optimal amount of time. This includes: the right amount of friends, the right amount of family, the right amount of drugs and alcohol, the right amounts of playtime, etc.

You can tell just from looking at the baseball players that they are not happy that much. They try hard, and if you get a hit 30 percent of the time, then you are successful. That means that the other 70 percent of the time, you are really not that happy. In football, how many teams are successful each year to go along with all the drama throughout the year? One team can win in each sport every year, so how happy does that make that competition? My question is, how do we remain happy more often when we are dealing with the everyday struggle of life and all of the elements that it contains?

How weather can change your mood—it is an old theory and it is actually true these days that depending on how the outside weather is, your mood and mind can change. It is pretty simple. If the weather is nice outside, then chances are you will be in a good mood. If the weather outside is shitty, then chances are you will be in a bad mood. This is especially important for people with mental illnesses. The fluctuations in the weather can also change your physical symptoms, not just mentally. Furthermore, your back pains can get worse or your flu could get worse. Those are just some examples.

Another problem/solution that occurs is when I open up my e-mails on my phone. If there are, let's say, five e-mails to be opened, and I open all of them, then that could be five lives that are lost. If I open up another five or ten, then those could be five or ten people that are happier with whatever was going on in their lives. This was something I figured out last year, in 2016, when six people died after I opened up six e-mails. It is what it is. They were on the wrong side of fate, and it didn't really treat them well. But on the positive, negative things are now or will soon be happening less frequently, so this will be a bonus to all of us.

I thought of this when I was sitting in my living room, but maybe the date 7/24/18 is the date that things start to change in the world for the better. I know there are still a lot of terrible things going on in the world, but perhaps if people could put this into a plan, then things will start to get better. If Jesus was resurrected, he was going to start to take over the world at the age of twenty-four. I am not quite sure what the 7/24/18 means, but it could mean something from the Bible. I know people have been praying for change, and hopefully these changes come soon, so I figured I would mark down 7/24/18 for that date. I have marked down several dates, such as 7/1, the date I moved from New York to Virginia, and Morgan Freeman's birthday, 6/1, when people's lives would change. But I marked down 6/1 for 2017 for when I thought the forever young thing would actually take place. I hope this works 'cause I would rather spend the rest of eternity on planet earth than in heaven because there are still too many unknowns about the afterlife.

Frozen in time—so I was watching the Miami college football game with my family and friends on Becka's thirtieth birthday party, and the weirdest thing happened to me that night. I was standing in the kitchen, and I saw everyone in the room get filled with excitement because Miami had just scored a touchdown. Then all of a sudden, the world felt like it was over, and I went up to my bedroom and felt like the devil or God or some other force was rocking my world. I got up after my mom was calling my name and went downstairs. Miami actually ended up punting on that possession and losing that game. My cousin, Kristen, is a big Miami fan because she went there for law school, and that is where she met her husband. My mind was all sorts of f——ked up, and I still do not know how that happened to this day.

Nicki Minaj mentioned being frozen in time in her song "Young Forever," and there is a movie called *Frozen*, but I do not know what that might mean. I also believe this was a part of my turning point in my crazy life. I ended up staying up until around 2:00 that night, drinking with my sister, family, and friends, so maybe that could also mean that it was a turning point for the world, with or without people knowing about it.

I was at Allyn and Steph's Halloween party when I was twenty-eight years old with my ex-girlfriend, and I had dressed up as Wolverine that year as she dressed up as Storm. I ended up winning the award for best costume, even though there were many great costumes there. Kevin Pearson, one of my other good buddies, also won for best costume. We both received goodie bags for our achievements. She said I was the life of the party, something I wasn't really known for the previous three years of my life because of everything I have had to overcome. This was a really fun night, and it was meaningful because she meant a lot to me. I was hanging out with my friends, and for the previous two years, I was fighting off apocalyptic conditions. Now that those are pretty much under control, I began to do what I was born to do: save the world.

This time it was Kim Le's thirtieth birthday party. I drove there with Becka, my older sister. Again, I was the life of the party. She had her party at a winery about thirty minutes away from where I live. I felt like the twenty-one-year-old Will Coakley again, going balls to the wall. It was with great company, all of Becka's friends, who I have steadily become friends with over the years. I was not too drunk until we met up with Michelle's Aunt Betsy who gave us a sampler of the different types of wines. Then it was game on.

I was on the opposite side of a rope that separated the smokers from the rest of the people. I tried to be like Superman and jump as high as I could into the air and land my jump. Well, that plan did not quite work out. I ended up falling pretty hard on the ground and got a pretty big scratch on my leg. It was funny because Becka and Kim could not hold back their laughs and thought it was so funny. On the drive back home with Becka, there were a few cars that were being obnoxious toward Becka and myself, so I started spitting outside the car toward the other car, and she started laughing. If anyone was watching me, they probably thought it was the funniest thing in the world. It reminded me of Roberto Alomar spitting at the umpire for not getting his way.

I play fantasy football every year with nine of my fraternity brothers, and I had taken a year or two break because of all the challenges I had to face. I ended up finishing in last place and as a league; we all came up with a rule that the last place team had to face a punishment. My punishment was to walk around Fair Lakes Shopping Center in Chantilly with a sign asking for money because of my last place finish, dressed up as a homeless person. I walked around with my boys Allyn Scott and Ryan Owens for about an hour and got some good laughs from people, and other people thought this was a creative idea and funny. I thought this would be a good story, so I did not care about the punishment and put this under the fun category because I had a great time making a fool out of myself with my friends.

To add to this section, I thought I would mention on some of the championships that have been received in this league. I believe that good things come in either twos or threes, so Kevin Pearson and Eric Shaker both won the league two times in the nine or ten years of its existence. This was definitely fate or destiny being thrown in their way to help them achieve these championships. Romy won last year, in 2016, then he quit. He said he wanted to leave when he was on top. If that works for him, then that's cool, but he could have definitely followed that up with another championship at some point if history repeated itself because Shaker and Pearson both won two championships. There have been other winners, but I wanted to mention these five.

This year is up for a toss-up. There are plenty of teams playing for the playoffs and teams competing for playoff position. My team is currently 5–5. I won the league in my cousin's league last year and collected about $400, which was pretty cool. Right now, in that league, this year, I am in third place. My friend, Andy Lee, invited me to join his league, so I am currently in three leagues. In that league, I am in fifth place, I think, so I am in pretty good position to make the playoffs. Anything can happen the rest of the season, but hopefully, I have fate and luck working in my direction to overcome some barriers that might make my team fall off. However, I like to stay optimistic and think my teams can get better for the rest of the regular season.

One of my best friends, Jeff, and I have taken up a hobby of playing bowling each week or every other week. We have both gotten incrementally better each time we play. Last time, I averaged a 125 over five games. I hope to make certain improvements to make that average go up. Jeff averaged around a 135–140 throughout those five games. It's fun because we go there and we drink some beers, relax, and just have fun and bowl. My mom is in a bowling league that she plays in every Tuesday and Thursday morning. She is working with the same tools since she was younger and averages about a 150 each week. However, for my own game, I hope to make improvements to further along my game. We have also been talking about starting a team in a bowling league. I think this would be fun and friendly competition against other humans and maybe even meet more people.

To add to the bowling section, I have been consistently going with my friend, Jeff, for the last year starting in 2017. Every time we both go together, we get better. Jeff is better than I am, but one time we went, I was in the zone, and I bowled an average of a 162. I ended up with a high game of 200, which was the highest bowling average that I ever did before. Two hundred is what the pros aim for, so I was pretty satisfied with this accomplishment. Part of the reason for this accomplishment was because my parents had just bought me a pair of bowling shoes the Christmas before, and this really helped me achieve a 200 game.

I am not a big gambler unless it comes to sports gambling, but I was at the craps table with Jeff, and he was able to go on some pretty extreme luck binges. For a streak of about a half hour to an hour, he would rely on the luck inside of me to make the dice hit in the right way. He ended up winning about five times and thanked me every time and was super-excited that it was actually working. I like to think of myself as a good luck charm, so this was pretty electrifying to see how well Jeff and I could work together as a team. Hopefully, one of these days, I'll have enough money so I can start gambling myself and learn some of these games. Until then, I also have another method I can work on at my home to help out other people that like to game.

I use my technology, and on my phone I have a song called "Paper Planes" by MIA that is based on people winning big at the gambling sites. I play this song, and luck just somehow comes to these people, and then strangers start to win big. It works fool-proof, and you can't really discount this mythology. It can also work when people bet with sports or with horses.

When I was in New Jersey with my friends for my friend Steph's birthday, I was talking to Jeff about how sports betting should be legal in the US when we were outside, smoking a cigarette. Within a six-month period, the Supreme Court, eliminating a 1992 federal law that had prohibited most states from authorizing sports betting, enabled states to legalize sports betting. I had even had conversations with one of my other best friends, Allyn, on this subject. He was more pessimistic about the idea than Jeff was, but regardless, sports betting is now legal in the US.

So I had some revelations with connections with the stars and God and things of that nature, and I am not sure if this was in my head or not but I thought this was important to mention in this book. I was playing card games with my parents, and I noticed that maybe this was because everything happens for a reason or if it's because this life is more than just a read-through, but the games we were playing seemed fixed to me. The games seemed as if whoever was destined to win was going to win any given game, even if the opposing player thought they had the better hand.

This is most likely true for the NFL games and probably people that go to Vegas or Atlantic City to play cards and craps and games of this nature. I also noticed this same concept when I was playing rummy cube with my grandparents and my aunt and uncle. It was a lot of fun playing these games, and my dad was usually upset because my mom would normally win the games, and I was trying to figure out inside my mind and my subconscious how these games were fixed, and sometimes I would win, but my mom had Mother Nature working with her most of the time for these games and would come out on top.

Talk about high school fun. When I first moved here from New York, I was a loser from sixth grade until about tenth grade. In tenth grade, I joined the JV baseball team and met friends this way. We were a close-knit group of people, and we would hang out with each other after school, after practices, and on the weekends. I actually did my first drugs and starting partying with these guys, but it didn't throw me off my game until senior year, when I was like, "F—k it, I will be in college next year anyway."

During the summers, we would go to the batting cages and practice our game on the fields. There would normally be the four of us that would practice every day together. The guys I would practice with were Carlos Yasuhara, Adam Burdell, Rollyn Lynn, and myself. We would always use my car when we would roll together, and we used these methods when we were trying out for the varsity team the next year. Also, I went to something called Explosive Performance, which was a training facility to help with agility and speed and other things to improve our game. I would go to Explosive Performance with Eric Slesinger, Stephen Hurley, and Rollyn Lynn. This was crucial for me to make the varsity team as well, and if I would have thought about it more carefully, I would've cared more about the money my parents were putting into this program so that I could progress my game.

There are so many reasons why we need to have the full potential theory go in effect by 2020 or 2021. One of those reasons is so that none of us are living in regret. I believe it is in progress, and people are thinking about it irregularly. Once it becomes more of a regular habit we can put all our stresses aside and come together in unity and have fun competing against each other. Nevertheless, all this hard work would pay dividends because I did make the varsity team as a junior in high school with all the guys I was training with. However, I didn't play baseball as a senior. I instead opted to play soccer, which wasn't such a bad decision.

I made new friends and had a hell of a time talking with these guys, and even though my skills in soccer were diminished, I would still hustle and compete every day for some playing time. I made the team easily, but it didn't work out too well when I injured my groin before the season even started. It hurt for like thirteen months, so I wasn't fully healthy throughout this entire time. There were guys like

Brian Powers and Spencer Wood who I became close to, and they were soccer fanatics.

My best soccer days were up to when I was sixteen years old. I played on a travel team with guys that I also became really close to. Some of those guys were Ryan Bullock, Evan Hill, Randy Devine, and Greg Garrison. There are other names, but I just decided to name a few. I was probably the best player on the team and helped our team move up to the second best division in the metropolitan area before deciding to quit. I was fed up because we were good enough to make it to the best competition division in the area, but the team just did not try hard enough for us to compete at the next level. With the full potential theory, we can all put the past behind us and just primarily focus on the future. There are so many things we can all do together and unite us as one.

The Nationals play on the field is going to end the gnat problem in the world. There are a few reasons for this. One is because I made up that rule because no one likes those annoying creatures to intercept our outdoors fun. The second rule is because the Washington Nationals are destined to win the World Series at some point, so why wouldn't I create that rule? This year, in 2017, people have already noticed how much better that problem has become. The reason for this is because I keep on bringing on weird weather situations from the sky, and I wouldn't think that most people would have a problem with that. I can see Mother Nature and know how to control her productively as I started to figure out how when I was twenty-nine years old.

I haven't felt as strong as I do today on my boy Jonathan's thirty-first birthday, May 15. I have been having tendencies to work out for like three to six months, and then I will take about two to three months off. Every time I start up my body again, someone gets stronger than it was before. It is a part of evolution, and believe me, evolution has done some pretty damn good things for me. If it wasn't for the path that I have chosen, then I wouldn't even be able to write this document. I take in all the advice that people have given me across the years, and now, in my prime, I feel ten years younger and look the best that I have probably looked throughout my entire life. The difficult part is making sure that we all stay in our prime forever.

I picked out Jonathan's birthday because he has been my best friend since I was three years old, so what better date than his birthday? I have also figured out that you don't need to take all those supplements to be physically strong. It also takes a well-balanced diet, and with the right support system, you can achieve your goals as long as you stay motivated. Right now, I am using a machine, one that you would see at a gym and working out three days a week for a month has enabled me to gain five pounds of muscle, compared to the skinny guy I was becoming again. Now I want to shape out my core and my nucleus so I just simply look like a beast.

I was born and raised in Long Island, New York, until I was about eleven and a half years old. During these years, I was one of the most popular kids in school and hung out with the "cool" kids. My best friend throughout these years was Jonathan. I also had a bunch of other friends in my click that I was very close to, even after I left New York. I am still friends with Jonathan to this day, and we will always be close and remain best friends forever. Since my groups of friends were the popular kids, we also hung out with the popular girls at the school. I had a crush at a young age with a girl named Michelle. She was really cool and pretty, and we had a lot in common. When I moved to Virginia before sixth grade, we would still write letters to each other to keep in touch. I am a friend with her on Facebook but do not really talk to her that much anymore. I was also on a soccer team with a bunch of guys that became my friends.

In New York, I mostly played defense. I was very good at stopping the forwards from scoring, and I couldn't really score myself, so they would put me on defense on my travel teams. We were really good and had a bunch of talent on our teams, so I was always on the A team in the city, and we mostly remained in Division 1. It wasn't until I played soccer in Virginia where they stuck me on outside midfield because of my speed.

I remember every time from, like, third grade to, like, fifth grade, with my group of friends in school, every time we were put in the same class, we would always get in trouble for just being childish and doing stupid things. I was never really good at following directions and paying attention, so this didn't work out in my favor.

I was also in the band at school, since it was mandatory in Long Island to play an instrument in elementary school. My friend, Mike, and I would play the trumpet, and we were probably the best two trumpet players in the school, so we always played the harder parts. During free time at school, my friends and I would play those Magic games and things of that nature and involve the girls in those games so that we would all get along. I was the most athletic kid in school because I would always win the awards when we were tested during gym classes and when we had end-of-the-school-year competitions I would always come in first in my class in the athletic department.

When it came to grades, I was also very good during elementary school. My parents would force me to sit down every day and study so that I would get As, and that is what I pretty much did. It was very sad when I moved to Virginia due to my dad's job relocation. My younger sister and I had a party with about fifty people there, just playing sports and hanging out together. We both had so many friends there from school and from soccer that it was hard to leave everybody. My family's house was the house that all of us would always hang out at, so when I left, it kind of crushed my self-esteem, and thinking about having to make new friends was pretty hard the first few years in Virginia. I would make trips back to New York for my first three years in Virginia as much as possible to hang out with my friends back home. I just really didn't fit in until high school, but middle school was definitely not a time period where I wanted to live in Virginia.

I know a lot of people have a hard time fitting in places when they first move. It took me three years before my self-esteem stopped becoming an issue, and I felt great joy once I found a solid group of friends in Virginia.

When I was twenty-four years old, my boy, Jeff, got a party bus for his birthday with a bunch of our friends. This was during my prime-time drinking years, so I went all out this night. This might've been the only time I have celebrated Jeff's birthday with him, but it was great. It was all of our friends on one bus, hitting up a few bars in DC and pretty much having the time of our lives for one night. Back when I was twenty-three to twenty-four, I spent a lot of time hanging out with Jeff. We would always go to Bagel Buddies, I would take

Adderall, and we would hang out and play video games and prepare for our futures. We were in school or working and took out time to work out together while still hanging out with our other friends.

It was actually before I thought of all these ideas that could change the world, and once we can put everything in this document into play, then I think a lot of us would benefit from this life, and we can all believe in something again.

When I was twenty-three years old, ten of my fraternity brothers decided to take a trip to Florida for spring break in Siesta Key, Florida. We decided to drive down there, and it took approximately fifteen hours. We spent a whole week there and had an amazing time. There were around eight guys and two girls, and we all had a bonding time that couldn't have been a better time. We would play drinking games at night and get drunk, and during the day, we would go to the beach. At the beach, we would throw the football around, and we played a lot of volleyball. It was a complete shitshow the entire week, but it was well worth it.

Back then, before I started to become more business-oriented, one of my key goals was to have the time of my life and to just get wasted with my buddies. I am not going to say exactly who I was there with, in case they want to remain private, but this trip defined us as a group of people that could be easygoing, relaxed, and talking to one another as if we were best friends.

In college, when I started dealing with depression issues, my best friend, Adam, was living with three friends, whom I didn't really know at the time, and he decided to help me out. I was twenty years old at the time and living at the fraternity house. The three other guys were Andy Lee, Eric Vogel, and Dan the man. They were all very welcoming of me living with them, and it ended up being five guys living in a three-bedroom apartment. I actually had a very good time during these nine months that I was living here. We set up a mini-basketball hoop inside, and we would play horse and have indoor basketball slam dunk competitions. Sometimes, it would get really competitive, but overall, we would have a great time.

At nighttime, we would watch TV shows or they would let me watch my Yankees play. Adam was obsessed with *Gilmore Girls*, so sometimes we watched that show, and I would get sick sometimes, and one week, I watched the entire series of *Dawson's Creek*. I kind of put my fraternity on the backburner because I was dealing with mental issues, which I found out when I was twenty-four that they can actually be cured. Now I am still best friends with Adam, and Andy Lee is one of my best friends too. It would be a blessing to reconnect with Dan and Eric again as they were very nice and friendly and some of the best roommates I have ever had.

One of my best friends, Adam, and I experienced great times together when we really didn't have anyone else to rely on when we were twenty-one and twenty-two years old. After we moved out of the house with Andy and Dan, we moved into a place with our friend, Eric. At this apartment, we wouldn't really go out that much and hang out with people. Instead, we would take our prescription drugs that made us feel really high every day and watch TV and movies. We killed the entire *Entourage* series in about a week. We would take Seroquel and Ambien to cure our anxiety and sleep symptoms every night. We would have the greatest bonding times together and wouldn't take any of it back. Not only that, but we would also act like we were drunk and act pretty stupidly while sitting on our couches at night.

Of course, we were both going to school back then, so we were both taking Adderall every day as well. We would sit in the living room and study during the day, go to our classes, and try to be good students. To calm down at night, we would also take clozapine to ween off the Adderall and not feel the side effects of this medicine. Our friend, Eric Slesinger, would visit us from James Madison like twice a month, and we would smoke weed and watch TV at night, and that was a lot of fun as well. Back then, I would act crazy when I would smoke weed and sometimes be paranoid, but we were all acting pretty f——king funny at the same time. I wouldn't replace these times with two of my best friends from high school with anything in the world.

Now that I am older, I have to start taking things more seriously, so I can't be f——king around anymore, and I try to be successful in life now. However, back then, this was exactly what I wanted to be doing. Sometimes, we would go to the movies high as hell and just have a blast with the two or three of us.

Like I mentioned in the previous paragraph, I lived in the fraternity house my sophomore year in college. This was arguably the best year of my life. I was constantly the life of the parties we would throw, and I was living with two of my best friends at the time. One of the guys vanished from the face of the earth for a while, but I am still really close to Shaker. I was drinking that year approximately five times a week, and we would constantly invite the pledges over to drink with us. We wouldn't haze them. It was just that they were more fun to us than some of the brothers were. One of my best friends, Allyn, was over there every day and would party with us every night. We would get belligerently drunk and do the dumbest shit. We would wrestle wasted in the backyard, which seemed like every night. I would also always invite two friends from high school over, Tim Cogswell and Bobby Eibert.

The four of us—Tim, Bobby, Allyn, and I—would play beer pong and wrestle each other every night. We were complete shit-shows and didn't care who knew it. Some of the other guys that would come over were Alex Shalak and Brian Platt. They were pledging at the time, but that didn't affect our relationship with them. The pledges in that class loved us because we treated them as if they were already in the fraternity. I didn't really believe in hazing too much because I wanted these guys to feel as if they could trust us and just show their value as a member of the fraternity to us. There is no need to overdo it and act superior because many people do not respond to that kind of treatment very well. I still cared about my schoolwork, but I mostly cared about bonding with the pledges, hanging out with my fraternity brothers, and just, plain and simple, having great times that year.

On the negative side, there were a few things that happened during this sophomore year at the fraternity house that I only told to brothers, and I know that my life has been crazy, so I thought I would add this to my book. I was living in this house with Rico and Eric Shaker, and we were living with f——king ghosts. I am going to tell a few stories that I have regarding ghosts in this house.

One time, I was so f——king high, and up to this point in my life, I was never paranoid or anything like this with weed. I had just smoked with the roommates and a few others when I decided to take a shower. There were voices that were coming into my system, saying, "Will" on f——king repeat. If it was people f——king with me, then that's another story, but we are just going to assume it was ghosts for all intents and purposes. I finally got out of the shower like thirty minutes later and was able to regain control over my body and lived the rest of the day as if nothing had happened.

Again, the next story I am about to tell, we are going to assume it was ghosts, but if it was people f——king with me, then for all intents and purposes, we will leave those names out. I was passed out in my bed, and it was like six in the morning, and I heard people knocking on my door, and it sounded just like my roommate and his girlfriend. All I heard was loud knocking and a girl laughing. It sort of sounded like a mixture of a twelve-year-old girl and my room-mate's girlfriend.

The next morning, I was hanging out with the two of them, and they said they were passed out until we started chilling this morning. I was like "What the f——k?" and then was kind of scared to fall asleep the following week. So while I was living in the fraternity house, the ghosts would only come out and play when there were three or less people in the house.

The next story I am going to mention in this section was when my friends, Allyn and Ryan, were over and hanging out, shitfaced. We were like, "Let's go in the basement and see if we have any occurrences with ghosts." The three of us decided to sit on the couch in the basement, and then all of a sudden, we heard cats above us in the ceiling, making cat noises, and it was scary as f——k. The three of us were like "F——k this" and went upstairs. This wasn't as scary because the three of us were pretty f——ked up, and this was one way I managed to live throughout this year was getting drunk every day.

The last story is pretty scary too. I was sleeping in my room, and all of a sudden, I heard loud banging from the ceiling above. It sounded as if someone had just fallen, and I heard a guy screaming. I am not sure if anyone else in the house had heard it, but I have been a relatively light sleeper on and off throughout my entire life, so I heard this shit pretty clearly. I am convinced that it was ghosts because they say bad things happen in either twos or threes, and the ghosts only came out when there were three or less people in the house. That means that people kept on coming and haunting us after they would die and bother us when there were three or less people around.

There was something else that happened in the fraternity house that does not happen on the regular. The SWAT team came one morning to pay us a visit. So, three weeks earlier, police came knocking on my friend's door while I was chilling there with him and his girlfriend, asking us if we knew anything about a robbery at the 7-Eleven down the street. We were like, "No." We had no involvement in whatever the f——k they were talking about. They were quizzing us for about twenty minutes and pretty much said they would bust up our parties if we were not honest with them. We said that we really did not want that to happen and we had no clue about anyone robbing the 7-Eleven down the road.

Three weeks later, I was up all night studying for a test, and my two roommates were sleeping. One of them was passed out on my couch in my room, and the other one was sleeping in his bed in his room. The SWAT team busted down our front door, and this was at around 5:30 in the morning, and the next thing I know, my door to my room was busted wide open, and I saw pairs of like eight guns pointed directly at me. They yelled at me, "Take your f——king sheets off your body!"

I quickly did this and raised my hands in the air, and they were yelling at my roommate, and he was still so f——king drunk that they started aggressively tugging on him and pulled him on the ground.

First of all, they were being such dicks, and we didn't even do anything wrong. In the other room, my other roommate was dead asleep and thought it was Rico and myself f——king with me, so he elbowed the butt of the gun that the officers were holding, so they took him and threw him across the room and kind of hurt him. I had a f——king exam at around 7:30 that morning, so I was like "F——k, how am I going to get out of this?"

They kept us in handcuffs while they were searching our house for about five f——king hours and did not find shit. They came into our house with weapons of force and couldn't figure out why they had done what they had done to us. This is just another example of police brutality that has been going on longer than people really realize. My one roommate was not listening to anything they were doing and put his handcuffs in front of him and to myself. I was just thinking about my test and how these officers had f——ked up my chance to ace this motherf——ker.

They ended up leaving around 10:30, and then I e-mailed my teacher and explained to him what had happened, and he fully understood. I ended up getting a B on that exam after I was up all night studying for it and dealt with this unnecessary SWAT bullshit.

When I was twenty years old, I was at George Mason University and living with two of my fraternity brothers. I was a sophomore at Mason, and their basketball team was having a fantastic year. It seemed like Coach Larrinaga had done the right recruiting and picked up the players that were great pieces to his team. They ended up losing about four games the entire year and lost in the conference championship game to Hofstra. On selection Sunday, all of us at Mason were very anxious to see if Mason had squeaked in to make it to the tournament that year. When their eleven seed was selected, everyone was going crazy in my fraternity. We would watch every game together, but sometimes I would watch them at home with my dad because I would come home once a week to hang out with my family. They played so goddamn well and ended up beating teams like UConn, UNC, and Wichita State to make it to the final four. Everyone that I was a friends with was going to Indiana to make it to the tournament, so I called my dad on the phone to persuade him to buy me tickets to take the road trip with my friends.

We stayed at my friend Rico's place, and we were completely drunk the entire trip. It was one of the best years of my life, and the entire year, all I was doing was partying. His dad was very cordial, inviting all of us to stay at his house, which was about thirty minutes from the stadium. When it was time to get ready to attend the game, we were all dressed up in Mason gear and roaming the streets with the other big name schools that were also in attendance that year. Some of those included UCLA and Florida. We were facing Florida in the final four, which was led by Joakim Noah, who ended up becoming a very good player at the NBA level. I was actually so drunk going into the game that I blacked out while the final four game was going on. I don't remember much of the actual game, but we were never meant to be there anyway, so we, as a school, were never meant to be there.

The rest of the trip completely sucked, and I ended up leaving, going back to Northern Virginia with my boys and back to the real life. Overall, this was one of the best road trips I have ever taken, and I am hoping that Mason can regain that success that they had in 2006.

Allyn and Steph's wedding—Allyn and Steph, two of my best friends from college, received a great marriage when I was around thirty years old. It was a great time to reconnect with old and new friends, and we were all so f——ked up. I always thought the best part about weddings is when everyone is on the dance floor, dancing with their own personal moves and connecting with each other through our movements. This was definitely a destiny wedding because these two are definitely soul mates, and we could all tell ever since they met, pretty much. Although every couple goes through their ups and downs, they were able to overcome all the adversity that was thrown their way and are one of the happiest couples that I have ever seen. Steph has never been anything but sincere and friendly toward me. If there were a thousand more couples like Allyn and Steph, then I think the world would be a better place.

The table that they placed me in was perfect. I was with two of my other best friends, Jeff and Eric, and Niket, whom I always thought was a great person and someone I would like to get closer to in the future. Anna, Jeff's girlfriend, was also at the table with us, and she has been nothing but so nice toward me and also a great friend toward me ever since I met her. The table next to us was filled with our fraternity brothers, and I have been on and off close to all of them throughout the years as well. I hope that we can all become closer to each other, like we used to, in the future. We aren't quite as crazy as we used to be, since we have all matured, but all of us were pretty drunk, and I think the wedding was a great success.

The one thing that I don't like is that since I was actually going through hell ever since about senior year of college, I wasn't invited to many of their weddings, and I wish that was different. Since all my turning points, I have been more involved in life and the understanding behind it all, which led me to writing this book.

Ten Percent Animals/Kids

Animals are just as instrumental to all of this as any other category. They are the backbone behind what makes us happy every day, how we deal with loneliness, and how we interact with others. Pets as seen on TV are tricky to understand. There are people in the world, including myself, that have had many pleasurable experiences with dogs that aren't seen on an everyday basis.

This all started when my dad bought Chloe, my parents and my dog, six years ago. I have noticed different tendencies, adaptation, and the pleasure she gives me each and every day. If you observe the outside life as I have, you can see that most animals operate like the survival of the fit. They want to be more welcoming to humans as long as we are accommodating to them. We go into pet stores and try to pick out the best pet that we assume will respond to us the best. Through their eyes, they do the exact same things to us and guarantee that this relationship will be long-lasting.

This might only be my personal belief, but I do believe that dinosaurs existed in the past, and I think since the world's return that dogs are dinosaurs from the past. I can tell from their mannerisms and by their actions that humans can relate to dogs just like the smartest humans back then were able to defeat or relate to dinosaurs. Dogs make people happy on a regular basis and help people get through tough times, and I believe that through evolution, dogs are the better version of dinosaurs that we hear of in movies and the stories that we are told of from way before any of us were born.

Personally, I have had several moments when Chloe and I have bonded and seem like we are inseparable. One time, I was in the car with my dog, and my dad and Chloe just randomly started doing like a dog dance to the music. At first, I thought that was just in my head, but people confirmed that Chloe actually danced to the music. Other times, it is like we are reading each other's minds, and the bonding is insane. Like when I described earlier when I had one day when I was literally in heaven on earth, I swear that Chloe was right there with me and was acting as stupid and happy as I was. It was by far one of the best days of my life so far. She is definitely one of the reasons why I am so happy most of the time.

It bothers me when people try to boss dogs too much, like dogs do not have feelings just like humans do. I do not really name names in a negative way, but there are too many people that act like they own dogs like they're their property. I do not believe dogs should be treated that way, and it is really bothersome to me. I think that is also why kids rebel against their parents because they do not want to be told what to do all the time. Nevertheless, dogs act the exact same way. They pick and choose their times to rebel against their owners if they are acting inappropriate toward them.

Another dog that entered my life with great surprise was my sister's dog, Rocco. She was talking about getting a dog for a long time, and she ended up receiving the perfect dog for her. He bonds with Chloe very well and is one of the most enjoyable parts of my life. He lives with Gino and his two dogs and my sister and gets along with those two dogs very well. I have had the opportunity to bond with him a lot because when my sister goes out of town with Gino, she will drop Rocco off so that my parents and I can take care of him. I help her out by feeding him and taking him out for walks, and he likes to cuddle with me on the couch and loves when I pet him. He comes into our house like he owns the place and always takes Chloe's bones to play with them. He is such a good dog when I ask him to come to me so I can pet him or before he gets into mischief and when he is asked to go into the crate because we are all leaving our house, then he will listen with no problems.

He has a known problem for destroying our houses when no one is home, so we have no choice but to put him into the crate. This was a great pickup for Rebecca, and I look forward to many more years of happiness with Rocco.

My friend, Jeff, has a dog whose name is Binx. He is still very young and very enthusiastic every time I come over. Once he gets a little bit older he will calm down, but he loves to play with me as well. I love seeing Jeff and Anna taking care of this little guy, and it also brings joy into my life. If Jeff ever asked me to take care of him while they were out of time, I would do it without any hesitation since they have been really good to me. They have taught him many different tricks, and he does them with no problems at all. They have done a really good job training him, but he loves playing with me. He gets a little aggressive sometimes, but it is all in fun, and it is actually pretty funny as every time I see him, he gets more accustomed to me. He has really inspired Jeff and Anna and he is a really great treat to have in my life.

My friend, Adam, also has a dog that I have become close to throughout the years. Adam's dog is named Brooklyn. Adam received Brooklyn about three years ago, and she is such a pleasure to be around. He has trained her to perfection, and because of her love for him, it has also given me a reason to maybe get a dog of my own one of these days. They say dogs are a man's best friend, and there are certainly no exceptions in this case. Brooklyn likes to play with me, very similar to how Binx does. He will come on the couch where I am sitting and try to lick me; he is so friendly and he has really calmed down now that he is around three years old.

Brooklyn is also a good guard dog for Adam in case anyone wanted to intrude on Adam's privacy. Brooklyn is definitely the dog Adam was destined to have, and I am looking forward to many good years in the future, bonding with Brooklyn.

I have also had moments with birds, geese, and a fox. The birds, I feel, are like an instrumental part to the ecosystem. Birds like to fly around in packs and hopefully hibernate in the winter months. I have a connection to the wildlife, so birds intentionally would hang out in my backyard and switch off days, months, or years of targeting me in a friendly way. They would sing in unison to capture my attention.

One time with geese, they were moving across the street in unison as they usually do. However, this time was different. They kept on looking at me and pretty much telling me that they owned the street and would do whatever the hell they wanted, and my mom and I were laughing so hard in the car. There has been a fox that people have been terrified of for a long period of time, but when I was in fear of the atmosphere, the fox was in my backyard and wiggling his right ear, just like I used to do as a child. It was a moment when we were connected to each other and I was a part of his family. I really hope the fox is still around my neighborhood somewhere and is doing his thing.

Kids are so instrumental to all of us, and somehow I gained the ability to talk to kids a long time ago so that they would get smarter at a younger age. Kids of all types and of all ages. They fit into the system, but at some point, that system is going to have to break down if we all want to stay forever young. Kids have had the ability to learn the ins and outs of life at such earlier ages than the rest of us, and most of that is because of me and whoever has been teaching these kids the fundamentals of life while they are still in freaking elementary school. They just get it, which is scary.

I have figured out a system. Since at least half of the reason we were born is through evolution, it means our parents have aged this much, and others that don't have kids because our generation is pushing them out of the world by our movements and the words we say out loud. And even now, many people are talking shit to people underneath their breaths. I want some of them that keep on saying "F——k him then" when they don't get their way to confront me, and we can have a friendly conversation as to why they don't like me. Am I going to change? No. Most people like how I am, but I will f——k around in their heads a little bit if they don't stop.

Regardless, if we can reverse half of our actions, then the best half of that generation will survive all this terrible shit that we've all had to deal with. It will work out with the best. We'll say 60–80 survive, the best 40–60 survive, the best 20–40 survive, and the best 1–20 survive. We cut everyone else out. No more bullshit, just real mature and immature people.

In this section, I wanted to talk about some memories I have had with my little cousin, Grace. Well, she's not that little anymore.

She is around twelve years old and around middle school age, I am assuming. She is really into ice skating and had dreams of going pro for a while. I used to always talk to her about her experiences in her competitions, and my cousin, Kristen, used to always show me videos of her playing. She is very, very talented, but the competition is fierce to make it to the Olympic level. However, the important part is that I would take time out to make sure she was doing great and she was on point with everything she was learning. She would also show me her teachings at her school, and I would try to help her out to the best of my abilities, and that was actually an entertaining day. At the same time, I was relearning things that I used to know in school that I guess we all forget as we get older. Now it's time to relearn those things!

My other cousin, Colin, who is now about six years old, has had some great memories with me so far as well. Whenever I go to Roanoke, over to cousin Chris and Tara's house, we are always playing sports outside or I am swinging him on his swing. When he was about four years old, he used to show me his style of clothes that he wears, and it used to be similar to mine in terms of matching colors with our outfits. Sometimes it feels like *Big Daddy* with me being Adam Sandler and him being the kid that Adam Sandler was taking care of. We would go outside, and I would let him beat me in football and soccer sometimes, but sometimes I would win so that kids do not think that they can win in everything. I think this is a good lesson for kids to learn at a young age. My only possible regret is not spending enough time with him, but since time is on our side, I do not think this is much of an issue.

Francis was a foster kid that my parents held under their care for about a year. I would play different activities with her like soccer and basketball, which was always fun. I would also take her to Chucky Cheese with Becka when she was having the time of her life. She would play those games, and Becka and myself would cater to her needs and babysit her, and she would just be enjoying herself like she was in heaven.

The best memory of our activities was when I took her to Disney on Ice. I showed up thirty minutes late because I used to do that all the time. I used to always show up late to places just so I did not have to wait there impatiently for other people to get ready. But anyway, again, she had the time of her life watching the skaters do their thing in front of the kids and thanked me so many times afterward. She told on me for showing up late, but I thought that was funny.

Antonio and Darnesa were a brother and sister that my parents held under their care for approximately six months. I used to always go outside and play soccer with the two of them, except Antonio had that personality when you would just want to beat him (he was like five years old), so I wouldn't let him win that often, but it was funny to see his reaction. He would change the name of the game for him to win more games.

With Darnesa, I would help her with her homework because she had a little ADD, but who doesn't? We took Antonio and Darnesa to my cousin's wedding, and they had a blast. Antonio was showing off on the floor his entire dance move collection, and it was a great time that we all got to experience as a family. They both ended up getting adopted, and we have not heard from them since.

Kenny was another foster kid that my parents held under their care for about a year. He was a bit of a troublemaker. He would light candles in his room, and the kid was about nine years old, so my parents were constantly worried that he would set the house on fire. Anyway, I would play video games with him all the time, and he would love the fact that I was so good, and he was trying to be in competition with me, which was great to see from a little boy who already had a troubled life. He looked up to me, and I gave him the best advice that I could. I would play basketball with him outside in the front of our house and let me win most of the time. He was another kid that my parents took under their wing so that he could benefit in the future.

Another little kid that I have enjoyed their company is Sandra's little girl, Ava. I was blessed to be able to attend her first three birthdays since she's been alive. I haven't been able to spend as much time with her as I would like because of the greed of certain other people in my immediate circle. The fact that Sandra invited me to those three birthdays meant the world to me, and even though I was still dealing with a lot on my own, I still made sure that I would attend all of those birthdays. Sandra has been one of my older sister's best friends since college, and they have remained close friends for a long time.

As time passes, I see how my life has changed, and this has led me to have a great relationship with Sandra, even though she is living in Spain now. Hopefully, it doesn't last forever and we will see her, Ronald, and the little one sooner than later.

Ten Percent Music

Music is something that brings us all together to unite us as one. When going into a conversation with friends and strangers, one of the most common questions that is asked is, "What kind of music are you listening to these days?" You find common and abnormal answers to these questions, but on a general basis, you can understand many common areas and distinctions that can bring friends together and relationships.

Music has revolutionized my life because it can help with stress levels and anxiety. When you can relate to a song, it makes those particular songs more enjoyable to listen to. If you want to have a bunch of friends over for a gathering, music can bring laughs and smiles to our lives. Music can also help you forget about the everyday stress that people bring to your lives.

Artists release their music, hoping and believing that people can relate to their lyrics. The most popular artists have this collective hope in common, but the underground artists are also as impressive because they did not have as much to work with and still released ridiculously good music.

There is a new study out there that the best therapy after back surgery is music therapy. I believe it because music makes people happy and can sure be a part of cures for diseases, back problems, chronic issues, and things of this nature. This study came out after I was living in a lot of fear of the elements of society, and my back was in a lot of pain. I would fall asleep three nights in a row with soothing music on my laptop, with back pain, and all of a sudden, my back was fully cured. I figured whoever the beast is can fix the back problems. It goes with the connections, B to B.

Personally, I have also enjoyed throughout my entire life going to ballparks and arenas and seeing how momentum can be gained based on the music that is being played. At hockey arenas, you usually hear rock or pop music, and at basketball games, rap and pop are usually played. Whether it is between plays or at half time, the music gets the fans pumped up and the players focused on their games to keep the flow of the game going.

Music is very instrumental to movies as well. If the scene is going to be intense, then the music that is being played is more demanding and kind of sinister. If the scene is a happy scene, then the music we hear is more of a welcoming theme or more enthusiastic for its viewers.

Empire is a show based on a Black family that struggles with personal issues but has also formed an empire based on the musical skills in the family. It is very drama-packed, but it shows how music can be different, like one kid is a pretty hardcore rapper, and the other kid is an R&B singer. But the way all of them relate to each other with their musical talents shows how blessed they are to becoming as great as they are and how competitive the music industry is. You have to bring it 24-7 if you want to make it big with music, and you have to have the right connections as well. I have watched every episode so far, and I think it is brilliantly done. It is now in its third season and is as entertaining as any other show I have ever watched. It shows a little bit of gangster stuff, some crazy family issues, and music that has been brilliantly made.

The best part of *Empire* is the lyrics of the song. They talk about the ghetto, the Mafia, and other important points that need to be discussed in this world. It's funny how I am talking about the show *Empire* right now because one of the first times I could relate to music in movies to my senses was watching *Empire*, just as I talked about in the paragraph above.

Over the past month, in May of 2017, I created a YouTube playlist with some of the songs that are most meaningful to the population and to the artists that created these songs. They relate to me, obviously, but in terms of the big picture, we need to put these songs to practice to keep the momentum going strong. Right now, I have about fifty songs on my YouTube playlist, and the list is all songs that have helped lead the world to the point it is at right now. If I am the person that people want to lean on, then I have accepted that responsibility full throttle, and life will just keep on getting better and better. I can just sit in my living room, put my headphones on, and do my concentrated power of Will stuff and play these songs, and if anyone is watching me, then they can enjoy themselves, and if they want to rock out to any of these songs, then let them do it!

I was listening to Mac Miller's song called "Knock Knock," which is a song he came out with to let people into Hollywood, and one of the parts of the songs he mentioned is "still setting trends." Furthermore, one day, I was out on the porch with my mom, and I was talking about going skydiving, and she sort of shook her head no, as if it was a bad idea. The next thing I knew, within a six-month period, Michelle Rodriguez and Michael B. Jordan were skydiving on the news. If what I said on the porch wasn't setting trends, then I do not know what is.

Twenty Percent Endless Connections/Signs

Okay, so I am thirty-one years old now, but when I was about twenty-seven years old, I started just thinking to myself about one problem. My father and my best friend both had back problems. So I assumed they were connected somehow by fate. Then I started diving into other friends, family, girlfriends, athletes, and different observations across the globe into the connections that we all have in common that keep us safe and secure on a daily, weekly, monthly, and yearly basis. They are endless.

I read a book saying how if a hockey player is born in January–March that they have that much of an advantage in making it to the big leagues. I ran even deeper tests with my mind, and the athletes that aren't as fit, strong, or as skilled as the professional athletes make it to the big leagues every year. I figured if I get enough support from the right people, we can make it possible for lower leagues to get that same or similar support from fans and in compensation to those "superstars" of the world. It can work, and I believe that it should in the next few or several years.

Another example is friends groups, mental clinics, and people with addiction demons. In friend groups that you develop over time, based on people's personalities, you figure out who is most trustworthy, who is more reliable to go out with on the weekends, and who are the better friends that you hang out with (those you can have serious one-on-one conversations with). In mental clinics and people with addiction issues, you build trust because you are there for more than to get healthy and live healthier from here on out. You are also there to notice you are not alone in the fight for a more beautiful life.

Caring about others is also essential to this. If you listen to other people, take in other people's problems, and put them into action to the best of your ability, these experiences can really make you prosper and make you a better person for going through difficulties that many people cannot relate with.

It is really pretty crazy how I have gotten this far, and I could not have done it without the help of many people. A lot of people were lighting up the inner demons inside my body to help with my own life and with theirs. Adam Seaman and his sister used to do this with me all the time and random people and other people in my immediate life. Everything is happening for a reason a little bit more every day and to see the world's progress as far as we have come as a human race makes me happy every day. I feel a lot better about myself these days and feel like none of the negative things that have happened to me have been by a coincidence. Once we get all the puzzle pieces together and put in all our work and effort into a common sense of knowledge that we will all form one, then I think peace will be attained.

There is one theory I have been working since 2016, and that is for the athletes of the world and how it relates to their lives, fantasy owners, and gamblers. There is a number and word association pattern that plays into this. Okay, so the word association part is pretty simple and can be based off a players season and career stats. For the players to monitor their on-the-field performance, you can categorize yourself with players with the same first initials of your first and last name with the same first initials of players within 1–3 rankings as you are.

So, last year, in fantasy football, Ben Roethlisburger and Drew Brees were in the same categories as NFL quarterbacks with very similar stats. If you look at it from a team standpoint, the three main players at the skill positions for the Steelers all start with the letter B. Ben Roethlisburger is the starting quarterback for the Steelers, Leveon Bell is the running back, and Antonio Brown is the starting wide receiver on the Steelers. I am also going to work in this theory to kill all the Bs in the world with the killer Bs on the Steelers.

The Cubs professional baseball management are working on this theory, and they started last year in 2016. This year, they acquired John Lackey from the Cardinals. They have two pitchers with identical names in Jon Lester and John Lackey. The Cubs had Jason Hammel and Jason Heyward on their team last year, two players with identical names. Additionally, there is a ranking of the 2017 best *Sports Illustrated* basketball players, and I am sure they pointed out who their predictions are based on past performances, but I just wanted to say that Lemarcus Aldridge and Demarcus Cousins were back to back at eleven and twelve, and if you look at their first names, they are strangely similar.

There is another theory categorizing guys that are aging that are athletes. Dwayne Wade of the Chicago Bulls and Dirk Nowitski are numbers 31 and 32 on this list. Both have the letter D with the starting initials in their names and are both aging superstars. The Yankees had Robinson Cano as their second baseman for a long time starting around 2009, and now they have Starlin Castro as their second baseman. Both of these players have last names with the letter C and are the Yankees' second baseman back-to-back, and they are both Dominican. I am not sure if this is a theory or the process in the world's evolution.

On my fantasy baseball team in 2017, the connections and signs are very obvious on the players on my current team. My 1B and my SS both have first and last names with the same initial. Those players are Edwin Encarnacion and Carlos Correa. My second baseman and third baseman are both Spanish and have last names that start with an S. Those players are Jean Segura and Engenio Suarez. In my outfield, I have two players that have back-to-back last names. One player's last name starts with an O, and the other player starts with a P. Those two players are Chris Owens and A. J. Polluck.

For my other outfield spot and my utility spot, I have two players that have first names that start with the letter J. Those two players are Jason Kipnis and Jose Bautista. This theory is still evolving around our eyes, but this is an example how I have been able to put the pieces together, and this lineup has arisen over the draft and first month of free agency pickups. My two best starting pitchers both have the same starting initial in their first name with an M. Those two players are Max Scherzer and Masahiro Tanaka. Also, I believe these two players might be facing each other in the World Series this year. My two relief pitchers have back-to-back last names if you look at their last names with N and O. Those two players are Bud Norris and Roberto Osuno.

The last four players on my roster, besides my catcher, all have connections to their names as well. The first two players of those last four again have back-to-back last names with the initials V and W. These players are Vince Velasquez and Taijuan Walker. The final two players on my roster that I am going to mention are Mike Leake and Marco Estrada. Both of these players have the same first initial in their first names with the letter M.

Being a fan of New York sports, I have already witnessed my fair of championships with the Yankees and the Giants. However, I would love to see a championship for my Islanders and my Knicks. I was talking to my shrink during the off-season before the 2017–2018 Islander season. To go along with my point above, I do not know if this is fate or concentrated power of will, but there are two connections I would like to discuss, one of them being that the Islanders have two players with the same first and last initials. Andrew Ladd and Anders Lee are both wearing an Islanders uniform to this date. Furthermore, Casey Cizikas and Cal Clutterbuck both have initials with CC for their both and last initials. If I want to dig into this further, CC Sabathia has been a Yankee starting pitcher since 2009.

It is just further proof that everything is really happening for a reason and to go along with all the analytics it goes to prepare for a season when you are managing or owning a sports franchise. If you look at the theories I have presented, it makes for great competitive play in franchises across the globe.

The MLB Home Run Derby in 2017 is using a format where it's a head-to-head with eight different players in the first round. They are using my theory of evolution for the players to compete. We have Giancarlo Stanton versus Gary Sanchez in the first round.

Both players have initials with GS. There is Mike Moustakas versus Miguel Sano with both players with the first initial M playing each other in the first round. On the opposite side of the bracket is Aaron Judge versus Justin Bour. Aaron Judge's initials are AJ, and Justin Bours are JB. AJ and JB connect through this theory in evolution. The last two some is Cody Bellinger versus Charlie Blackmon. Both of the initials on these two players are CB. This should make it very interesting, and I am so intrigued to find out what the results will be after the first round and who will win the title for the 2017 Home Run Competition.

It is not a coincidence that all eight of these players are having the years that they are having and that the names on the sheet coincide with one of the recipes to saving this world. So, the recap, in my opinion, was that Judge just dominated the Home Run Derby. He won by a landslide in the final matchup against Miguel Sano. Sano had just plain and simply run out of gas, and with Judge's power and height and youth, he was able to perform with great expectations in the finals.

In his first round, Justin Bours gave him a good run by hitting twenty-one or twenty-two home runs. However, Judge edged him out by hitting one more home run. Gary Sanchez surprised Stanton and hit around eighteen homeruns in the first round. Stanton is the defending champion, so many people around the globe expected him to be in contention with Judge throughout the entire night. Sanchez brought his A game in the first round but ran out of steam in the second round and lost there. Cody Bellinger is the third rookie who played in the game. He made it through the first round but lost to Judge in the second round. Miguel Sano silenced his critics by having an upset over Moustakas in the first round and then beat out Gary Sanchez in the second round. I know all of New York was hoping for New York finals with Gary Sanchez and Aaron Judge, but again, Sano brought his A game last night.

I was watching the NBA rookie and sophomore game which they made the teams as the USA versus the world, and the USA won this year in 2019 with the score of 161–144. Since Satan's number is 44 and *not* 66, this score made perfect sense to me. To their surprise, this was just my doing, and you really can't make this up because the losing team ended with the exact score of a 44 in it. Therefore, both teams were trying with minimal defense but putting on a good display for their fans, and 61 is Andy Lee, but I have the magic inside of me, so the final score of the losing team ended in 44.

I love creating upsets in the sports world, and when I was watching the three-point contest, Stephen Curry lost to Joe Harris, even though Stephen Curry was trying his hardest. I love this because I think the playing field in all sports should be equal. Joe Harris is a great player and is having a great year, and he just happened to outperform Stephen Curry in this matchup.

Watching the NBA games, I started analyzing some of these games a little bit. On Wednesday, February 28, I was analyzing all the games that ended with 125 because if God was alive right now, then he wouldn't age past the age of twenty-five. But then Sum 41 came out with that "Hell Song" that everyone's got their problems, everyone says the same thing to you, and it doesn't matter how you solve them. So the Wizards won their game against the Nets, 125–116, and this was all of my doing because I am everything with 25, and I am trying to connect all the signs and symbols into one dimension. The Wizards haven't been good this year, but they won this game, 125–116.

I am all about creating upsets in the sports world, and the Heat beat the Warriors, 126–125. Dwayne Wade outdid Stephen Curry and hit the game winner. I do not want to see the Warriors win again, but then again, I do not think anyone does. They have already won enough, and it's time for a new champion. This is good news that it proves that anyone can beat the Warriors if the Heat can. I believe it might have to be a team coming from the East if they want to upset the Warriors, but maybe they can be upset before the finals. We will see.

There are plenty of good teams in the NBA that could pull off this magic. Nevertheless, I put the good in the good life, and I was able to come through for the Heat this night. The last NBA score I wanted to mention for this night was the Lakers game that ended in 125–119. Again, the score was 125, and age is just a number for us because behind all of our backs, they are working on a solution for the human race, using me as an example. The Lakers haven't been playing up to expectations this year, and Lebron hasn't been able to bring his team to that title level, but he is trying. The competition in the NBA is better this year than it has been in previous years. I know that the Warriors have five guys in their starting lineup that are all-stars, but you never know when upsets can happen. I was able to come through for them, but when I am busy focusing on other things, then the games are decided by fate or by other people who have more say in this world.

Maybe we can designate it by cities or countries or states to regulate these responsibilities. We cannot rely on the government. We need to take the power back and do it ourselves because the government is corrupt, and I'd rather just do it myself. The Lakers can still make the playoffs this year, but they need to play better and better as a team.

We can even look at some of these theories to fix real-world problems. I came up with this theory for the 2016 college basketball season that is based on Luke Kennard's performance on the Duke basketball team that my boy Andy Canards problems were going to be fixed, speaking in loose terms. I thought if this is halfway through the year, and I haven't seen Andy Canard since then, hopefully everything has worked out for him.

In terms of fantasy owners, I have been working on an ongoing theory about comparative stat analysis. For instance, on my fantasy basketball team, Will Barton of the Denver Nuggets and TJ Warren of the Phoenix Suns are both averaging exactly 13.8 points a game in my semifinal matchup throughout the entire year. It is also not a coincidence that one of my players has a first name that starts with a W and the other player's last name starts with a W. On my other fantasy basketball team, J. J. Redick, the shooting guard on the Los Angeles Clippers, and Jordan Clarkson, the point guard on the Los Angeles Lakers, are both averaging 18.3 fantasy points per game. Both of their first names start with J.

If you want to look at this solution from a matchup standpoint, I have Aaron Gordon of the Orlando Magic facing Pau Gasol of the San Antonio Spurs. Both of their last names start with G, and both are having similar seasons. Aaron Gordon has sixteen points, and Pau Gasol has fourteen points after the first day of the week of the finals. Therefore, if this theory becomes fool-proof, I win the matchup by having Aaron Gordon instead of Pau Gasol.

The next day, I picked up Marcus Morris as a free agent, and my opponent scrapped up Shabazz Muhammad from the waiver wire. Marcus Morris had seven points and five rebounds and two assists, while Shabazz Muhammad had two points and two rebounds. Both with similar stats and both start with the letter M, but Marcus Morris obviously had the better stats, so my team has a better chance of winning for the week.

I was analyzing the stats of the NHL players for the year and noticed some good comparison analysis. I notice things with words and numbers, and I wanted to talk about the points category for the NHL and where certain players were. At fifteen and sixteen, Brad Marchand of the Boston Bruins and Mathew Barzal of the Islanders sit in these respective spots. One of their names start with a B and end with an M. The other guy's name starts with an M and ends with a B. I thought this was interesting, and they are back-to-back in the points category as of 1/25/18.

Sidney Crosby of the Pittsburgh Penguins and Alex Ovechkin sit at twelve and thirteen. These two players have been the NHL's two best players for the past several years, and in my opinion, this was very interesting that they are back to back as of 1/25/18 in the points category. The third comparison I wanted to discuss is Jonathan Marchessault and Jonathan Huberdeau who are back to back in the point's category at twenty-eight and twenty-nine, with both names being Jonathan. The fourth one I am going to discuss in terms of the NHL points category is Johnny Gadreau and Claude Giroux. Both of their last names start with G, and they are both respectively at five and six.

Things like this are interesting to me and help me to understand the system of how everything in this world works a little bit better. Another connection I noticed was numbers 40 and 41. At these numbers are Tyler Seguin and Eric Staal. Both of their last names begin with an S, which I thought was also interesting and ends to the endless signs and connections that I observe throughout the world. At numbers 43 and 44 stand David Perron and Artemi Panarin. Again, both of their last names begin with a P, and they are back-to-back in the points category. I think this is great and may help people understand sports a little bit better with different terminology being used.

Sitting at numbers seventy and seventy-one are P. K. Subban of the Nashville Predators and Nick Schmaltz of the Chicago Blackhawks. Both of their last names begin with an S, just like Seguin and Staal, but these two are a little lower on the points category standings.

In addition to the comparison analysis I was doing on the NHL stats, I also looked into college basketball. The first thought that came to mind was Tai Odiase and Tariq Owens who are 6 and 7 in the rankings on February 17, 2018. Both of their first names start with T, and both of their last names start with O. I thought this was interesting, and they are back-to-back on the blocks category. Next, I looked at the eight, nine, and ten rankings, and the names are as follows: Anas Mahmoud, Austin Williams, and Kenny Wooten. I thought this was interesting because both of the first guys' names start with A, and both of the second guys on this list's last names start with W. The next set of names I wanted to mention is Isaiah Brock and Brandon Gilbeck. Both of these players have names that start with a B and the other starting initials in their names are G and I. I know that H is skipped on their initials, but it is still close enough to mention in this section.

Furthermore, at sixteen and seventeen are Namdi Okonkwo and Pauly Paulicap. Both of their last names contain an O and P, which are back-to-back in the alphabet. Again, these are very interesting trends to me. In addition, at twenty and twenty-one, are JaKeenan Gant and Philipp Hartwich. The next set of names sit at thirty-one and thirty-two. These players are Johnny Hamilton and Khadeem Lattin. Both of their first names are J and K. Again, they are back-to-back in the alphabet with their first names starting with J and K.

I have also thought about how the professional athletes and college athletes compare to the people I have met and still are friends with in real life. One of my friends is Andy Lee. There is a player who sits at thirty-three on the blocks category. His name is William Lee. I thought maybe his ranking compared to the conversations I have had with Andy Lee in the real life.

There is another comparison I wanted to mention here. These players are sitting at fifty-nine and sixty. Their names are Joshua Patton and Jontay Porter. Both players have the initials of JP, and they are back-to-back in the block category at fifty-nine and sixty. The next two players are sitting at sixty-five and sixty-six. These two players names are Kyle Alexander and Brandon McCoy. This comparison is different, but I think it is also relevant. Kyle Alexander has the last name starting with A, and Brandon McCoy has his first name starting with B. The players are back-to-back in the blocks category and have similar names. Furthermore, at sixty-nine and seventy, the players that are listed here are Ryghe Lyons and Elijah Minnie. The first initials in their last names contain L and M, which are back-to-back in the alphabet. I thought this was interesting to mention here.

Going along with what I mentioned above with the name William Lee, I wanted to mention Marcus Lee. I have a friend named Marcus Walker, and I have a friend named Andy Lee. Combine those two names together, and we come up with Marcus Lee. To go along with this last concept I had just mentioned, I wanted to mention the name Mitch Lightfoot, who sits at eighty-seven. I have a fraternity brother and old friend named Mitch Miller. Both of their first names are Mitch, and their last names start with L and M, which are back-to-back in the alphabet. This is relevant because it just adds to the endless signs/connections that I have developed over time.

Nevertheless, sitting at eighty-eight is Albert Owens. I have a friend named Ryan Owens, and my uncle's name is Albert. I thought this was relevant to mention because sitting at eighty-eight in the blocks category is Albert Owens. The last two names in the blocks category for the college basketball stats are Christian Mekowulu and Aboubacar Diallo. Christian's first name starts with C, and Diallo's last name starts with D. They are back-to-back at the last of the rankings, and their names, respectively, are C and D, which are back-to-back in the alphabet.

I was watching the Xavier versus Villanova game, and Villanova was favored, but Xavier won the game, 66–54. I put money on Villanova, thinking they would cover the spread. I have the magic in me, so when the score was 44–44, I took a pee, hoping it would turn the tide for Villanova. Instead, Xavier went on a massive run and was up by a whole lot. They eventually won by twelve, but the fact that the score ended with the number 66 doesn't make me as mad. I just wished it were for Villanova and not Xavier. Anyway, hopefully karma catches up with me soon.

On Sunday, February 24, there was a game that was playing between American and Army, and the final score was 77–66. It takes two to connect the dots, and the other person happens to be my cousin. The score ended with 77–66 because of whatever Ray and I were doing during this time. A seven-nation army couldn't hold me back, and that is why I have the 666 in my phone number. A seven-nation army meaning the sevens. But people on the West Coast have figured out that 444 is the devil's code, not 666. Ever since then, I get very mad when things happen ending in 4 because I worked so hard to get to where I am right now, and Jeff doesn't deserve any of this credit. Not only because of the fact about how bad he's been disrespecting me but also because he hasn't been through jack shit compared to what I've been through. Anyway, the score was 77–66, so that was obviously my cousin and I.

I was watching the Auburn versus Kentucky elite eight game, and it takes two to connect the dots, and the final score was 77–71. I like to make things interesting in this world and prove the analysts and people who think they are smart wrong, so Auburn ended up upsetting Kentucky by six points. The other person, like I have mentioned in this book who is connecting the dots with me, is my cousin, so they ended up scoring 77 points. My dad had Kentucky going to the finals and winning the entire thing, which would have been nice, but I am so sick of everyone's greed in this world, so I was rooting for Auburn, and Auburn won the game. It is what it is, but I am a different person now and don't like when people are being selfish and greedy.

I was watching the Michigan State versus Michigan game on February 24, 2019, and the final score was 77–70. Like I have mentioned in several sections in this book, it takes two to connect the dots across the world. The other person is my cousin, Ray. So whatever my cousin and I were doing in this game, it resulted in the final score being 77–70. It is very simple math, and I use this math to put it into play into the sports world, and we never know how the outcomes will be. I have been really close to my cousin since we were little, so it makes perfect sense. All grounds are covered with the information that Hollywood has given me, and they started at the end, so now it's about execution and finishing what we started to build this new world that we are trying to build.

I was watching college basketball on February 26 and noticed that the twentieth seed and twenty-first seeds won the games with the final score of 77. This means that whatever Ray and I were doing made the teams win by the score of 77. I put money on the Virginia Tech team to beat Duke, who was ranked third in the nation, and Virginia Tech won. This seems like a recurring theme with college basketball how a lot of the scores are ending in 77, but it just makes perfect sense to me. If the fake were to die, then I would be a lot happier because it would eliminate a lot of the people that are cruel in this world and people that just don't understand life the way it's meant to be understood. I only write about facts in this book, and for people like Jeff, it is impossible to see the big picture because they are so f——king fake.

To add to the previous section, LSU beat Texas A&M 66–55, and again the final score was 66. This was all of my doing since I stand for the sixes in the world. LSU is the thirteenth best team in the nation, and the fifty-five stands for my dad, so this score makes perfect sense. Like G-Eazy said, I put the good in the good life, and they only pray for more ends while I hope for the best. So, hopefully my sports betting continues on the upward trend, while I take care of the people who are trying to make this not happen for me. I am taking down names of as many players as I can in college basketball so to get them to have more say in the world, but this all runs through me.

I have been through all of these tests for a reason. Someone in the world decided to put the bad in the best people in the world. Now my list is at about 34,000 people, and I don't plan on stopping that list ever. It is important so that we have all grounds covered all across the world. We can't rely on the government anymore, and we have to give the power to the people to make this work the right way. Again, this all runs through me since I get life better than most or maybe anyone in the world.

Peyton Manning said he was going to put me through that exact same game again, and ever since then, I have understood life a lot better, and even though I got stuck deeper, there is always a means to an end. This score was just one example of the good I have done for the world.

I went to the Mason game on Wednesday, February 27, and the final score of this game was 77–63 in favor of George Mason. It takes two to connect the dots, and the other person is Ray, so the final score ended in 77. I have the magic in me, so I just took one pee during the game for it to end in 77. I actually put money on this game for the spread, so I lost, but still, it was progress since the signs all pointed to Mason scoring 77 points in this game. It was all good, and I am just happy that things are falling into place again. Mason will be good again soon, and on the NCAA radar, they are making the right moves in recent memory to put them in a good position to be dominant again.

I went to this game with my dad, but sometimes you have to take matters into your own hands and just make things happen for other people. I am doing pretty well with my sports betting, but it was more important for Mason to win this game.

I was watching the college basketball games on March 13, 2019, and wanted to point out a score that struck my interest. Boise State won 66–57 against Colorado State. All the sixes in the world is my doing, so I was able to help out Boise State to win this game against Colorado State. I am proud that I am able to help out people around the globe, and as G-Eazy said in his song that I put the good in the good life, I was able to help out Boise State this day. I don't care if people think this is the devil's code because most of my life, I never believed in a god, and I am trying to do whatever I can every day to get back on track and to help out as many people as I can along the way.

When I was looking at the scores for the games that happened on March 12, 2019, the score of the Northern Kentucky versus Wright State game was 77–66. It takes two to connect the dots, and the other person is Ray, and he is the sevens of the world. Therefore, the final score of this game was 77–66, and this makes perfect sense, and if we are trying to connect the dots and make things equal in the world, what two better guys to rely on than my cousin and I? I'm sure the players are happy that they can see someone who is trying to help them out on a regular basis.

Everything I am doing for other people goes beyond sports, though. I can help homeless people off the streets and I can help people get jobs and heal their injuries all across the globe. I love seeing the output for the input of my work in this world. I just hope that people realize what I am doing for them. I made certain moves to make sure the world keeps on progressing, and the people that are holding us back we will just eliminate.

Iowa State beat Baylor 83–66, so when the equalizer comes out to play, he will kill the seventeen people that made the Iowa State team win this game by seventeen points. The sixty-six points should be the winner unless the top score is seventy-seven. Everything in this world should be equal, and I put money on Baylor to win, so I am not happy about this score. Florida beat Arkansas 66–50 on this same day on Thursday, March 14, and this score makes perfect sense because Florida is trying to make the tournament, so if I can help them achieve this success, that would be great. I am going to start doing three-game parlay's to win more money, and if Jeff can get the f——k out of my head, I will be a lot happier. I hate that kid so f——king much. He is going to pay the ultimate price because he did that bullshit to me (that indecent exposure).

Furthermore, for fantasy owners and even maybe general managers and owners of professional sports owners, when looking at a matchup and trades, you can count the number of letters in a players first and last name, and if they match up perfectly, and the numbers are similar, then these two players could be of equal value. When competing against that opposing player, you would want your player to outperform their player, and you could come out with a victory.

I have also been looking at why certain teams win every year in the playoffs and what gives them the edge besides how people look at the obvious trends. So I am doing FanDuel right now in 2017 for the NBA playoffs. You are allowed to pick up nine total players, so I picked up one Spurs player and one Wizards player for the sixth game for each team. Celtics players and Rockets players rounded out the other seven players. The Spurs already won their game when I picked up LeMarcus Aldridge, and now we will see tonight on May 12 if John Wall can come up with a victory for the Washington Wizards.

So John Wall and the Wizards won the game, so this theory was proven correct. Going into game 7, on Monday, May 15, I thought I would do some comparative stat analysis for the two teams to decide who I think is going to win the matchup. I analyzed the stat leader in the main five categories for the playoffs: points, rebounds, assists, steals, and blocks. The Wizards are clear winners in all five categories. John Wall has averaged 27.9 points a game, while Isaiah Thomas has averaged 25.1. For rebounds, Marcin Gortat has averaged 11.2 rebounds per game while Al Horford has averaged just 7.6 rebounds per game. John Wall is averaging 10.3 assists a game, while Isaiah Thomas is averaging 6.0 assists a game.

In terms of steals, John Wall has the edge with 1.8, despite the efforts of Marcus Smart at 1.6. When it comes to blocks, Marcin Gortat is averaging 1.6, and Al Horford is averaging just one block per game. In conclusion, the Wizards should be clear favorites to win game 7. Let's see how it plays out on Monday.

Well, I was trying to end the curse of the fact that the Wizards didn't make it to the Conference Championship since 1979. Oh, well, there's always next year.

In game one of the Spurs and Warriors game, I did another lineup in FanDuel. This time I had two guys going for the three teams (Wizards, Celtics, and Warriors), but I had three guys going for the Spurs. Right now, the Spurs are winning by fourteen points. We shall see how this plays out for the rest of game 1 of the semifinals. The Warriors actually ended up winning the game, and I did the same comparative stat analysis on my own to see whom I would predict to win the series. With this analysis, the Warriors would win the series because they control four of the top five spots. When it comes to scoring, Kawhi Leonard has Stephen Curry edged out with average scores of 27.8 to 27.1. For rebounding, Draymond Green of the Warriors beats out LaMarcus Aldridge with margins of 9.1 to 8.0. In terms of assists, Draymond Green leads in that category with 7.3, while Kawhi Leonard of the Spurs has 4.7 assists per game. Draymond Green wins the steals category averaging exactly 2.0 steals per game, as Kawhi Leonard is averaging 1.7. When it comes to blocks, Draymond Green is averaging 2.7 blocks per game in the playoffs, and Pau Gasol is averaging just 1.2. In conclusion, if you want to draw up who my predictions are to win this series, it would be the Warriors.

I have been analyzing the final scores of baseball games for some time now and seeing how the signs add up and how I can benefit these teams that are winning. I like to mostly look for the teams that win with the scores of 6 and 7 since 66 stands for me and 77 stands for Ray. On Saturday, June 15, the Red Sox beat the Orioles, 7–2. Since Jeff is always on the other side of what I am trying to do to improve the world, he stands for the 2 in this scenario. The 7 stands for Ray and myself, and since one of the best pitchers (Chris Sale) was pitching, we were able to provide him with this victory this day. I actually put money on the Orioles, but the Red Sox ended up winning since they had the advantage, and Chris Sale was pitching. I would have liked if the Orioles won 7–2, but that's just not how it turned out.

On this same day, the Astros beat the Blue Jays, 7–2. The Astros had the advantage since they were favored, and Ray and I again were able to bring this victory to this ball club. I know players are mad that they are still dealing with injuries, but that will be fixed over time. Anyways, this was another great accomplishment as the Astros won with the score of 7–2.

The Phillies game this day was interesting because they were down 5–4 until they overcame with the score of 6–5. I don't like when scores have the ending score of 4 since Jeff is my nemesis, but the

Phillies came back this day and scored 6 runs. This is another great accomplishment, and I hope that I can keep providing for these teams and the individual players so that their stats can be in a good place.

Another theory that we could work into the system for fantasy baseball is how many of every nationality we have on our teams. This year, I have about five Spanish players that fit into my system very well. This could also work well as we all revolutionize over the next five years and see how we spread the wealth in terms of diversity. I am looking at the signs from two of those Spanish players in tonight's games, May 3. Engenio Sanchez, my second basemen, has one hit, one run, one homerun, and three RBIs. My short stop has three hits, one run, one homerun, and one RBI. So the two Spanish players have three ones and one three in the four offensive categories that I am looking at right now. I thought of this theory right after I saw the players I drafted and am viewing not only how far Blacks have come in baseball but also Hispanic players.

Does anyone even know who the first Hispanic player was? I think that is also important in our history. I read in the *ESPN Magazine* that it is actually Roberto Clemente in the 1960s. I wasn't much of a historian until I was given all these tests, and then I saw how much history means to many of my friends and family and people around the world, so I am going to dive into the history of the world in a little more detail in the next year.

I was looking at the stats for the MLB batting average, and Jackie Bradley and Jay Bruce are back to back as of April 4, 2019, at sixty-five and sixty0six. Both of their names start with J and B and are back-to-back where my sign stands at sixty-six. This is pretty cool to see because I know this is my doing since I am in this maze and am trying to figure out how to get out of it, but at least now I know more about the world and why we are alive right now than most people do. When I was looking at the pitching stats, there were two Jakes that were back-to-back. Jake Arrieta and Jake Odorizzi are both really good players, and they are nineteen and twenty in ERA standings.

To go along with what I was saying about baseball stats, I was looking college basketball stats and I was looking at the assists and how the signs match up. Jared Harper and Jalen Harris are back-to-back at twenty and twenty-one, and both of their names start with J and H. They are both great players and did well in the NCAA tournament. I'd like to see the full body of work, but the examples I give in my book are good enough for now.

I was looking at the scores of the MLB games on Sunday, August 4, and there were a few scores that caught my eye. The Yankees beat the Red Sox, 7–4, to complete their four-game sweep. It takes two to connect the dots, so the combination of Ray and me helped the Yankees win 7–4. Jeff is always on the bottom side of things, so when the losing team has the score of 4, that is usually a good thing. The Orioles beat the Blue Jays, 6–5. My soul sister is Amber, so I get happy when the Orioles win and I am able to help them out. Six stands for my number, and five stands for my dad, and there are people in this world that are still one-upping me to show their love for me since I have had it as hard as I have had it. Maybe some of them were in Baltimore so the Orioles were able to win this game 6–5.

The next game I wanted to mention was the fact that the Indians beat the Angels, 6–2. I was able to help the city of Cleveland once again by helping them beat the Angels with the final score of 6–2. You never know entering these games who is going to come out on top, but in this particular case, it was the Indians that were able to outperform the Angels by a four one difference. The next score is pretty cool because it takes two to connect the dots, and the other person is my cousin, Ray, who stands for the sevens, and the Rays won this game, 7–2, against the Marlins. I know that parity is crucial in the future and the Marlins will be better again in the future, but for the time being, the Rays wrapped up this game pretty easily with the score 7–2.

Furthermore, the Reds beat the Braves, 6–4, in extra innings. This is cool because like I previously said in a previous paragraph, when the losing team ends with the score of 4, this is progress. When the final score ends with 6–4, this means that I was able to defeat Jeff again, 6–4.

To add to my previous paragraph, there are a few more scores I wanted to mention. The Cubs beat the Brewers, 7–2, and as I have mentioned several times in this book that it takes two to connect the dots, so the Cubs were able to beat the Brewers with the final score of 7–2. In addition, the Rockies beat the Giants, 6–2. You never know which teams are going to come out in front, but this time, the Rockies were the better team and won this game, 6–2.

When I was looking at the NBA stats for the playoffs, one stat caught my eye. It was the NBA field goal percentage and the positions for 139 and 140 with Danilo Gallinari and Danny Green. Both of their initials start with D and G, and they are back-to-back on the stat sheet. I find this interesting because I play the simple as song to eliminate some of the population, and it has to do with the alphabet as well. When the stars align and the names come into formation and align with each other, it just makes perfect sense to me.

I put money on Tigers versus the Red Sox game during the afternoon of April 23, 2019. The Tigers ended up winning this game, 7–4, and this was the team that I wanted to win. The Red Sox have been struggling this entire year, so I figured this was a good bet to place. Four stands for Jeff, and he is my nemesis and the person that Hollywood really doesn't like, so when the losing team scores four runs or four points, then we all know that this is Jeff's doing. When the winning team scores six or seven runs or six or seven points, then we all know that this is my doing. This kid continually disrespected me for the longest time after I was helping him out, so I don't care what kind of consequences he faces in the future. He played games with my mind and controlled me to do things that were against my free will with the help of the CIA, so whatever he faces in the future is fine by me. Every single day, I want to see nothing but progress, and I will keep everything moving forward, except for the times when I chill out during the day.

There is also a worldwide competition thing going on, so I decided to put this into action on various different levels. In my current fantasy matchup in March 2017, I have James Harden on my team. The first week, my team played against Russell Westbrook and blew him out of the water with his stats and my team's victory. The next week, he played against Kawhi Leonard and blew him away with his stats and my team's victory. Now, in the finals week, he is playing against Stephen Curry, and in the second day of the week, he his exploding with his stats against a weaker Stephen Curry. Now I did not face Lebron James at all during the playoffs, who has been underestimated the entire second half of the year, so the analysts are not really mentioning his name in the MVP candidacy. This has all unfolded this way because I took it in my hands to go out on a limb and put my personal fantasy matchups into play with the NBA, NFL, and MLB players as it coincides with the new rules that have been placed on society.

I also have a tendency to place bets on sports, as do many people around the globe. In March 2017, I put money on the Kings and the Jazz. The Kings' home record is 14–22. The Jazz's home record is 22–14. The records are exactly opposite, and if you look at the signs, everything matches up perfectly.

To take a break from sports, I figured I would throw this theory out there. It is signs and symbols and connections and that sort of thing that I am going to discuss. I think if everyone in the world could list their fears in order from A to Z and try to overcome them and make progress every day, then people's lives would be better. For instance, my D fear is dying, and my B fear is Bugs. My M fear is meeting my maker, and my L fear is luggage being misplaced at the airport. I think this would be a good thing for people to accomplish and overcome. Another one of my fears for S is staying on my meds for the long haul without coming out with a suitable solution for them.

My N fear is not finding a solution for the human race, and my I fear is introductions to the famous people in the world. My P fear is people forgetting my name, and my A fear is Alzheimer's. These are just some letters that I thought I would mention right now. They are unique, and everyone has fears. This is also derived from the book series and movie series *Divergent*.

Divergent. I wanted to talk about how they came up with this script. Well, in one of Flobots' songs they talk about how we are building up a new world, kind of like Noah's ark, but it's different because we are living in a whole different era. So we are trying to build a new world where there are blue skies all over the world, and like I said in will.i.am's world, everyone gets a say in the world, but it all runs through me because I am the one that gave up my twenties and teens to build the world that we need to live in for the rest of the eternity.

In the *Divergent* series, they build up different personality types and form them into different groups, and they learn from each other. I believe they put Jeff as the bad guy in this movie, and I am the guy who saves the world. I am very complex, so I don't fit in with any particular group. I am trying to do things right in this world and put it back on the track so that we can focus on the full potential and my perfection. Jeff is the asshole who constantly goes against the cool guy who goes against the rules and is the rebel trying to break the rules since they aren't fair to everyone.

Age is still just a number to me, and karma needs to pick up soon, and I believe it is soon. Now, in the movie, they cast several characters, and they are around the world because they have the scripts written. Amber was a nightmare, so they try to separate me because everyone has been underestimating me, but that's going to change once everyone sees all the good I am doing for the world. The bad guys in this movie are the ones that are trying to control everything, and he goes against their rules, and that's why in real life, these guys don't like me. However, they know how valuable I am, so they try to keep me protected from the people that are looking for answers for the fallen people in the world.

The Maze Runner—well, I have been in this maze that I cannot escape for several years now. I need to escape this hell and get back to being myself again. This includes feeling my alcohol and meds the way they are supposed to be. *The Maze Runner* has several characters, and the one that he is closest to is Asian. This character is Andy Lee. We are very similar, and he pretty much resurrected my life and came in and helped me out so much. There are good people that went down in this movie, but I don't know how that relates to the real life. Again, he goes against the people that are supposed to run the town and is the rebel in this movie. He falls in love with a girl who has done him wrong because she joined forces with the people that are trying to control everything in the world. However, she has a great personality, and there is a reason why he is in love with her.

There is another group of people in this movie that come to save them from this hell. I believe that's why Twenty One Pilots said, "Wait for them to ask you who you know." Those are the people that remain in the background but play instrumental rules in all of these transformations and why I am going to make it big one day. They are cool, down-to-earth people and want to f——k the system up. Adam just doesn't belong in this new society we are trying to build, so they sent him packing back home. However, I love all people the same, so I would welcome Adam back into my life, but he needs to be more consistent and be a better friend. My other friends have done me good, but he was just dragging me down.

The people that are trying to kill the main character and his friends are my enemies. I can easily remove them from society, whether they are kids, adults, or the elderly. It's a revolution, so we need to kill the flesh. I am not a fighter, but I know how to defend myself, and I have learned how to protect myself from outsiders that are weird and are trying to f——k up what I am trying to accomplish in this world.

Transformers, the first two movies—I wanted to talk about how this relates to the military and all the signs that connect and how I have been going crazy after I've been hearing symbols or whenever symbols enter my brain. Well, people in the military rely on me every day to know how to proceed overseas based on what's going on in my life that day, whether it is signs that I see or signs that I relay to them. The war overseas is going to end one way or another with a lot more blood or not that much blood. This originated from the movie *Transformers*, and in the second movie, Shia LaBeouf constantly goes crazy when he sees signs and symbols that are given to him by aliens or extraterrestrial creatures.

In real life, I am Shia LaBeouf, and I remember the first time it happened, I was in therapy and was freaking out because of the aircrafts I was hearing when nobody else was even really seeing them or just playing them down like they were a part of everyday life. This started happening on the regular for a while, and then it stopped. This was when I was twenty-four years old, and I was still in college. It took me a while, probably until I was about twenty-nine years old, to make these symbols and signs productive and put them into play and put them into practice.

It is pretty simple. From whatever planet they are from, they just kind of hand them to me, and I make it real. Whether it's in the real life for professional athletes or for people in Hollywood, it works; we just have to develop our methods to progress the human race.

Silver Linings Playbook—this is another movie that was primarily made so I can pick up on all the signs in the movie. The first one I am going to discuss is that my shrink is an Islanders fan, just like I am. In the movie and in the book, this was the case with Bradley Cooper and his shrink, and they ended up going to a Philadelphia game together. In real life, my shrink and I have talked about going to an Islanders game together plenty of times, and once we start breaking more rules, maybe this can be a possibility. Also, like I mentioned in another part of this book, I was destined to be with my ex-girlfriend for two of her birthdays and one of mine. The signs were all there so that I can start healing her life, and this movie was also released so that we can start protecting people.

I figured since I went on that drive to Pennsylvania (no coincidence because Philadelphia is the main city in *Silver Linings Playbook*) that we would start protecting people as a society. It started with yours truly, then it went to the simplest forms, and my mom had to be second, and that's when our true revolution started. Other people started making *Silver Linings Playbook* relevant to their lives, and sometimes I felt like it was a worldwide comedy show because of this f——king movie. They did not know how this was going to play out. The first reason was to make my life funnier and heal *me*. After that, it was all going to be a game and for us to heal ourselves.

This part of the movie is still sort of going on in my life, but they are playing out the girl character as my mom, and she is so goddamn funny, which makes my scenes a little bit more hilarious.

When I was hanging out with Allyn, Jeff, and Romy, watching the NBA All-Star game, I was thinking about *Silver Linings Playbook* and how Eminem and Rihanna released the song called "Monster." In this song, he says that these voices are driving him crazy, which was part of the movie *Silver Linings Playbook*, and the girl in the movie was telling him to not let the voices control him and to not let people in the past get to you. This happens to me a lot because I have so many terrible memories that pop into my mind since there have been many people that have been very cruel to me, and I figured retribution would be a great payback, but maybe I shouldn't hold any grudges against the people that have done me wrong in this life.

The monster he is talking about is Jeff because he is the devil and keeps on wiping me off my feet and destroying my life for some reason. I don't know, it all started when I was battling that entire world ending stuff. Will Smith said in his song "Switch" that before the scripts were written, and they pretty much hate Jeff because he is part of the reason why the world isn't progressing. Everything that I have been through seemed so f——king simple, and it is pretty annoying that I am still living in fear, and when Peyton Manning said that he was going to put me through that same exact game, I pretty much haven't stopped since then in doing what I was born to do, but still, I am stuck pretty deep. I cannot wait for all my fears and worries to go away.

While I am in the process of analyzing all these movies that Hollywood puts out, I thought another way that we could come together would be if some of us could form into a group that can relate to the kids still in school. In this paragraph, I am talking about the movie *Old School*. From analyzing this movie, I am going to say that my friend Jeff is Will Farrell, my friend Allyn is Vince Vaughn, and I am Luke Wilson. We can add others to this group, but in the movie, they have three main characters. To me, it seems like kids in college still need a sense of purpose and motivation. If we can add Shaker to this mix and a few other kids, we can help kids out a lot in the future and branch out to these kids. The whole concept of us forming together and forming one originated from the Bible and we, as a society, are trying to duplicate these efforts, but I need my best friends by my side throughout this entire process if it's going to work to perfection.

When I was twenty-five years old, and I had just started to go through hell, I had heard my first voice. The voice was, "It's the CIA." I don't think it was a coincidence since I was born to fix the world.

Due to our process in evolution, our memories start to fade when we turn twenty-five years old. Every day, I work to cure our memories to get them back to normal. Was it the CIA? Only time will tell, and I also think it was a combo of a few different factors that lead to me leading the life that I did not choose to lead but accepted as the process kept on getting longer and longer. The reason why I am bringing up the CIA on a negative standpoint is because they were following me for about a week when I was twenty-four, then all of a sudden, I was standing in my bathroom, and I heard a voice saying, "It's the CIA."

Who could have even said this to me? When I was twenty-nine years old, they started following me again by car, and the sun was beaming down on me pretty hard, just like an incident that I haven't described yet in this book. This happened for two consecutive days. After all those years, they were still bothersome to me. There is only one way this is going to end, and it's not going to end like the assassination attempt on John F. Kennedy. For some reason, though, the second time was different. It was just like a movie, obviously, but I had people blocking their paths to my car so that they couldn't follow me as intense as they were the first time.

College basketball—In 2016, I started to look up the signs and connections on the RPI (Rated Percentage Index) for all the college basketball teams across the nation. I started noticing a lot of similarities between the rankings and the teams that were really close in the standings. For instance, teams ending with A and M were generally grouped together with at least of those two aforementioned schools together. UVA and Virginia Tech were pretty close the entire year, and there are many more examples of this theory. Also, when looking at particular matchups, you can see a lot of similarities between the different stat categories.

For example, if you look at the strength of schedule and their actual rankings, you can grab a pretty good grasp of how teams might perform against each other, and with some other factors you can throw into this, then you can have some pretty good forces thrown your way to win.

The University of Connecticut women's basketball team was on a 111-game winning streak that started on November 14, 2015. I ended the UConn college women's basketball streak so that another team could step up and win. UConn Women were on a ridiculous winning streak, and they would blow out teams every single game. I figured that streak had to come to an end because it wasn't fair for the other three hundred teams that are fighting for a championship every year. The team that upset UCONN just happened to be South Carolina. I say "just happened to be" because I was rooting for their men's team in 2017, but the women's team is the one that came out on top with a championship.

It was impressive, and for myself, there are a few key points I can take away from this. First off, the winning streak started on the day within my sign (Scorpio), and it lasted exactly 111 games. The one stands for me for being the best of them, and the eleven stands for Adam being my best friend and the second best of them who are not in the national spotlight.

The WNBA championship ended in a win for the Seattle Storm over the Washington Mystics, 98–82, and that was because I put the good in the good life, and since Seattle deserved to win this championship, they won. Washington had already won two championships this year, so winning another one wouldn't have made any sense. It's great for a western team from Seattle to win this tournament and hopefully sometime in the near future, more people will start following the WNBA.

Scorpio, my sign and TV show—they are saying that my sign is important to our existence, and my birthday actually lies on the last day of the Scorpio sign on November 21. The show involves a group of five or six people that try to figure out solutions every episode. In real life, I feel like every time my parents watch an episode, there are exactly two solutions being figured out. The Killers also came out with a song a few years ago saying that my sign was vital. After this song was released, Hollywood came out with a show called *Scorpion*. My ex-girlfriend, Amber, used to say how important our signs dictate our personalities. I wasn't sure how much I believed this, but it could be important, and I am intrigued to watch the show and find out the dilemmas and situations that these masterminds figure out every week.

Here is a fact that I wanted to state, and we can understand the meaning of it later. Dwayne Wade of the Chicago Bulls lost his cousin this year, and Isaiah Thomas of the Boston Celtics lost his sister this year. Both accidents happened in the same calendar year, and if people can figure out the main causes behind these accidents, we can finally come up with the traffic solutions and problems that I mention later in this book. They were playing each other in the playoffs this year, but the Boston Celtics came up with the win. I can imagine how bad the losses to the world could be, and it is unfortunate that these two key living legends are living without family members now.

There is a hair removal gadget called the Remington, and I had told my mom to buy this because of the devilish character on the *Blacklist* named Raymond Reddington. I just found a connection there, so I thought this would be a good buy for my mom, and it has worked out great for her and I am sure many other people around the globe. They worked out the scenes and episodes in this series based on the people and problems I would have to deal within the real life.

I have also been observing and experimenting with the connections based on all of our personalities. In the earlier section, I had said that we are all the same and different in so many various ways. For instance, my Aunt Mary and my father are very similar, and my mom and my Uncle Ray are very similar. I combined my Aunt Mary and my dad's personalities to help the Yankees win on Sunday, April 30. My mom and my Uncle Ray are similar because they are both easygoing and have the same viewpoints on many subjects. My dad and my Aunt Mary both don't like scary movies and have always meshed together with the same personality traits. My cousin Ray and I are similar because we both see the big picture. We are both easygoing, and we are both super friendly.

My cousin Chris and my big sister, Becka, are similar because they both are so freakin' outgoing and like similar things with fashion and marathons and shit like that. My cousin Kristen and Meghan are both similar because they both received the book smart genes of the family. They know how to teach others well, and both stay low-key to a certain extent very well. I can also mash all of the ten of our personalities together to come up with different rationale as to why I am similar to the other nine and vice versa. I have found the same connections with other families as well and as to how they mesh with my family. I feel like the Zayas and the Coakleys are both anomalies, but as a society, so many of us carry the same personality traits.

I was doing research into the movies and TV shows and how they relate to my life. So in the show *Friends*, Phoebe is Lauren (Ray's wife), Rachel is Rebecca, Monica is Meghan, Joey is Jeff, Rodrigo is Ross, and I am Chandler. All of our personalities match up perfectly, and the connections are all there throughout the entire series. In *Seinfeld*, Rebecca (Elsie) is Elaine, Gino is George, and Chris (my cousin) is Kramer. Once again, our personalities match up perfectly, and it is what it is. A lot of our conversations have gone these ways throughout the years like the script was written for the names I mentioned above, and we just live our lives as these characters. There is much more, but that is coming soon.

There is a show called *It's Always Sunny in Philadelphia*, and back when I was twenty-four years old, my friend, Keith Mann, said that the characters in the show reminded him of Allyn, Eric Shaker, and myself. The more I look at the episodes and the way they betray the characters, the more it makes sense when the three of us are hanging out. Furthermore, I guess the girl character would be Steph, Allyn's wife. The show is supposed to be a comedy, but they bring up some very good points. Like I mentioned earlier about the crisis in Nigeria, they bring up environmental issues, and they also talk about gun violence. This show should have higher ratings, but people don't usually get the main concepts of shows like this, and also, it is on FX, so I am not sure how this affects the ratings system.

Furthermore, there is a show called *Bloodline* on Netflix where there are four siblings that have a lot of drama with two parents that are pretty crazy as well. The show has some comedy in it as well. I figured I would designate the characters in the show. Well, there are three guys and one girl. So the girl that is very demanding and needs to have it her way and is a lawyer is my cousin, Kristen. The guy who seems to be the most stable and the decision-maker of the group is I. The guy who is always trying to make money and has anger problems and can't grasp with the idea that he needs to be a bigger part of the team is Romy. Lastly, the character who is always getting the short end of the stick and is attention-driven and relies on the character that resembles myself is Adam.

Another show that Hollywood has come out with in the last few years is called the *Blacklist*. It is about a guy with a mastermind that has beauty to it at the same time. This is also in OAR's song called "Wonderful Day." The character's name is Raymond Redington, and since I am the star of this whole show, the character is based off my mind, but I also think it is based off my cousin's actions in real life. The two combined forces with my cousin and myself can create a dynamic team, and this also relates to the business we are trying to get underway. Nevertheless, if anyone gets in our way, they become a number that is on our blacklist. It is pretty self-explanatory; in other words, you do not want to be on my bad side because then we will have some issues that need to be determined by fate.

The character named Denbo is a character that they created based on my dad and my uncle. He is the person that Ray and I rely on for our business sense and how we proceed with life. They have given us all the power in the world to make it big, and pretty much, our dads are our second in hand.

In the show and movie *Entourage*, they display four guys who were childhood friends, and one of them is really talented with acting. The guys' names are Johnny Drama, Vince, Eric, and Turtle. To get my points across to the mainstream, I would have to become famous and be good at something to make this happen. So the writers in Hollywood and myself thought that the best and easiest way for this to become a dream would be if I perfected my acting skills. I never really thought of this, but they developed these characters so that my crew and I could move to Hollywood. They can see progress in the world, and thanks to the song "Remember the Name," I can make this a big dream and make this happen within the next three to five years.

If you want to look at this from the signs point of view, they came up with Eric because of Eric Shaker, Johnny Drama because of Jeff, and turtle because of Allyn. Vince and Will are in common because W follows V in the alphabet. I pick up on everything that Hollywood comes out with, but dreams don't happen overnight. So give me three to five years, and I will live out my dream of becoming famous one day. Every episode is meant to be meaningful and have comedy in it, with guest appearances from many famous people involved. If we were all to form one in the next few years, I would have to be in Hollywood to make this happen for everyone. It is the easiest way to get my message across, unless I was the president of the United States, but the easiest path is to be in Hollywood, trying to get everyone to collaborate as one.

In *Designated Survivor*, the show that just came out around the time Donald Trump was elected, they use his first name as Tom in the show. To go along with the signs that I realize, Tom and Trump both start with T, and they need to connect these signs in this show, and if this show gets cancelled, then in another show that I haven't watched yet. Trump is just dealing with so much drama, and it was inevitable, so they made a show that is loosely based off that. Plots are different, but if you look closely enough, then you can see why the show *Designated Survivor* even exists since I am trying to make everything real time. Personally, I have dealt with some drama with Russian hackers myself that dates back to 2010, before people even knew that Russia was even a problem to the USA. Nowadays, they have hacked into Yahoo accounts and whatnot, but it's nothing that the USA cannot handle.

There is a reason for everything in life, and what Donald Trump is dealing with definitely has an underlying reason for it.

In Donald Trump's first year in office, he has already accelerated the stock market, and they are reaching marks at astronomical areas.

In terms of employment rates, I feel like starting now, until for the next year and a half, we will see vast improvements in this process. I believe that Americans need to be more patient and trust the process that Trump is foreseeing for all Americans. He is also trying to get rid of the debt that has been accumulating throughout the years. If we can get that debt down to minimal areas in the next four years, I think he can consider this presidential opportunity as a success.

In recent months, I have been looking and regulating the stock market, especially my stocks that I placed with my friend Romy on Robinhood. I am Mr. Robot, so I know how technology can run our world. Anyway, my stocks have gone up a total of $200 since I put money into Robinhood within the past year. I also like to see how my Scottrade accounts are doing from time to time. They are up about $2,000 within the past three years. I had withdrawn about $3,000 in the past year from Scottrade, so if I never withdrew that money, then I would have probably doubled my money over that time.

When I wanted to buy a new training machine for my basement. I asked my dad to do research for me to see how to buy this machine. We ended up going to a place that was on Watson Street. Another sign/connection thing I have been working on is the names of the streets that I visit every day or every month or every year. Watson is the last name of one of my friends who I was friends with back in college and met up with her when I was dating my ex. I think this is significant because it shows that life is continuous, and this was the machine I was destined to use.

It is May 2017, and within the first month of using it, I have already got in much better shape and continue to make this progress in my steps to becoming myself again. These are all signs that people should be aware of, and I know in the bottom section, I put that Kevin Pearson lives off a street that has the name Amber in it, and they are both dealing with Crohn's Disease. I am going to save this world, and this was just another step in the right direction.

Ten Percent Intruding into the "Stars" of the World

So one day I was on one of my godly levels, and I just started spitting out different verses from my own created songs and mixing in some of the signs and connections I was talking about earlier and putting this into the real world. Part of this process included getting the famous people involved. I would communicate to them on a daily and monthly basis to make sure that we were on the same page. This goes for the professional, collegiate, and Hollywood superstars. The communication would go back and forth until the middle class and the upper classes were closer to being on the same page.

One role model I learned this from was Tom Coughlin. But instead of trying to get the Giants on the same page, I looked at it as a human race issue and formed different groups based on people's needs and criteria. This is and will continue to be a work in progress until I can perfect the art.

An example is when I was interacting with Lebron James, the NBA superstar. Nobody is perfect, and fans pretty much speak their minds when they are watching the games at home. Well, I said a comment that the Cavaliers were only doing good because Lebron James was not playing at that current moment, obviously just joking around because of the connections that I had already developed with these superstars. He said, "Will, we ignore you when you say shit like that."

Again, obviously just joking around. This started to become a trend for many of these players when I said things that might be out of line, just so we can remain peaceful and prideful.

When I was intruding into the stars of the world, the NBA players would joke with me that I was the laughing stock of the NBA, and I think Carmelo Anthony was hearing voices that resembled Lebron James' voice, so then randomly, Carmelo tackled Lebron in a game when they were facing each other. I thought it was cool because I was branching out and felt a connection to Lebron and Carmelo because of this. This happened when I was around twenty-nine years old, and within the next two years, they had a commercial with the guys from *ESPN First Take* when Max Kellerman said something like, "He is the laughing stock of the NBA" but was not naming any names in particular.

Another funny thing that happened with Max Kellerman was when I was in the plane traveling from Virginia to Florida, during a commercial break, he did a sign that a plane was about to crash, and then he was like, "And this is what's going to happen to Tom Brady."

I am not sure where these guys get this information from, but they put this commercial on air to make people laugh, and it was pretty funny to me because I was like, "Dude." Right after I said "Dude," he was like, "And this is what's going to happen to Tom Brady." Of course, this is all just humor, and nobody wishes any harm upon Tom Brady.

I feel like this also goes under intruding into the stars of the world, but it also relates to playing video games. One time, I was watching Ray Allen play for the Miami Heat, and he was trying to draw a charge. He was so far away from the offensive player, and it looked so silly. He wasn't even close to drawing a charge. I don't know or care what was going through his mind, but that was the first time I've ever seen anything like that. I was watching the game with my boy, Shaker, and we were laughing because we both noticed it at exactly the same time.

When we used to play basketball on a regular basis Allyn, Shaker, and I used to always pretend to draw charges like this. However, to see this in an actual NBA game was priceless. Another funny thing that I wanted to mention is Joe Haden, the cornerback for the Browns, jumped so far off sides in an attempt to block a field goal in one game. He actually successfully blocked the field goal, but it was ruled a penalty since it was so obvious how far off side he was. I used to do this all the time in video games when I was just f——king around, and to see it actually happen in a real game was so funny to watch.

Another example is when I was hanging out at home and again just speaking my mind, but this time was Derek Jeter. He was at bat, and there was an inside strike that was called, and I said "Derek, you have to swing at that ball." It was actually pretty comical because he thought it was the third base coach talking to him. He took in what the third base coach had said, then someone told him it was just Will. He goes, "Oh, it was just will" and smiled.

To go along with this Yankees theme, again, I was just hanging out at home, and Mark Teixera, the former Yankees first baseman, made an error, and I said out loud "What the hell?" and he looked up into the sky. If only he was still playing, but ever since then, he is another person that I have been seeing eye-to-eye with. Non-coincidentally, he was in an episode of *Entourage*, which Hollywood is preparing for my group of friends, and when I arrive to Hollywood for the first time, believe me, it will be to stay.

Johnny Manziel, an athlete who couldn't really handle the press and the media when he was in the NFL, had said going into 2017 that he only really needs one man to believe in him for him to be successful in the NFL. He was talking about myself and because of all the support I have given to people; he is expecting me to have his back if all else fails. This shouldn't be a problem, but people are cruel and harsh, and for them to just turn on him because he had a few mishaps is inexcusable, and all I am saying is certain people in this world need to chill the f——k out. I look at Johnny Manziel, and I am like, "This kid has all the talent in the world, and he is going to let a few people, who probably don't belong in our new society anyway, get in the way, then he needs to grow up and be the person he was born to be."

Eun Yang, the NBC news anchor, was announcing the news one day, and this goes under intruding into the stars of the world because she is on TV every day. Anyway, she was saying how lonely she was, and then I said something really funny. I really wish I can remember what it was, but she started hysterically laughing and forgot her lines.

I said the same thing to Angie Goff when I was just chilling at home, and she started to laugh really hard as well. I needed to branch out to the news so that we can fix all these problems that keep on coming up on the news every day and so we can all reach our silver linings.

People reached out to me for help because their lives weren't going as expected. One of those people was Rhonda Rousey. This was after Hollywood recruited her to be in the *Entourage* movie and before one of the biggest fights of her career. Again, just like I said about Carly Lloyd, she said I was going to help her win. She thanked me as sin and knew she was going to deal with a lot of hate because of it but still was prepared for it. She ended up losing the fight as I was out drinking with my friends that night. I didn't look at it as a big deal at the time, but ever since then, in my opinion, this young girl has been looking at life from a positive angle and is making progress with her and with the universe. Her haters can find another job and leave her the f——k alone. She is someone who a lot of people still look up to, thankfully, and this is how her story remains. If she wants to fight again, and I think that she will, then it will be on her terms, and believe me, she will not be on the wrong side of it next time.

When Charles Oakley had visited Madison Square Garden this past NBA season, James Dolan, the Knicks owner, escorted him out for acting out of line and for, I guess, just speaking his mind about how f——ked up the Knicks franchise has been. It wouldn't have been a big problem, except everyone ended up knowing about it since he did it so publicly. I got pretty mad that day, and with all my powers inside my body, I took over the entire social media interface. There was a lot of hate for James Dolan and other NBA executives, so they had no other choice but to apologize to Charles Oakley, one of the key franchise players for the Knicks in the '90s. They made up and are acquaintances now. I am so pissed at the 1 percent, and now that Trump is trying to pass that bill that treats the upper class better, this isn't going to make my relationship with the stock market fags and others that represent this country in a positive manner. It's war, mother——kers.

Michael Jordan was on ESPN one day, talking about if he was in the prime of his career how he would love to challenge the likes of

Lebron James, Dwayne Wade, and Carmelo Anthony. I would love to see MJ in his prime playing against these guys one day. It would be a miracle to watch. A lot of the old-timers like to talk trash to the current players, saying how basketball was different and that the younger generation couldn't handle all the adversity that the guys from the '80s and '90s could handle, but I would love to see guys like Magic Johnson and Michael Jordan play in their prime again and would add to this friendly competition thing we have created.

Hollywood got the idea of *Legion*, the new TV series, from the skits that were run on me about three or four years ago. It is a great show, and I was sort of connected to my friend David's mind to come up with all this crazy shit inside my head. Now there is a TV show about a guy that has the power to read minds called *Legion* that's on FX, using my friend David's name. This was another part of my life when I was on another level and was just breaking free from the wraths of society, and it was honestly such a great time, even if I was just by myself for most of it.

The songs and signs that have helped the world and myself get this far in the process:

Fort Minor, "Remember the Name"—this song was written by Mike Shinoda and Styles of Beyond. This was part of the original plan which included 10 percent luck, 20 percent skill, 50 percent pain, 5 percent pleasure, and 15 percent concentrated power of Will. My book specifies how things turned out a bit differently. Also, in this song, it specifies how I am going to be a rap superstar. In my opinion, my best skills are accounting and acting, The two As which I talked about earlier in the "Endless Signs/Connections" section. I believe if people really believe in the full potential theory that there really are endless possibilities for all of us. In the original song written by Fort Minor in 2006, it was stated that I would be in Hollywood, rapping in front of everyone in 2014. Instead, in 2015, I made a rule with just Mark Wahlberg that it was going to take eight years for me to get to Hollywood to begin an acting career. With everything I had to accomplish and all the elements I had to overcome, there was no chance I was going to be rapping full-time in 2014.

I think many people figured out that I am a better actor than a rapper anyway, but I could probably manage to do both. I believe that Hollywood put 5 percent pleasure in this song so that I can achieve perfection when the time is right.

The Killers, "All These Things I've Done"—now this song has several key points in it. One of them being that if perfection was to be achieved by anybody that is currently living, then I am the one that has the highest potential with this. And to make this more of a group effort, we are all contributing to helping each other out, and so we can all max out while keeping our eyes out for the long haul. The last call for sin part is in play because that will become a part of our society when everyone is happily married with his or her soul mates, and I am the last one on deck. From watching movies, I think it is going to happen in New York. New York is probably the best spot for this; I was thinking at maybe Yankee Stadium or at Times Square, and this would be the best party to happen in mankind. Everything that I have talked about with everyone and all the endless possibilities, etc. will be in play.

Kottonmouth Kings, "Where I'm Going?" Two of the verses of this song were written for me. The best part of the song describes how me and others who know how to lead are going to have everyone dancing in unison across the globe. Another part of the song is how I am going to make a lot of money one of these days and throw it in the air. Instead of throwing it in the air, I am going to give it to people that need it to help the main causes in the world.

Another verse in this song explains how I am going to fix this mess of a world that we live in. I stopped working a long time ago, and ever since then, I have been answering prayers or people that are in need and people who actually deserve it. I make sure that people are on the right track to succeed in life and that the athletes are as healthy as possible every year. I also want everyone to form into one unit one day so I can fix the problems that I see on the news every day.

I wanted to add to what I already put in this part. In the first part of the song, he says we look to the sky for guidance. I know a lot of people do, and I don't, really. I know when I ask people to throw their backs on me, it is coming down from the sky. In one of Karmin's songs, she says that I control the weather. Hollywood knows there's nothing left to fix in the world, and it all boils down to me. There are a lot of people in the world that look to the sky for guidance, but Hollywood made it pretty clear that nobody is above us, and it will all come down to me once karma picks up with me.

Another example of this is the address at one of the golf places is 6625. The sixes stand for me, and if God was alive right now, then he wouldn't age past the age of twenty-five. They also came up with the human songs, saying that I am just human after all and that karma will catch up with me at some point. He says in this song my life is going north. Or is it heading south? For those people whose lives started heading south, it was because they were self-destructing, and if they ended up dead, it's because there was no need for them anymore in society. When people's lives are on the upswing, it's because they have figured out life and maybe found glitches in the system, and this made them prosper in times of being down. He says this for the general population to listen to, and it is a pretty positive song, so if you want to prosper, nobody is going to do it for you. You have to have that determination and motivation to do it yourself.

Of course, there are a lot of people in this world that are helping each other out, and Hollywood will be right through my war, and they started at the end, so before the scripts were written and they make this music for me to listen to, I am grateful for all the help I can get.

The next part of the song, he says I am walking a fence between wrong and right. I have walked this boundary for a long time since I got stuck as deep as I got stuck. There are a lot of people going through hell because of Mother Nature, and I can try to straighten that out so that people don't have to live in fear because of the storm makers. For me, I am trying to be a better person and a better friend by being by my friend's side, but a lot of this was out of my control. After the apocalypse was supposed to be over, Hollywood and the professional athletes made this way too hard for me, so all these deaths are pretty much on them because karma should've caught up with me by now. It will come, and then I will forgive all of them.

As I have said previously, Hollywood knows there's nothing left to fix in the world, and it all comes down to me. I have made a lot of bad decisions in the past, and when I get into my mindsets with my mastermind, and if you are on the wrong side of it, then that sucks for you, but the world is too overpopulated, so we need to eliminate the people who bring no more value to society. The next part of the song, he says I am trying to keep a level head and keep my goals in sight. I am trying to keep a level head with all the tests I am given on a daily basis and with all the information I am trying to take in about the world. I am trying to keep my goals in sight, so that means that I am aiming for perfection, and I am trying to make all my businesses work.

I am trying to play softball and play it great. I am going golfing and bowling with my dad and trying to play the best I can possibly play. I know that a lot of people think the pros and everyone else separate all of us from society, but I don't think like that. I believe that things will start to even out and I believe that at my best potential that I will be able to compete with them. I can't work right now because I am too busy focusing on other things, and I cannot have a girlfriend because I am too busy focusing on other things, but once these "other things" come together, then I will be rich and will finally get married to the girl of my dreams.

The next part of the song, he says friends I've known for many years started acting strange. He says this, pretty much talking about Allyn and Jeff. These two friends I have been friends with ever since college, they started disrespecting me and acting weird around different people, and I didn't know how to respond to that. These two guys are still two of my closest friends, and I have many friends and other friends that I will reconnect with in the future, but these two guys started acting strange, and now I think they are getting back to normal again. I am never going to be that immature, selfish guy that I used to be. I know a lot more about the world, and I didn't see any of the good and bad things that have happened to me over the past several years coming, but now I know exactly why they happened to me and I know how I can change the world and make the world a better place by just working with the things in my solution pit.

I was thinking about Lebron James yesterday, and then something was burning inside my skin, and I saw on the news today that Lebron had to evacuate his house because of the wildfires near

Los Angeles. This is pretty insane, but I am going to save the world because I hold the future of the world in my fingertips, and people are going to love me all over the place because of the magic and blessings I can give to them. The next part of the song, he says, "When does the train get back on track? When am I going to even care about that?" He says this because I go through streaks of being depressed and being very anxious. At some point, this trend will end, and I will be the happiest motherf——ker on the planet.

I don't drink as much as I used to that used to ease the pain of being nervous in social situations, but now that I am more real, I can see how fake people can be in different situations. This is why when he said friends started to act strange, he is talking about some of my friends starting to act more fake and just out of character instead of if we were just hanging out with ourselves. I lost track of my goals because I was busy helping out other people, but now in my solution pit, if the things I do for other people can also benefit me, then I will be very happy about that. I know exactly what I am doing, so I told Jeff to throw his back on me, and he ended up killing Jefe in our fantasy football league and put up the most points in the league.

Everything that I am going through is real, and I knew I was going to win in the two leagues that I was focusing on. I have the magic inside of me, so the two fantasy basketball leagues I am in are already fixed, and the best team in each league is going to win. I really hope that person is me in at least one of those leagues, but I have no idea.

The next part of the song, he says, "Why am I that always takes the bad cause, took the easy road, but now my life is hard?" I had everything handed to me in grade school and in college. I was on the right meds. However, things changed when I was around twenty-two years old. They put me on these stupid bipolar medications that actually made me bipolar. The stupid shrink and people at the hospital misread me, and these pills have really f——ked up my life. Nowadays, I am trying to make the best of it. I know I get depressed sometimes, and that's why I was on depression meds. I know I am ADD, and that's why I was on ADD meds. I know that I have anxiety, and that is why I was on anxiety meds, but I was never bipolar. All of my friends know that I am not bipolar, and nobody would be able to tell. They totally misdiagnosed me, and it really f——ked up my time in school and my time in the social world.

My life is hard because I am working this solution pit, and since I am the best person in the world, I had to go through the worst tests. Amber was a nightmare, but I was very angry. I was still going through the side effects of all that heaven and hell experience on my trip to Pennsylvania. All of my relationships could've worked out if it wasn't because of alcohol. Therefore, I don't really drink that much anymore, and with my next relationship, it will pretty much work out because I am a lot more mellowed out now and more calm. I need to be with a girl who is down to earth and who can see eye-to-eye with me.

Looking back in time, Amber was the best girl I ever dated, and she is my soul sister who I will reconnect with in the future, but some of the things I was going through was terrible, and I didn't deserve some of the hellish things that were happening to me. I don't think anybody does. In the Third Eye Blind song, he says that I should step away from the ledge, and everyone I know has a reason to put the past away. I have killed some of those people that put me through this hell, and now, sometimes, I kill the flesh, but it's all in the scripts that Hollywood has written. I am holding this certain balance in the world, and if you don't belong in that balance anymore, then you are definitely worthy of being eliminated.

The next part of the song, he says, "Still I try to make it work out for the best, and I know I have to clean up all this mess." I try to make it work out for the best because you can't rewind the past but you can make the future work out even better than the past has treated you. I pretty much know what I am doing, so anybody who is going through any hellish things, then I know that I can help you, and I am helping out millions of people every day, and those that still need and want my help, I am asking you to be patient. I try to make it work out for the best because the world is still pretty unpredictable, and I just quit the dating websites because I can't deal with these girls that are reading too much into what I am saying to them because I am harmless, and they need to understand that I want the same things they want, so they need to calm the f——k down. I have to clean up all this mess, and this means all the wars end.

People said that World War II was the war to end all wars. Then why the f——k have we had wars since then? Right now, this is the war to end all wars. The Killers came out with the song "Shadowplay." He says that I did everything I wanted, I did everything to end all the corrupt bullshit in the world. Katy Perry then came out with the song that I fell for everything and went from zero to hero. You can look into these two songs however you want, but I still hold the future of the world in my hands, and my solution pit tells me that we will be here forever, and this right now is the war to end all wars. I also need to focus on peoples little problems, and there will be nothing to fix in the next three years, so everyone's wishes will be granted, just like the genie that Will Smith played.

The next part of the song, he says, "If I knew where this all started when this all would end, I think I would probably do it all over again." When he says this part, he is talking about the wildfires and how this has impacted me and all the bad things that ISIS is wishing on me (the American God). I would do it all over again. Why the f——k would I ever want to be in the position of self-vulnerability that I was in the past. When they came out with "Spaceman" and "Crash Your Party," those were the two scariest things that I have ever been through. The beginning parts in both parts were both great, but what comes afterward were so scary and ended up with me being in the hospital. This is why I am on that f——king Invega. The Invega is the worst med I am on right now, but because I mostly stay evened out, it's not affecting me like the bipolar meds were affecting me before. However, people started to know exactly who I was because of those two hospital visits, and everything I was going through was real.

I delete all the Hollywood songs that don't matter because everything I have been going through has been real. They started at the end and when I was attaining all my goals and achieving perfection. They saw when I got rich and when all my friends were back. I think they actually saw when we were all united into one big family. This is all I am going to say about this song for the time being.

The Killers, "Spaceman"—this song pretty much describes how I was going through hell, and I was very lonely for two years. Then, when January 1 hit in 2013, a lot of evil and devilish thoughts came to my mind. I was thinking about the worst things possible, but at the same time, this experience was also breaking me free from the wraths of society, so it felt pretty good. This obviously ended in a hospital visit, but it meant more than just a typical hospital visit. I also started gaining my powers in the world, taking over the sky, and when the weatherman predicts the weather all over the globe. This started developing into something special, and it was breaking people free all over the globe.

Karmin, "Crash Your Party"—about three weeks later, I was sent to the hospital again against my free will. Since the CIA hates when people act as God, I was sure it was them this time around. "Crash Your Party" has many different mixed signals inside this song. The most important part is me paying a price for possibly being God and paying a price for coming into this world and saying other people besides me deserve to pay a price. There is another part saying there are people that think we are all equal. Now the realists of the world know that this is not true or else we would all be famous and millionaires. There is another part of the song mentioning how complex I am. Now I know this is true because people assume that I am going to act a certain way or say a certain thing, when in actuality, I do something totally different than expected. This is frustrating, but it must have been my personality since I was born. It is hard to tell sometimes because I have gone through so many transformations.

There were many great things that came from this experience. First of all, I got many people to start believing in the full potential theory where nothing is impossible. Also, I started taking charge and control over the world. These two things don't happen overnight and are a work in progress, but I have made some significant progress with both of them, and I believe that for the most part, people are happier on a daily basis then they were three or four years ago.

B.o.B, "Past my Shades, ft. Lupe Fiasco"—Once again, this song has many different meanings to it. The first one that I want to address is that I am ahead of my time, just like Albert Einstein was. That is evidence of this book that I was able to put together and put it into play in people's lives. The other point I want to address is that people have been trying to dissuade my thoughts so that I can't reach my full potential in sports and smarts, pretty much since I was born. That must be the CIA doing this because I also picked up on the mixed messages from the movie series called *The Bourne Identity*. I have been telling myself within my own private thought process that I was born for a reason since I was in seventh grade. I also use this song to kill ISIS and to bring the troops back home.

Sum 41, "The Hell Song"—this song was made for everybody who fears growing old and for me to fix that problem. Pretty much, there was a point in my life where everywhere I would go, people were complaining about growing old and blah, blah, blah. There is one man that can fix that problem. That man is me. So with a little more time and patience, this problem will be fixed without too many problems. Whoever I am, whatever I stand for, I will provide this problem full throttle for everyone.

We came up with this solution thing called the solution pit. If people have problems, they throw it my way, and within a certain period of time, I guarantee I will be able to fix this problem. It is simple math, and with my movements and how I do what I do, it is classified but also efficient every day. The synopsis is that we will all be forever young. This was never what I chose. The choice was Adam's so that we would all believe in God, and he put me through all these tests so that we could make this world as a country and a world.

Another part that I wanted to mention in this song was that he said "with all these pictures" crossing my mind. I had one vision that I thought was Amber, but it ended up being Cardi B twerking on stage somewhere. I thought it was Amber, but it ended up being Cardi B, which I thought was interesting.

Atmosphere, "Hope"—this song is all about hope that is needed in this world, and it all comes back to me. I am finding all the signs to connect and putting them in this document. I am reading my favorite book every day since I was twenty-six. They are making more sense now. I did quit rapping and decided to get a life with my friends and family, which has turned out great. I watch the news every day and make sure that we can solve as many problems as we can as quickly as we can so that these issues are maintained. Also, the ways we wake up every day can change the outcome of an entire day.

In one phrase in his song, he put "I hope you have a great day, and I hope its tomorrow." So I try to get the most productive days possible every single day since I have gained my powers. There is another part of the song that says, "I hope you can let the star go." I believe he is talking about the north star which is the devil's star. It's scary to me, but believe it or not, I have dealt with a lot of terrible demon problems, but I am taking care of this every day by just simply answering prayers and helping others with their demon problems.

Shwayze, "Corona and Lime"—this song is about a brother and brother-in-law that might not get along, and if he does not like the way he acts around his sister, then we can settle this as men. I joke around that this song is about Gino and myself. We get along great, so this isn't a problem as I get along with most people pretty well. However, there are people that have significant issues with their brothers-in-law and sisters-in-law, but if they can just get past their flaws, I think they would enjoy life a little bit better.

Chiddy Bang, "4th Quarter"—this is a song that Chiddy Bang, the rapper, made in 2010 so that when I was starting to get life, I could play this song to motivate certain basketball players to pick up the pace during the crunch time of the NBA games in the fourth quarter. This worked hardcore this year in 2017 for many of the players. It worked the best for the MVP players, such as Isaiah Thomas and Stephen Curry. These two guys were built to pick up their play in the fourth quarter, and with proven efficiency this year, this should continue for the years to come. This theory is also going to work to decide games for football this year during the last two minutes of the game when the game is on the line. It was cool how it all started to work and how it played out.

Killers, "From Here on Out"—what this song pretty much talks about is that I was conquering a world of fear. As in like the movie says, "The sum of all fears" for my entire life, and once that trouble is gone, we will all reach the promised land in this lifetime. I was listening when my boy Ryan Bullock was talking about it and when Doug Baldwin, the wide receiver on the Seahawks, had their rationale for why we could all reach the promised land. This song also describes how friends are going to be hard to come by. I already have my base of friends, who I talk to and chill with regular enough. But this is also another obstacle for the human race for all of us to become friends with each other. We get closer to these goals every day that we are all alive.

What he means when the group says "from here on out" is that we are all destined to live for a very long time. Furthermore, there is a part of the song that describes how a "little birdy" had said that. This means whatever that godly symbol means, we all have to conquer this to be on the pursuit of happiness and to get what we all want. Literally, it is all within reach, but we need to grab it within ourselves to go the extra mile.

Fun, "Some Nights"—this song pretty resembles the struggles I have gone through since I have turned eighteen and the struggles of others. When he says, "This is it boys, this is war," he is talking about the Mafia, the 1 percent, the CIA, and the others that have been controlling us for all these years. Well, at least since we were all born. When Fun says, "Here they come to jack my style," he is talking about in all aspects of life. It is nothing I cannot overcome, and since I have the future of the human race at my disposal, it is actually pretty easy. A lot of it has to do with executing the baby steps as we all have to learn to do as a society. When the music group explains how I can use some friends for a change, it kind of coincides with the "From Here on Out" song by the Killers, saying that the little birdy said friends are going to be hard to come by. Friends are important to all of us, and I would like to believe that we are all friends living on the earth for the same reasons: to form one group of amazing people.

Offspring, "You're Gonna Go Far, Kid"—there is a reason why I was never concerned about making money after I went through all of my transformations. A lot of this reason was because of this song and the future that people in Hollywood saw for me. There are many points to this song. The first point is that I am indeed going to make a lot of money and have a great time doing it and will share it with my family, friends, and people that need it. The other point is the fact that the only reason George Mason went to the final four in 2006 was because of me. I guess it was the fear I was living in that I would have to dance in front of all the Greek life at Mason and my superhuman mind led George Mason, the underdog, to go to the final four that year.

The dancing part is a competition that is held at George Mason every year, and I volunteered myself to do part of the dancing part. I had mastered the dance, but I knew I would get stage fright when I saw all the people that were going to be watching me. The third part of this song that is important is developing trust in people. Nevertheless, the part of the song that says "Trust N'Sync" is there because they were going to have my back in this war for humanity and all of its elements. One of the more important parts of this song is the fact that he mentions if you cannot get what you want, then it is all because of me.

What he means by that is that since I was the one given the cure and the future of the world, I am going to work my ass off to help people out every minute of the day and supply my powers across the globe, and this is part of my job. The last part I wanted to mention is that Offspring says "It is a scene about me" because since everything has been proven to be for me, they made story after story with scenes after scenes of everything that I will and have accomplished and the funny parts of my life.

Ace Hood, "Get 'Em Up"—he is a rapper from Hollywood who released a song for the competition in the world that my cousin and myself were going to be going through in terms of making money. I figured that I would take care of the dirty parts, and he could be the guy going out there and selling the product. Life isn't fair, but I don't play by all the rules, so why would I care. I am gunning for those that are purposely making this process more difficult than it ever needed to be. My life is getting better every single day, but no excuses for us not making that much money when we have the perfect game plan.

Blink 182, "Wendy Clear"—now this is going to happen in one of two ways. Either we let North Korea get their way and build and use nuclear missiles or Donald Trump does what he does and I do what I do with the "Wendy Clear" song, which talks about tampering with nuclear missiles, and then it's an easy win for America. I still do not know who the Wendy girl is, but we will use her to the best of our abilities to make sure America is still safe. We have ships in the safe zone far away from North Korea to keep South Korea safe from North Korea, and the president of North Korea was complaining and said that he will take action against the US if they do not remove those ships. With how unpredictable we have been, I wouldn't do that if I were North Korea. Also, since I am the one with the future in our hands, I am pretty confident that North Korea would get f——ked up.

Katy Perry, "Last Friday Night"—this song is another song that has a lot of meaning to it. The first I wanted to illustrate was the fact that through everything everyone was going to go through that we still had to enjoy ourselves on the weekends, which has been inconsistent for all of us, but we still have friends that we are building over time. The second point I wanted to make was that it takes two to connect the dots. So all the connections that I talk about in this book are that it takes two people to do it the right way. I still have not figured out who the second person is, but it might be my fraternity brother, Dan Kortan. Since I have become as smart as I am today, it does not really matter who it is, but Kortan will work out fine.

The third point is that Katy Perry mentioned something about an epic fail since we were all given a bunch of tests to build us stronger character and morals for the future. Mine have been the hardest since I am the best, and one of my fails was telling Amber's roommate the second day of hanging out with her that there are too many ghetto Black people to play hoops on the courts in DC that she wanted to play at. I only said it because her roommate and her roommate's boyfriend said they judge other people and were happening to judge a Black person at the time.

When I do not talk with a filter, I never know what's going to come out of my mouth. Either way, I am looking at it as an unfair test, but Katy Perry mentioned that one in her song because there was no foul on my part, but it might've had consequences to other people's lives. Katy Perry also mixes in other parts in this song about her life and about potential in other people's lives in my immediate circle.

Watsky, "Sloppy Seconds"—again, there are a bunch of points in this song that I wanted to discuss. The first point is that Jonathan and myself need to clear out all the evil elements in the sky and replace them with beautiful elements and around our minds and so on to reach all of our goals and everything I talk about in this book. The second point is that no matter who you are or what you have been through, I will still love you when I start meeting new faces, and even with the people in my immediate life.

We have all made mistakes, but it's nothing that cannot be fixed with a little bit of Willpower. Watching the music video made me think of when the Detroit Tigers were a powerhouse in the Major Leagues. It could still happen again, but there wasn't much like it back in the day when Zumaya was throwing his 103 mph fastball that couldn't be touched and brought his team to the World Series that year.

Kid Cudi, "Day 'N' Night"—in this song, he is talking about myself and Adam. His main points in this song are that I created life, and Adam is the lonely stoner (Jesus) that was separated from society dealing with demon problems that he can't get past and only really trusts me in this world. Furthermore, Kid Cudi mentions that I created life and how cool I am and things of this nature. Kid Cudi also says that I cannot shake the shake, and involved in this shake is the new world we are trying to bring across to the people that believe in freedom and in God's free will. I can also try to control the weather, and sometimes I can do it with pretty good success. I can also hear when people pray to me, and sometimes I know who the person is, but I do not know what the prayers are, so I'll just do what I do to get it done, and *bam!* Their prayers are answered.

American Authors, "Believer"—in this song, they talk about the optimistic things in life. In one of their verses, they said that when "we were talking about getting older," it was bringing me under. It was one time when Shaker said, "Do you think your planter fasciitis is a forever thing when we were around twenty-seven?"

I kind of rolled my eyes and looked to the right, so my answer was going to be insecure. Anyway, my planter fasciitis will not be a forever thing. He also says in this song that I am a little bit sheltered and a little bit scared. I wish I had more opportunities to leave my house and hang out with friends more often, but until those opportunities arise, I will just keep on plugging along every day. But when he wrote this song, I was very sheltered and very scared. Now my fears are pretty much going away, and I know how to manage them now, and I am more active with friends and family than I was when I was twenty-seven and twenty-eight. Another line he input into this song is that "I am a little bit nervous I am going nowhere." I have been working on business plan after business plan for the past three or four years with minimal success. I am still very hopeful and optimistic that they will work, and I can overcome this adversity and make it in the real world with all these big expectations.

Next, he says I am a little bit jealous, slow, and hurtful. I can be hurtful when I talk without a filter and say things that I really don't mean. I am a little bit slow because sometimes it takes my mind and my brain a few seconds to register what the person next to me has said, and to respond, sometimes you need quicker reaction speed. Lastly, he says I am a little bit jealous. I am jealous sometimes because people have been living their lives while I am at home, not doing much on a Friday or Saturday, and I am jealous that I do not have a girlfriend, but these things will get better with time, so it's nothing to really worry about.

To go along with my last point, he says "I get a little bit angry when everyone's around, but I get lonely when no one's out." I get lonely when I am out and about at night, but when no one is around, then it sucks. He also said, "I get a little bit angry when everyone's around" because I am upset that I haven't been able to feel my alcohol in the right ways since I was twenty-five, ever since I started dealing with my first demon issues.

The third point has to do with cars. There is a solution that the 1 percent or the CIA or even the Mafia have in mind for us. This includes enjoying cars for their main purpose. These include: road trips, family gatherings, and other necessary things. This does not include adding all this unnecessary bullshit that people love to put on their cars just for the hell of it like rims and tinted windows. The fourth point of this song is that in order to be a part of this new society that we are created for, you need to have a story of some sort. Mine is clear, and this book is the clarity for that. However, everyone else needs to step up to the plate and have a great foundation for the future based on what they have been through.

The last point goes to that whole solution thing. Who is doing things for the right reasons and who isn't? Watsky says, "Everyone and their mom can hear the drama that's happening behind these thin walls." It doesn't matter whom the other person or group of people is, but people need to be aware of these types of things.

Starley, "Call on Me"—this song originated when we started looking at all of our fates when I was twenty-six years old, and I was sent to the hospital against my own will. One point of this song is what do we do when the help doesn't come? Then are we supposed to suffer? I started making this more of a group effort every single day that we are all still alive, but I am still the main focal point behind all of this. So we need to find a way to cheat and keep the right people alive forever with everything that we have at hand.

The signs that connect and the people that are responsible for helping me out are key to all of this. The second point in all of this is that I am the one people can rely on when they need someone. She says, "Can't stop their tears from falling down." I have gone out of my way so many times to help people out, and I know how thankful they all are that I am still alive and I have the ability to do what I've been doing behind the people's backs that have been living healthy this entire time without seeing the pain that I have been seeing. The part of this whole experiment that I do not like is that it has been bringing me down every f——king day. Every day, things are still getting in my way, but there is nothing I can do about it because I have the power and strength to answer to people, and I cannot just leave them stranded.

POD, "Youth of the Nation"—what this song resembles is the fact that all of under, say the age of forty, are part of the youth of the nation. We need to unite and stand up for everything that we stand for, including our flag of sin, which is a saying in another song that was in *Pitch Perfect 2*. The people that I have formed connections with over the past thirty years and the outsiders that I have formed connections with over the past five years need to unite, and we need to start acting as if we don't give a f——k and f——k all the rules that people in our society try to put on us. I believe in all the freedoms that we are given, and nobody and no group of people and no other countries have the right to take that away from us. This is all part of us unifying into one big group of people that have passed all these crazy tests that we have given.

This part I wrote before, I started opening up my mind and seeing the endless possibilities. I am going to add to what I already wrote in this song. The first part I wanted to mention in this song besides what I already wrote was "call me blind," but I didn't see it coming. He is talking about all those tests that were run on me when I was twenty-four or twenty-five years old. When Johnny Richter said, "Look a man in his eyes and never, never say die," he is talking about when I ran onto my driveway when people were terrorizing me when I was playing video games and my dad was in the room. I ran out to my driveway and said something like, "You wanna f——k with me? Come out and show your face."

The next day, the worst day of my entire life happened. The invisible pains started inside of me. I had my mom call the ambulance, and they didn't detect that anything was wrong with me. It was invisible and nondetectable. It was like things were wrong with me, but nothing in the system could detect that anything was wrong. I think that Adam did this to me, and then he forgot all about it. It went away that night after I was in the hospital for about five hours, and they kept on quizzing me about my bipolar and depression symptoms.

Looking back at all the crazy things that were happening to me back then, it seems insane, but now, I know that it was all real. Nowadays, people in Hollywood are like, "Maybe karma will catch up with him." I am stuck pretty deep, but I think I know what do to with my powers, and I had once said, "Fix me, and I'll fix everything else." The things in my solution pit are all real, and I delete every one of Hollywood's songs that don't make sense to me or just don't make sense to the world. Jeff will lose it all, and so will my dad. Once karma catches up with me and I surpass Jeff and my dad in back-to-back years, then we will see the light at the end of the tunnel.

The next part of the song, he says maybe this kid was reaching out for love, or for a minute, maybe he forgot who he was, whatever it was, I know it because, he leaves out certain things in this part of the song. Maybe he forgot who he was. He is talking about being God or Jesus. I can't believe because that is one of the biggest sins of the Bible that if Jesus was resurrected, you're not supposed to admit that you are him. There are so many people that thought they were, but none of them went through the apocalyptic things that I went through. This is why Atmosphere put in his song that Will admits that it's not that complex, just a big popularity contest.

Apparently, I did win that popularity contest, so mission complete. I can't believe because it is a sin to the world. The next part of the song, he says, "Little Suzie was only twelve and was given every chance in the world to excel." He is talking about my ex-foster sister, Susan. She was around twelve when we took her in, and my parents almost adopted her and Donald if their aunt didn't get in the way. Their dad committed suicide when they were in our care, and the things that Donald was going through back then were so scary, and his whole body would be like fainted or paralyzed because of the pain he was feeling with the loss of his dad. He ended up joining the military, and I think he is doing really well now with two kids and things like that. I talked to him through social media a few years back, and maybe we can connect at some point in the future, but this is what POD is talking about when he says this part in the song.

The next part of the song I wanted to mention was that he said he crossed a line and there's no turning back. He is talking about me again. When I started getting stuck deep and saw how overpopulated the world is, sometimes I'll take chunks out of my day to kill the flesh. Nothing's going to stop me but divine intervention. I am sick and tired of the way things have been, so if you are in my way, then get the f——k out of my way and let me fix the world and put you inside your grave because you have been deemed worthless to society. There are too many people that don't bring anything to the table, so why the f——k are they still alive? They are just wasting valuable resources in the world, and we don't need your bullshit and nonsense in this world anymore.

I started eliminating people who put me in that devilish game, but now it's just fun because I feel a certain adrenaline rush when I go into those mindsets when I play "Bye-bye-bye" and "Complicated" and "X" and "Simple As." It's a rush that most people would never experience in their lifetime, but whatever, I am in control of the world, so if you don't bring any value to it, then f——king die. I never chose this path, and I never thought that I would get stuck this deep, but I know the heavens are right above us, so if anyone tells me (Jeff) that it depends on what you've done, then you are wrong because you are the only heathen in the world, so f——king leave me alone. I mean, like, get the f——k out of my life.

The next part of the song, he says, "Who is to blame for all the life that the tragedies claimed?" This is a tricky part because I don't blame it on me, obviously. I don't blame it on my dad and I definitely don't blame it on Adam. If anyone is to blame, it would be Jeff. He is the easy target because of his personality, and the three of us bring way more to the table than that devil does. They came out with a lot of songs that somebody is going to pay, but that somebody will definitely not be me. In each song, they put out people's names, but the most common name they put out was Jeff. I think he played the key role in playing games with me in the past, so I think that Hollywood says that he is to blame.

The next part of the song, he says, "I'm tired of all the lies, it's the blind leading the blind." When he says I'm tired of all the lies, it's because once Hollywood made this way too hard, and then the professional athletes made this way too hard, there were a lot of lies that were flying in the sky and through people's mouths. I was lied to a lot in the past, but a lot of lies were done to my face. Jeff and Allyn kept on saying that Romy is a liar, but he's never lied to me, so I have no idea what they are talking about. Adam lied to me a lot also back then, so maybe he is to blame as well. When I said underneath my breath that you dug your own hole, lying to a dude, he scratched his face. I can catch people with their lies and especially with their truths because I hold the future of the world in my hands, and nobody is going to take that away from me until the world is perfectly fixed.

I had no idea, but Amber even played a role in this devilish game. She said she gets confused with her yesses and nos, and she was throwing up a lot. I was being shaken with my head, yes and no, a lot back when I was younger, and she was obviously a part of that. She was throwing up because she was also making me throw up in the past. I don't know who else was putting me through this hell, but those are the specific people I wanted to mention.

Hopsin said in his song that he is ashamed, and he played his role in this devilish game. I hate that fun song when he says, "This one isn't for the folks at home" because a lot of people did much of this bullshit to me to make me go through all of this hell. When he says, "It's the blind leading the blind," this all comes with the fact that you can't teach an old guy new tricks, and some say we are never meant to grow up. It's two idiots or three idiots devising plans to save the world, just like they had in many movies. One of the movies is *Dumb and Dumber*, and another one is the *Night at the Roxbury*. Those are just two examples.

I was never too smart of a guy until recent memory. Sometimes I still act stupid and don't really like when people take themselves too seriously. Adam thinks his whole life revolves around himself, and that is part of the reason why he is always by himself. People with creative minds can write a document like this, and that is why I was about to write this book which will be two hundred pages long, and then I will save it, put it on my external hard drive, and continue writing on another document.

The next part of the song, he says, "Will it ever make sense? Somebody's gotta know, there's got to be more to life than I thought exists." Somebody's gotta know what the f——k is going on in the world, and that is evidenced by this document. There was another movie they came out with called the *Book of Eli* and another movie called *Silver Linings Playbook*. Those are two movies that called out it was inevitable that I was going to write this book. There has to be more to life than I thought existed. He is talking about heaven on earth and the limitless possibilities. The one day when it was just Chloe, my mom, and me at home, I experienced heaven on earth. Like I put in another part of this document, people said that in heaven, it's something like one minute is like a thousand years, and a thousand years is like one minute. That is exactly how I felt that day.

When G-Eazy put in his song that I am on some kind of drug, he is talking about my uncontrollable laughter. It has something to do with our systems and the environment and the clouds and how it's all interconnected with our bodies to put us on those other levels. Ludacris was on TV on *SportsCenter* and was like, "I am living my dreams, are you guys living your dreams?" Then he pointed at the screen and he said, "Are you living your dream?" He was talking about the movie *Entourage*. The Imagine Dragons came out with this song afterward, "Who do you think you are, dreaming of becoming a big star?"

People said that Vince isn't the hottest out of the four in that group, but he is the star. They made this script because I am the one of the group that makes sure that everything is interconnected, and Ludacris is one of the people in the world who is making me.

Taylor Swift, "Out of the Woods"—this song has a special meaning to it. The message she is delivering is to help out those in need, whether it is a soldier in need over in Iraq or someone in debt with loan sharks, to help them out with a little bit of willpower and songs and telekinesis. She also mentions in this song how we were meant to fall about and come together again. What she means by this is that as a society and as friends and former friends, we should all reunite to be one again, hopefully sometime in the near future.

B.o.B, "Airplanes"—there is corruption in the sky, whether it's the CIA or the Mafia, but they fly planes at night to survey the population. I use this song, "Airplanes," to answer wishes from people. Whether that is with sports betting or for a new car or for a new raise, I am here for people if they need me. One part of this song explains that you sit by your phone and hope the "never" people call you back. I've been dealing with evil people calling me for some time now and am patiently waiting for it to end. Anyway, this is a good tactic to push the world in the right direction to answer these different wishes that people have, and I answer the prayers that are more necessary first, then put the other ones on the backburner.

Jason Mraz, "I'm Yours"—in this song, he further explains why Billy Joel had said that only the good die young. He mentions that our name is our virtue, so I believe the cut off age for this is sixty-six. If you make it until you are fifty-nine or sixty, then you know you are doing something good with your life. He also mentions in this song that inside my heart, you will only find love, unless you disrespect me, then I have no guarantees you will pass the tests needed for the future of the world. I want to further elaborate on this last sentence. He mentions certain people's parts in my world in this song. He says, "Well, you better done me and you better have felt it." He is talking about my dad. He put me through some hellish tests when I was younger, and I am not sure if he even remembers those tests. I think that I am actually God because my dad doesn't understand the meanings of things and the exact reason why we are here on earth right now like I do. He has been through a lot in recent memory, but that will all change once I start to take control over life, and he gives it up because he and Jeff just don't deserve to stay in the world like I do.

I don't think either of those two are real and can't open their eyes and see the world the way that I can. "I tried to beat you but you're so hard that I melted." He is talking about Adam. I am not sure if this is entirely true, though, because the next part of his song, he says, "I fell right through the cracks, and now I am trying to come back." Who else could he be talking about bedsides Adam? He is the lonely boy from *Gossip Girl* and really doesn't have anybody else he can turn to besides me.

These two parts of the song I think are mixed messages, and in my opinion, Hollywood laid the lice in me, and they know there is nothing left to fix in the world. I think that Adam might have done some of those devilish things to me in the past, but I think a lot of people did. I thought I was the devil until one of their artists said, "Maybe karma will catch up with him," and they came out with several other songs that said that karma is going to catch up with me.

The next part of the song, he says, "Before the cool run, I will try to give it my bestest." In this part of the song, he is either talking about Allyn or Shaker. I have known these two guys since college, and it was always the three of us conquering the world together and getting drunk and doing stupid shit together. There were always other characters in my life that added spice, but when Jason Mraz came out with this song, he was talking about these specific people. I think that my friend, Tim Cogswell, also plays a part in this song. Maybe he is the one who is trying to come back, and Adam tried to beat me. I think that Adam looked me in the eyes and told me to die several times, and I do not think I am wrong about that. I think when he says I am trying to come back, he is talking about Cogswell.

There are several songs that say that Adam is going to die at some point before this is all said and done. Sia even said that it is hard to lose a chosen one, and she is talking about Adam. I am pretty sure that he is the only person in the world who tried to beat me. I don't think anybody else in the world would wish harm on me besides maybe ISIS because they would be attacking America's God. The next part of the song, he says, "Nothing's going to stop me but divine intervention." All these probably unnecessary deaths in the world were caused by me. I look at the world, and I see a lot of people walking and talking without a purpose. I am still eliminating people in the world who dealt with me or are still dealing with me so I can win in fantasy and so I can win in other aspects in my life.

Atmosphere put in one of his songs that nobody befriends the beast to pay rent and make ends meet, so I have been eliminating some of those people, and Adam even once said, "I am still going to be friends with you," so I am pretty sure that he tried to beat me. I know what that Jesus bullshit is all about, and sometimes I just really f——king hate it. The statues built inside of us are f——king annoying, and when I try to laugh, sometimes it's like a sin to the world because Jesus is a f——king statue, and he just stares at us. When he also is talking about "Nothing is going to stop me but divine intervention," it also means the drama and the conflicts that people try to bring into my life.

The next part of the song, he says, "Open up your eyes and see like me, open up your plans and damn your free." This is what I was talking about before. They constantly bring me down, so I am looking forward to all the people who have one-upped me because they love me to see me shine and not let them two bring me down anymore. When he says open up your plans, this means that the people that are currently in my life and other people from the past who are going to enter my life will have me on their go-to list, just like they did before because I never chose this path, and I didn't realize what I was. In "The Hell Song," Sum 41 says everybody has their problems, everybody says the same thing to you, and it doesn't matter how you solve them. I guess maybe I am God because I don't think anybody else in the world is. I am looking forward to not being so lonely all the time and my friends coming back into my life instead of living at my parents all the time.

I made a list of my favorite people in the world, whether this is a friend of my current and past, athletes, people from Hollywood, or outsiders that I meet in the streets or outside my house. This list was originally devised my connecting the dots and signs that I came across in my solution box, and another part of this was to give these people more say in the world. This list also includes random people I have seen on the news to give them more say in the world because the people on this list actually get more say, in my opinion. I want people to keep in mind that none of this is happening randomly, and this is part of the keys to the future of the world. To continue on this paragraph, it says we are just one big family, and it's our God who says love, loved, love, loved. When he says loved, he is talking about Jeff, and that is why I keep on disrespecting Jeff. It's not my fault, but he was disrespecting me pretty badly, and he lost all that respect from a lot of people in the world because of his own actions. I stopped making that list because I was sick of people overriding my say in the world when they didn't go through the shit and have no idea what the f——k they are saying when I am more right than they are.

Therefore, he says, I won't hate because Jeff is all hate, and I am all love. I will stop hating on people, but I have really been through hell and fell into this rut by mistake. Jeff is the devil, not me, so he should have paid the prices that I have been paying. He lost it all, and everything he does in this world doesn't mean anything.

Kid Cudi, "Pursuit of Happiness"—this song relates to me because I feel like I have been on the pursuit of happiness for a long time now. Making it by rebelling against the system isn't easy, and I have had hopes and dreams of becoming a millionaire/billionaire for a long time now. With the help of the people around me, especially

Romy and Ray, whom I expect to make it big with, I hope to reach this millionaire status in the next few years. We have come up with a lot of different unique ideas that can further our dreams and make us rich if we would just follow through on them. I need them because I am not really good with selling products, and they can bullshit with the best of them, so I am expecting them to get out of their own way and help me make this happen!

I wanted to add to this song. In Sum 41's song, they said some say we are never meant to grow up, and it is too late to live with faith, and time is up to make your choice. Kid Cudi obviously picked me instead of Jeff. So, in this song, he said you don't really know about anything, talking about Jeff. He also said that you don't care about the trials about tomorrow and you'd rather lay in your bed full of sorrow. A lot of girls have done different things in my presence to meet their soul mates and find their partners, so that pretty much covers the fact that I am laying in my bed, full of sorrow.

Will Smith said that the scripts were written for the general population to enjoy, but they were also loosely based off my life. So I have been on the pursuit of happiness for the longest time. Now it's time for the people around me to come through for me and hopefully sooner than later.

Kid Cudi, "Simple As"—this song was written so that the athletes could prosper, and the people that were causing conflict in the world would be eliminated. Every time I play this song, eight people die. Whoever they are is determined by fate, and we get the rewards of these people not being alive anymore. They added Common in this song, saying, "As our hero seems to be dreaming in peace." Common was talking about me and that these people are useless and are deemed to be not needed in our new society that we are creating.

Timbaland, "Throw It On Me"—this song relates to me because people can throw their problems into my solution pit, and I can try to resolve these problems as soon as possible or I can make it happen for people right now. If there are problems in people's lives, I believe there are solutions that can be made to solve these problems. I am a man of miracles and also believe that science can solve problems, so if anyone has anything that needs to be resolved, you can throw it into my solution pit, and I can help you out with your issues.

Grits, "Ooh Ahh"—let's just say that I am, in fact, Jesus, and the Grits put out a song pretty much talking about my life. He talks about the price I have had to pay since I was reborn. The prices have been pretty brutal at times, like the highs and lows that I have experienced and things of that nature. He also talks about fingertips. I think he is talking about getting rid of the demons of the world by me cutting my nails. That was the only thing I could come up with for this part of the song. Since a lot of people are unpredictable and I stay evened out, he also mentioned that people should be more like me. I wouldn't have any problems with that because sometimes people aim to impress too much, and that's not me. I always just try to act like myself and be kind and nice to people. He also talks about how explosive I can be. I have had anger problems that have calmed down over the years, but that's in the past and now. Like I mentioned earlier in this paragraph, I try to stay evened out.

He also mentioned in this song about the tears of feeling what love once was. I went about eight years without a girlfriend. So when I connected with Amber after not being with a girl for a long time, it took me a while to understand how love works again. The last part I wanted to mention about this song was that he says, "Here comes the boy from the capital city." A bunch of the songs that Hollywood has put out includes us forming one in the future. I am the key for all this to happen the right way. So I can do this from the stages in Hollywood, and I think this might be the only way for everyone in America and even to get other countries involved for us to form a united front.

Pink, "Please Don't Leave Me"—I just play this song to save lives of people that are in danger and that need help. Every time Pink says, "Please don't leave me," I save one life that could have been lost. I found this a good activity to perform during my free time instead of wasting time drinking or playing video games. I also like to read books to learn more about the world, and I read books on all sorts of different topics. Nevertheless, I have saved countless lives by just playing this song. Whether people have cancer or if kids are in need, it still works.

Spose, "Alternative Radio"—I was put through a test where I was living in fear, and the radio was pretty much killing my mind, and I was in fear of dying because of the devil. So I created this game based off Spose's song called "Alternative Radio" that when certain songs are played or certain people talk on the radio, it saves lives. Furthermore, every time he says the words "Alternative Radio," it saves someone's life. I thought this would be a fun activity to do during my free time, and it works very well.

Will Smith, "Switch"—I use this song to regulate people that have had car accidents in recent paths. There is a key part to this song that says, "Hit it," as in hit the brakes so that you can avoid getting in more accidents. The switch parts that our personalities are intertwined makes it so that people can tolerate each other without getting in fights. There is too much animosity in this world, and life would go along much smoother if people got along with each other better. I like to exercise my mind when I play this song and just let the music do the talking. It's a fun exercise for me, and I think that people have benefitted from me playing this song.

Jason Mraz, "Remedy"—the definition of *remedy* is a medicine or treatment for a disease or injury. I think the point of Jason Mraz releasing this song was for a cure for the human race. Nobody has had it easy, and I believe that as a society, we can fix our problems with science and faith. Science can push us in the right direction, but if our prayers aren't being answered, then what do we all stand for? Maybe by releasing this song, he also meant that we can stay forever young, and this is the cure that we all need to make this happen. Let us die young or live forever.

Kid Cudi, "Alive"—I use this song to get the world in the right direction each night. He says that I am a "beast" in the night, meaning that he takes over the nighttime fears in people. But it's not like the devil. Think of this as like a Superman character that fixes issues people are having by supernatural effects. If people can't see it, they can't prove it. I also use this song to fix the games of the MLB. Furthermore, if the scores end in four or five, then the result is because of Seaman or my dad. If the game ends in five, then it is because of my dad. If the game ends in four, then it's because of Seaman.

I know there is a rule that says "Deal with the devil at your own risk." So if people are still doing this, then I use this song to remove people from society and shrink the population a little bit. At some point, people need to learn their lesson that what comes around goes around, so tough shit if bad karma hits you.

B.o.B., "Nothing on You"—this song talks a little about my past and my current life. Some of the games that were played on me in my past were "for better or for fun." Another part was that Shaker used to be like me and only wanted one woman instead of being a womanizer. He would purposely go out to meet girls, and that wasn't my style, so I would just stay in. A third part was that Adam ended up with no money, which made my attempts of making money harder because he used that against me, and the timeliness of everything have to be perfect for this to work the right way, and Adam sort of f——ked that up by being greedy, and he is still broke. The last part of this past and future that B.o.B. mentions in this song is that I ended up losing my own personal bets and in my own life because I was doing so much for other people who weren't really returning the favor, so at some point, I am going to start focusing on myself again so that I can be happy.

They say that people that do the most for other people end up lonelier when they go out of their way to help others as opposed to the more greedy people in the world. Another part of this song focuses on when the scripts were written by Hollywood with me being the main character in most of them, and this has to with Wonder Woman. She is going to help me end the war overseas, but in the meantime, I can just do it on my own. This is so important because we need world peace, and there are people in the world that do not make this easy, and these people need to be taken care of in other forms. The last part of the song I want to mention is that three old people die every time I play this song because they are probably just wasting their time on the planet anyway.

Hallie Steinfeld, "Let Me Go"—I use this song to kill eleven old people that are just wasting their time on the planet. This world is too overpopulated, so we figured we would just kill the flesh.

Brittney Spears and TI, "Gimme More"—this song has a few different meanings behind it. First off, they mentioned that I know how to act now, so if we are still aiming for the full potential theory, then I can be a decent or a good actor when the time is right. Another part of the song mentions that if Christians are on a mission, then you have my permission to spread the Word of Christ. The next part of the song mentions that I got rich, so instead of working the nine-to-five bullshit work, I went off on my own and ended up getting rich besides all the adversity I have faced to get to that point. I am hoping to start up something with Ray, Romy, or Adam, but it will pick up at some point and last forever. Furthermore, they say that they are believers because Fort Minor came out with a song that I would be in a maze that I can never escape, and I have been fighting my way to escape this maze, and it's working every day.

Every day is a success that we are all still alive, and I work my ass off to get out of the maze; not like Adam ever cared about what I was going through because all that kid cares about is himself. So I am happy that I am hanging out with people that actually care about me now. Additionally, me and Marcus are going to play two-on-two basketball against other people in the world, just like the scripts were written with *White Men Can't Jump*. I think it would be cool if we could get a tournament going that would last across the United States and maybe even in the entire world.

Sum 41, "Makes No difference"—this song was released to let me know that it makes no difference to me whether I am Jesus or the devil. I deleted that "Some Say We're Never Meant to Grow Up" song because I was stuck so deep that I realized that I wasn't the devil. So Sum 41 released a song saying that it makes no difference to me. He said in the song that "I am missing," as in God is missing on his targets, and I am supposed to clean up this mess because we have the power back. He said, "You're all wearing thin" in this song, meaning that everyone to me seems fake at some point because of the fake sarcasm and the way people act around other people. At parties and when strangers enter people's lives and larger groups, people start to act differently, and it is really annoying to me since I get life and I don't act fake or deal with fake shit anymore. The pains that I have been feeling have not been meant to hurt me but to cure the human race.

Like what Danny Elfman said in his song, "I have a box full of tricks at my disposal, and I have the human race under control." In this song, Sum 41 also mentions that there is nothing left to fix. So nothing's ever been perfect in human history, but we are going to take this way too far, so that I can understand what is going on in the world and will at some point, hopefully sooner than later, have nothing left to fix. He also says "You can't ignore" as in for the people who have witnessed all the pain I've been through to help me during this time of adversity. For example, I am kindly asking people to help my meds work the right way again and put me on my path to perfection.

Furthermore, he said, "Now that you're older, there's more weight on your shoulders." What he means by this is that I was too young until I turned thirty years old to realize what the main problems of the world were. Now I get things a lot more clearly and can fix some of these issues that couldn't be resolved before. He also says in this song that I can't seem to keep things so perfectly straight as in I self-destruct about two times per day. That is noticeable to an outside audience or to the people in my life. This can be fixed, but it just needs more time, I guess. Another part in this song is that the songs they release are so basic because there was another rapper who said that shit's getting deeper and that people are paranoid to avoid the Grim Reaper. They started at the end of this cycle, so they don't want me to be in pain or fear anymore and that it has nothing to do with trying to avoid running into me. I downloaded the live version of this song, so in this song, when he was performing in London, he said, "Everyone, look behind you." And the crowd looked behind and saw me. After this happened, they all cheered, but I was clueless at the time, but now I get it.

Xzibit, "Spit Shine"—He says in this song, "Fight the good fight, don't need no help" as if we have the power back from the highest power. It all started with how Hollywood and whoever else poisoned me and when I started thinking clearer. I understood what people's needs were a little bit better. He also says, "Defend your-selves" in this song, meaning for our soldiers overseas to come home safely. Furthermore, he says, "Move like I move and live life long." Again this was how I was poisoned, and because of all my transfor-mations, I am able to focus and work out and get my mind clear and, hopefully, we can remain forever young. In this song, Xzibit says, "Can't move up if your heart's not strong."

I created this list of whose had it the hardest throughout their entire lives and who brings the most value to society, and Xzibit is saying that you have to prove your worth to even be on this list. He says in this song, "Don't f——k with gay shit, so that means I can't f——k with you now." He is saying that I am Jesus, and Jesus was gay or something like that. I don't remember exactly, but I put that in his song so that I would realize what I might stand for in this society.

In addition, he says, "With the people involved in what I was going through." He says, "Let one nigga talk everyone getting caught for sure." He was talking about Adam and him coming clean when I was hanging out with him. He was also talking about his father and the empire that made me go through the chaos I was going through. They have been following my story for a long time now, so he says I should tuck my tail and jump the fence.

This happened when I was coming home from work that one day when I thought the KGB and CIA were attacking me, but I think it was the Mafia. Then he says, "The f——k never ran from it," meaning I am still alive and never left the area since then, but now I am so goal-oriented and focused on the future, so there really is no sense on holding grudges, but I just wish that Adam would be a better friend. I put Xzibit ahead of the list before DMX and Dr. Dre, so he mentions their names in this song, meaning that he belongs higher and more successful than they are. I believe this is the meaning of the song that Xzibit released that was on Eminem's *8-Mile* soundtrack.

Kid Rock, "Bawitdaba"—in this song, he says, "These are for the questions that have no answers." What he means by this is that if I was ever, which I think will happen, to talk in front of everyone or a big group of people that some things in life just don't have any answers. If your loved ones have died for any reason, don't blame it on me. He says "all the crackheads" which my therapist and I were talking about that if I was to give them money that they should use it for good causes that would benefit their lives, not on things that would make them self-destruct. Then he goes, "All you bastards at the IRS" because they take our money without any known reason, and they are just annoying to a lot of people because they take our taxes away, and people want that money. Next he says, "For the crooked cops," which is a very good point because there are a lot of them, and they are corrupt and shouldn't be doing the things that they are doing.

In this song, despite what Xzibit is saying, he says that Empires are full of love, so everything that they have done to and for me has been to make me a better person, not to cause intentional harm.

Furthermore, in this song, he says, "For the time bomb's ticking." What he means by this is the time ticking on the clock and how we can stop it. I think I know how to, but it has to be this year, no later than my thirty-fifth birthday. They also mention this in *Mr. Robot*, like the ticking time bombs he says in this show. Next, he says, "And DB Cooper and the money he took." I'm pretty sure he's talking about the CIA, and then he ran away, and they haven't caught him, or maybe they have by now. I do not know.

What I do know, though, is that they put it in the show *Prison Break* as a character that was on the run and never wanted to get caught. The last part of this song, he says, "For all the hate means war." He is talking about ISIS and whoever else in this world that brings hate to it.

Will.i.am. (Black Eyed Peas), "One Tribe"—this song is pretty much saying how our ship is sinking like crazy, but at one point, the eager was threatened by the one, which is me. He is talking about all the games that I fell for and how they created this new society that we are trying to build through me. In this song, he says that we are one planet, one race, so that everything in this world is equal and everyone deserves an equal say in this world, even if you're poor, rich, or what you've been through, as long as you are willing to make changes to better the world. We don't care about the color of your eye, the tone of your skin, or your face. There are too many judgmental people in the world and racists, so it's now 2019. It's time to get over the fact that people are different than you are.

Furthermore, all main ideas are connected like a sphere. So what he means by this is that the Internet connects the globe, and we can control the skies and people's lives by connecting within each other. He says there is no propaganda to upper hand us, so this means that the greed and antics of the very upper class like the fifty richest people in the world won't dictate how we live our lives and like the amatse won't control our lives anymore. Will.i.am. says, "Man, I'm loving this peace" because he probably saw after the fact that the wars overseas are over, and people are starting to unite into one big family. He says, "If I have had any enemy, then my enemy is going to try to kill me." This is why G-Eazy says we only pray for more ends while you hope for the best. The Twenty One Pilots came out with the song "Heathens," saying that we can smell your intentions. If you have bad intentions in mind, then we don't want you a part of this new world that we are trying to create.

Whoever these people are have told me that so many different people in the world are evil and to forget about all of this because they are all lies. I don't know who these people are, but I'm sure that he does. Additionally, he says that there are too many things that are making people forget to focus on the main cause. Some of these problems might be like your little miniscule problems that people things are big problems when you have people like me that are trying to save the world every day.

Another problem is that people are so greedy that they only care about their own self-interests instead of helping out other people because that is how we are supposed to be. He says, "Use your mind and not your greed." This is what I am trying to explain to my therapist every week. I have provided the needs of people all across the globe when they are in need. There are so many people that just care about their own lives and aren't adding value to this society. Then he says, "But we know that the one (meaning Will Coakley)" was vulnerable to these attacks by outsiders that wanted to get to know me better. So some people in Hollywood were trying to separate me from everyone else so that I can understand that we have a war to overcome and that we are going to be here forever and to not let people's greed and the evil inside of us get me down.

Freedom exists when we all become one, forever. Then he goes on to say that we are connected like the Internet, united, that's how we do. This gives a lot of people more say in the world, especially if I am following you or if you are following me. In addition, he says we need to overcome the complications because we need to. This is where faith comes into play. It's hard for me to believe sometimes because of all the terrible things that I've been through, but in my own personal life, I am really close to peaking at my age limit, and I am doing things right. The question is, though, are other people repeating my steps and doing what they need to be doing to make the world a better place?

You need to look in the mirror and see if you are doing things to better the society or if you are making the world a worse place. For me, he is telling me that we are all just people, so I shouldn't hold grudges if people don't meet my expectations and aren't as good as I am in the world. However, there are so many shitty things that people have done to me that it is really hard for me to trust people a lot of the time. Sometimes people are reliable and are there for me, but most times, I am by myself, and in my opinion, people just aren't meeting my expectations.

I'll start trusting people again when they've earned that trust. Until then, I will just progress for myself and do what I do every day to make sure that the world is on track for all these things to come together.

Danny Elfman, "The Little Things"—this song was on the soundtrack for the movie *Wanted* and for a reason. These guys that have been training me to be the person I am going to be in the future are working hard every day to make sure I pass these tests with con-sequences for people we do not want alive anymore and for successes for the people that are doing right in the world. In this song, he says that bad things come in twos. This is a true statement because it was always a lie that bad things come in threes. I know that the devil wants bad things to come in threes, but we are actually now trying to make bad things come in ones. Good things come in threes, and bad things come in twos.

Every day, it's a battle because you have to fight the evil to make things right in this world. In addition, he says but I never knew about the little things. Every single day, things get in my way, whatever those things are, but I am looking forward to more positivity instead of all these demons that are trying to steer me the wrong way. I don't know what it is, but it is really f——king annoying, and I am sick of it. I am not a fighter, but I want to make the person pay who is making my life so f——king hard. In this song, he says, "Someone has to pay for the little things," meaning that someone (Jeff) has to be for the people that have been casualties of society.

Next, he says, "I am through with the stars," meaning that I am no longer looking at the stars in the sky for help, and I am just relying on what we have in the real world because back in the day, when I was clueless about the world, I was roaming around my neighborhood, looking at the sky and following false orders from people who I probably shouldn't have trusted, and I am slowly finding out who did what, but I know that everyone has a reason to say, "Put the past away."

This was a part of song I just picked up on, that I am walking and talking. I have been spending so much time in my house and being antisocial, but a lot of that was because I kept on self-destructing and was only allowed to leave my house for a certain amount of time every time I would leave my home base. Now Hollywood has moved past that part, and I am a part of the community again and talking control like I was trained to.

Danny Elfman is telling me that it's got nothing to do with God. This would mean that the fear and my issues in life had nothing to do with anything that might be above us. I heard my first voice when I was twenty-five, and it said, "It's the CIA." For some reason, I do not think it was the CIA, and if God was alive right now, then he wouldn't age past the age of twenty-five. Hollywood has put out a lot of songs about karma catching up with me, and it will at some point, hopefully soon. People are throwing things inside my solution pit so that I will know exactly what to do with it and fix the world's problems. For instance, there won't be another war in human history.

Donald Trump is now good with North Korea, and that is not because of Trump. It's because of the scripts that were written and because of everything I am doing at my house. People said that World War II was the war to end all wars, but there have been more wars since then, so I don't know why people say that. Now there is a war with the Middle East, which will end at a certain point, but I just don't know when. Hollywood knows, and I think Carly Lloyd knows, but we will see when that war comes to an end.

Furthermore, Danny Elfman says, "I am through with the pairs." This means that we kill the flesh, and the pairs are irrelevant since there are so many things that can be paired, but he is mostly talking about people's names and how you can group two people with any situation you can think of. The next part of the song, he emphasizes on the part when there's nothing to fix, and it all comes down to me. This would mean that people need to train me on what it's like to talk to the media and what it is like to be in the national spotlight. People are, and I think I am, doing a good job at it. Nobody is controlling their own lives, but I still need to deal with these demons that I wish I didn't have to deal with on a regular basis. It's not necessarily me but the people around me. I know who the devil is, and I just wish he would just f——king die.

Also, Danny Elfman says, "Let the headlines wait." What he means by this is that the things that have been done to me in the past and me trying to make things right in this world means that people need to die, and when the time is right and people stop trying to find out who is ending lives in this world, then I can talk to people freely without worrying about people blaming this on me. I am doing my best, and the world is overpopulated, and there are a lot of people that bring no value to this world, in my opinion.

Another problem is that too many people are having kids, and it is such a f——king tired game because they are so f——king selfish and don't care about the progress of the world. They only care about the benefits that kids bring to themselves. Danny Elfman then goes on to say, "I can deal with fate," which are the songs that I listen to that are ending lives, which just happens to be fate that was created in my life. When my therapist was explaining to me that someone just ended their life with suicide. It was because I was listening to a song that ends about six to twelve lives with suicide.

There are other examples like N'Sync's song of "Bye Bye Bye" and Xzibit's song, "X," but people need to worry about their own issues instead of trying to blame their shit on Hollywood and me. Next, he says, "With a bucket of tears." Ever since I took that drive to Pennsylvania, for the longest time, I couldn't stop crying, but it was just the side effects I was going through from the other level I was on, and I really couldn't control myself. "I look into the sunlight and I feel no fear." This means a few things. Well, this has something to do with the universe and the moon and how the sun was supposed to collapse with the earth in the next five to ten thousand years. I am sort of connected to the world and Mother Nature, and once the fear of the sun goes away, then I think this issue will be on its way to being resolved and will be another example of how we are going to be here forever.

Danny Elfman then goes on to say, "A mountain of maybes and some Icarus wings." What he means by this is that people have been really unreliable to me and inconsistent. Once this ends, then I can start trusting people the way I used to, but once people pick up on the trends that have been going on in my life over the past several years, and we all try to stay evened out and consistent, then this won't be a problem anymore. Nevertheless, he says, "I am on with the delusions" which is happening now because we are living in the age of paranoia, and I am not scared of the things that are going on in my life anymore because the people that were playing games with me are starting to realize that these games are f——king stupid, and it is time to grow up.

Atmosphere, "Let Me Know that You Know What You Want"— in this song, Atmosphere hits several key points. The first one was that someone was born on the year of the razor blade, which was 1901. So that means that someone has been alive longer than any-one else and is in our generation. Next, he says, "We act like we got a whole lot of road left." This was when I started the forever young movement, and everyone kept on saying that age was just a number to them and that we are going to be here forever. I still believe this to be true, but it is so important that karma catches up on me first.

Additionally, he says "Earthbound" instead of one of the Imagine Dragons songs saying that I was "hell bound." I think Jeff is because all the signs that I have calculated makes me believe that he is hell bound, but I actually do good for the world and answer prayers and come through for people in need, so I am "earth bound." He says, "Aim for the soft spots." This means because of the situation I am in, I took control over who lives and who dies, meaning that I have sold my soul. When the people who are helping me out aim for the soft spots, it means that I can start to become myself again and don't have to worry about the side effects of becoming who I have become, which is a hero.

Atmosphere says a rich man still faces death alone because he is too busy making a name for himself and doesn't have time for a relationship, so we are trying to group them with other women who are single and are older.

Furthermore, Atmosphere says, "Get shone." This means that people can see me so that we can prove that there is an evidence of a god in our lifetime. Now I am in a position to take control over the human race, and if other people don't get it, then it's their loss.

Atmosphere says, "Wait for the right time" for karma to catch up with me. This means that everything in the atmosphere and the globe and the stars need to be in aligned and with the universe as well. This also includes Mother Nature so that we have all ducks in a row. Next, he says, "A lifetime to outlive the nighttime." He says this because there are a lot of people in the world that are scared of the dark, and we can overcome this by just uniting as one force and defeat the demons that we are dealing with every day. In his next verse, he says, "I keep bad on the back of my mind." This means that when I go into that weird universe that I go into and take away people's lives, this is not a good thing, and I wouldn't recommend it for anyone, but it has to be done, so I took this responsibility into my own hands.

Atmosphere then goes on to say that I am laughing on the inside because when he is watching me from Hollywood, he thinks that I am a funny guy, and I am looking for a life full of tests to end, and because of everything that he knows about the world and what I am doing to save it and what I do on a regular basis, he thinks it's funny. In the next part of the song, he says, "One nation with a capital I." This is what my therapist and I talk about a lot, and this means that we need to stop being so f——king selfish and help out others who are in need. People with power and people with resources need to help those who are less fortunate, and even if you don't have all these resources, you can still make an effort to be a better person every day.

Atmosphere next says that everyone wants to be the next to blow. Hollywood is taking down names of people and only lets certain people get appraised for their hard work so that only those people can reach the heights of singing in front of a group of people on the national and global level. Going along with everything else I have written with this song that has meaning behind it, he says, "Just to let you know, I can let you go." He was talking about me and my role in society that I can let anyone go if they are wasting our time and don't have a need in society anymore. He says, "Everyone is difficult and everyone is simple." Jeff is difficult, and Adam is simple, and everything in the middle depends on people's personalities.

I feel really alone a lot just examining what is going on in the world, but I am somewhere in the middle. This is important because you don't want to deal with difficult people on a regular basis. You want to be with friendly people who are going to respect you and not those assholes who think they are better than you are.

Gorillaz, "Clint Eastwood"—he starts out singing this song by saying, "Who, who, who, who, who." The haters in the world are multiplying, so this eliminates five of them by just playing this part of the song. Then he goes on to say, "I'm happy, I'm feeling glad, I got sunshine in a bag." I try to stay happy as much as possible, but since there is so much negativity around me, it is hard sometimes. Around most people, though, I am usually pretty happy and stay optimistic. "I got sunshine in a bag," which means that I am taking control over the light that is being formed outside every day all over the globe. I am feeling glad because I am looking forward to the future and I am usually a positive influence on others.

The next part of the song, he says, "I am useless, but not for long, my future is coming on." The things that have happened in my life probably seemed simpler than they were brought on to me, but there's no reason to dwell on the past and just move forward when the fears go away. My future is coming on because I am the only one with the power to make the future of the world come on quicker, and I am the only reason why the world is still going around in circles and why we are all still on planet earth. The Gorillaz say that I am useless because I am at home a lot and not showing myself in the real world as much as I would like, but this is mostly because of all the bullshit that I have been dealing with and all these tests I have had to pass. When I am no longer useless, then I will be hanging out with friends more often, and more and more people will start entering my life.

In several parts of this song, he says, "My future is coming on" several times because we own the technology now, and they make this music so that I will listen to it so we need to progress and none of us are getting younger, so this needs to happen sooner rather than later. He says, "Finally, someone let me out of my cage." I fell into this rut after I took that trip to Pennsylvania when I was on another level, and now I am trying to get back into other people's lives and am relying on certain people in the world to help me out and become myself again. The Gorillaz then go on to say, "Nah, you shouldn't be scared, I am going to repair." I shouldn't be scared of all the fears that I have had to overcome, and people are going to repair my soul because like I have said in other parts of this book, the world is simply too overpopulated, so we need to kill the flesh

He said, "I bet you didn't think so I commanded you to." He is talking about my indecent exposure that happened approximately a month and a half before I took that trip to Pennsylvania. Someone made me make that move, and I am going to find out and make them suffer. I still think it was Jeff, but I don't know yet. The next part of the song, he says, "All your different crews." I have had many different people in my life, and I am hoping they can reenter it at any point now, even though everyone is doing different things and everyone's busy, but we were seriously built to fall about and fall back together again.

When the Gorillaz say, "All your different crews," he is also talking about the athletes, the people in Hollywood, and the anonymous people across the globe that have been helping me out this entire time. The next part I wanted to mention is that Jeff thinks that all that Jesus stuff is fictional, which is sad because he is a coward and should rely on the people in the world that are doing work, not some invisible force that isn't showing his face. I am the one saving everyone's ass, so he said I might be the Son of God, but they started at the end, so we will find out exactly who I am at some point. Additionally, he says that you are too crazy. What he means by this is that I lose control a lot and I am not like anyone else in this world and act crazy a lot of times. He says, "Rhythm, you have it or you don't."

He says, "Corruption in the skies from this bucket enterprise." He is talking about the Mafia or the empire that put cameras in the sky to spy on people, but most people don't see these planes, but that is how people have watched me in the past, and I didn't care unless people were using that against me. These people are part of the people who have made me the person I am today. Without them, then I wouldn't be so prepared for the future like I am, and they are training me every single day to be ready for the future.

He says, "I am stuck inside your lies," meaning that since this invisible force is mixed in with the devil, when I telepathically talk to people, sometimes they are lies. He says, "You perceive with your mind," which is true because I don't have a choice but to defend myself, and I am doing everything in my power just to start living my life again, but it is hard because of these f——king tests that I have to test every day, and it is really frustrating because I don't think people get the amount of pressure there is behind this.

In the next part of the song, he says, "So you can survive when law is lawless." I have had to pass physical and mental tests to be prepared against the worst and best-case scenarios of the different and unique people in the world. Sensations that you thought were there were the feeling I had that I kept on complaining to people, but it was a mixture of all the elements and atmosphere and whatever else was thrown into my solution pit. Furthermore, he says, "No squealing; remember that it's all in your head." So they wanted me to stop complaining because of how people react to these types of situations and so that I wouldn't get in trouble anymore.

Wiz Khalifa, "Black and Yellow"—he starts out this song by saying, "You know what it is," meaning that in my solution pit and the problems that I am solving in the world are giving this godly figure more power and the devil less. I am filled with demons every day, and I get rid of them by walking and talking, and it doesn't make me any happier because this process seems to be taking forever. The next part of the song, he says, "You know everything to make me smarter than I was before but also under control." I do know more about the world than everyone else does, but that is just because of the training I have been doing behind the idiots backs of the world that bring no value to my future society. The pills help, and the prayers that I am able to answer for people help as well.

Additionally, he says, "Them niggas scared of it, but them hos aint." So I have been a scary person in the past, but I have calmed down since I was told to and to just go about my everyday business. When the full product is done, then people are going to be pretty scared by the guy that I will be in the future. He says here, "Them haters talk, but there's nothing you can tell them." People are quick to judge and hate in this world, but I am the one doing all the f——king work, and I have either sent to jail or killed many of them in the shootings that have happened or by other means.

The next part of his song, he says, "No love for a nigga breaking hearts," talking about Jeff because behind his radio or whatever the f——k he was doing on his free time, he is probably still doing it. He is f——king up relationships that should be everlasting. He is part of the problem of the world, not the solution. He lost it when he started disrespecting me on the regular, so now he's going to have to prove his worth to people that don't know his personality, and because he is fake, people will like him.

I don't like people because there is too much fake bullshit that is going on in the world, and people really don't understand the full meaning of why we are alive right now. My friend, Eric Shaker, gave me a reason, but it was bullshit. We are here to be forever young and to form into one big happy family. Jeff has already f——ked up two of my relationships; so once Anna says we are done whether they are married or not, then he will realize, "Well, maybe I should have done things differently in my past."

The next part of the song, he says "Not a lesbian, she a freak, though. I think he was talking about Anna because she has devised some plan to stab him in the back, and according to one of Kid Cudi's songs, the CIA is going to charge Jeff for what he has done to me in the past.

Wiz Khalifa then says I can't tell what the time is so that I can cure time and make us all forever young. I am now using this box full of tricks to figure out the best course of action for everyone in the world that fits the needs for us in the future. We are talking about if you are still alive in the next two to three years, then you are of value, and if you are dead, then you are no use. That is why we are killing the flesh so that the right people can enjoy peace on this world. There will be no drama and no conflicts and no rude people and no people that will cause me conflict. Moreover, he says, "Stay high like I'm supposed to do." He is talking about Adam because that is his own personal cure for himself, and maybe weed is a big part of the solution for the human race.

He says, "Can't get close to you" because of all the demons that are surrounding me all the f——king time. Our goal is for people to throw on to me their demon problems so that we are cured from death and from diseases for the rest of eternity. Next, he says, "But it's super mean that I said Wiz Khalifa, how's your sister doing after she died because she was f——king around with gangs?' I am sorry, but I know the population needs to get down, so I am happy when people die because it just means more gains for people that have more value in this world. He say's "real rap" because a lot of people think Tupac and Biggie were so f——king important in this world, but they rap and sing about my life a lot. Tupac and Biggie were just taking up space in Hollywood when these other rappers have obviously proved more worth than they ever did for me. Additionally, Wiz says, "She feels that." So one other girl in the world feels the pains that I feel. I don't know whom, but I would love to find out.

"Y'all should already know what it is. If you don't, you should by now," is what he says next. There are other songs where they say, "Don't confuse this with mountains," meaning that it's still like Jesus f——king Christ in this world as well.

Red Hot Chili Peppers, "Can't Stop"—the first part of this song I wanted to mention was that they said, "In time, I want to be your best friend because I can't stop" since I was destined from that trip to Pennsylvania, and perfection is my direction, and I am probably just going crazy because of the fear. I think that there are a lot of people that would want to be my best friend in the future, but I want to know what you are doing for me now that allows you to even be a part of my life in the future. There are a lot of shitty people in this world and people that are quick to judge others when you are not walking in their footsteps, so why don't we start judging you when you are hating from the sidelines?

He says, "Don't die, you know that you are the son, dude." This was just a description that was given to me since I was going through all of these tests and experiments so that we can cure the human race. I have been through hell, but a lot of it was also positive. I have learned a lot about life and the meaning behind it because of how strong of a person I have become, mentally and physically. Maybe I am the son, dude, but maybe I am not, but either way, I was destined, and things just never changed the way they were supposed to, so it's time for us to take matters into our own hands, and if I am not the son, dude, then karma needs to catch up on me soon!

In the next part of the song, he says, "Ever wonder if it's all for you?" If this was all for me, then why the f——k have I had it so goddamn hard? This is a question I need people to answer for me because I have no explanation for it. We are all getting older, so no more f——king games, and it's time to buckle down and fulfill our destinies. I don't believe this is all for me, but maybe down the road, it will be because I don't see anyone helping me out. People are so selfish and arrogant, and their beliefs in religion and politics have really made me not give a shit about those particular people and say that you have to prove your worth if you want to even have two seconds to get the chance to talk to me. There are a lot of fake people in this world, and I am not going to name names, but please develop a serviceable personality so that you can prove your worth to me.

He says, "Smoke rings, I know you're going to blow one" because it is a myth that cigarettes are worse for you than other things. Cigarette smokers have lived longer lives than other people that don't do anything bad their entire lives. "Only the good die young" isn't just a phrase, but it's probably a fact of life. He says, "Can't stop the spirits when they need you" because they are looking for God in the afterlife, and I am alive right now, so I can guide them to do the right thing in the afterlife. For instance, when I was at the movie theatres one day, I was saying a little prayer to myself, and the invisible force was surrounding me, which was the spirits of the afterlife. This was crazy and a miracle at the same time. I wish I could explain this to someone who wouldn't think I was crazy, but I know that Hollywood and my therapist would understand, so I will just keep it like that for the moment.

In the next part of the song, he says, "I am passing out, win or lose, just like you" because you can't win every battle, but you can win the war. I don't always win my bets or win with my unreliable friends, but I am still waking up the next day and doing it all over again. I can win this war overseas and I can be the best person in the world since that is what I am, but we need karma to catch up so that all this can be real, and I am actually happy that I am not talking to Adam as much because that kid was wasting my time and energy when I can take that time to spend it more productively on things that matter more.

Some of those things are the meaning of life, which Shaker was wrong about because I am aiming for perfection, not that garbage meaning that he was explaining. I can save the world, and maybe fixing me up is the recipe, but first, more people need to die so that we are not sitting in traffic, and there are a lot of terrible things that are still happening in my life that I am trying to get rid of. I need people to stop acting fake around me, and I need the blank stares to stop. Those two things are really starting to get really f——king annoying. Next he says, "Far more shocking than anything I ever knew, how about you?" He says this because my personality doesn't exactly show that I am Jesus because I am not fake and I am a real person, and that is why I get life. I am a little bit of an asshole and probably aren't the nicest person in the world, but whatever, I do what I do to help out millions of people all over the world, and I don't see anyone else doing this job.

The Red Hot Chili Peppers next say, "Right on cue" because everything happens for a reason, and when you can relate certain events in your life that define why this is happening right now, then you know you are doing something right.

In the next part, he says, "Your name is in the dictionary, and this life is more than ordinary." What he means by this is that "free willy" (Jesus) is in the dictionary, and this life is more than ordinary because we are crazy people that are all going through issues, and everyone has their problems in their own lives that they are trying to deal with. What I do not like, though, is that there are people that like to judge other people when they are not walking in their shoes. So many f——king people were judging me when they had no idea how hard I had it before they knew who I was.

I still need to know who gave me that indecent exposure so that I can move on from that devilish experience. One time, Mark Jackson, a person that a lot of people look up to, said, "Good, they are making sure he pays a price."

He thought I was the devil, but then you look around at other people in the world, and the things that I was going through were complete bullshit, and honestly, what the f——k is your value in this world if you want to be so ignorant to what the real-world problems are? The last part of this song I wanted to mention was that he said, "This life is more than just a read-through." What he means by this is that the people and things that happen to you are not by accident. Everything was destined for you, and everything that happens was not your choice. It is because of that evil man above us that many people hate.

Q-Tip, "Won't Trade"—he starts out this song by saying, "Now that I know what it is, boy," meaning that the maze that I cannot escape is just the devil playing tricks on my mind. This is for anyone who is trying to help me out and save and fix the world, including the empires of love. He says, "Niggas laugh," meaning that people around the world think that I am funny and that everyone will come to their senses one day and realize that they need me in their god-damn lives. My life throughout my thirty-three years have had a lot of comedy and a lot of drama and a lot of terror, so the funny parts are good, but the not funny parts I need to stop immediately because it's people that are ruining the world, and it probably has a lot to do with God as well.

The next part of the song, he says, "Do you believe?" I have been through hell and am literally conquering everything and don't want to put up with anyone's bullshit anymore. Everyone has to grow the f——k up and stop playing these dumbass games or else some-one that you love will die or get seriously hurt. I am done with the garbage that people give into this society, so that's why I kill the flesh and let the right people into my life and understand what is going on in this world, and somehow, hopefully, we can cut out the peo-ple we don't want in this society, even if they are still alive, and only allow the people that are worthy of my time to be in the future of the world. I look around and see people just walking like statues, so I don't know who I would exclude, but people really need to show me their worth or else they will die.

Anyways, I read on Twitter that God killed three million people, and Satan killed ten. That sounds about right if I am God because I am never going to stop, and whoever is getting in my way everyday gets eliminated.

In the next part of the song, he goes the Division 1 leader, who I don't know who he is talking about, but I don't think it's someone that is a good person, but maybe it is. Maybe it is someone who is getting in my way every day or maybe it's someone who is helping me get through this process. Furthermore, he says, "I mean, nah, he's good," I mean because I go through a lot of ups and downs through-out any given day and really need the downs to go away, but it seems impossible until Satan (Jeff) dies. Once Peyton Manning said that he was going to put me through that exact same game again. I have been stuck very deep, but I just can't stop now. I never stopped working out and reading and understanding life a lot better.

I am thankful for everyone who has helped me out because I can't do this on my own and need people's help. When I listen to this song, and in the next part, he says, "Franchise this, man," which is helping these athletes get the contracts they deserve to keep the world spinning, and it makes a lot of people happy. People love going to the games and watching them on TV, so it's good for the people who run the stadium, the management staff, and especially for these guys who work and try hard to be their best selves for the fans.

Additionally, he says, "Give him all the things you can" so that people can provide for their own futures and get wealthier, and just like the script was written for the *Hunger Games*, I can give people things that other people cannot provide, just because I was handed the future of the world in my hands. Once injuries start going down and I step back into the line, then I think everything will be better again. I have helped out so many people all across the world, and someone decided to lay the worst in the best to make us overcome all of this crap to become better in the future, but nevertheless, we become stronger people in the end.

I like doing things for other people that appreciate it, but I just wish that certain people would see the big picture and stop complaining about the little things that they are dealing with because there are some people like me that are dealing with way worse. Next, he says, "Think long-term plans" because sometimes people crash early in their lives because they decided to live hard for their early years and cannot maintain that lifestyle for a long time. This is part of the reason why I cut back on drinking because it was just destroying my brain cells and making me bloated and fat.

Now I drink a lot more water and eat healthier and work out all the time because of the help that I have received from outside resources. I once said that I would fix everything if people fix me. Atmosphere later released a song saying that he would fix me for free because there are people in the world that want to get paid when this is all over because they already know the future that is ahead of me and want to receive those dividends. I can't really blame them because I am the golden child, and I am trying to promise myself that it will never get to my head ever again.

Q-Tip then says, "Nicest nigga, kinda, sorta" because I have done some things in my past that made people not like me. However, I made a lot of changes in my lifestyle and work ethic and how I responded when Hollywood said, "Act like you're not alone." I try not to say the N-word anymore and am trying to be a good model civilian and not make the dumb mistakes that other people make. I earned my way back into this society and didn't have a choice because I was stuck so deep and had no idea why. I cannot wait until the fears go away and I can start living my life again. I will probably never be the same shit show that I used to be because I grew up and learned from my mistakes. I need karma to catch up to me so that we can be forever young, but anyway, I am not fake and will not pretend to be nice to you if I don't f——king like you.

In the next part of the song, he says will inevitably make a call because of all these spam calls that we are receiving. I wasn't receiving any calls before I made that trip to Pennsylvania and am pretty pissed about it, but hopefully, soon the calls go away. In one of Halsey and the Chainsmokers songs, they say, "Four years and no calls" because it was the demons that were holding me back, and the fours stand for Jeff.

In this song, he also makes this for the athletes that can listen to it and says when asked about the trade rumors, "I am just here to produce the best effort for my team." These guys are just following instructions and are outliers to the rest of the population, and that is why they are making so much money, and hopefully, they give back to the community. I know some of them are, but I think if this was more of a group effort, we can get more people involved. Honestly, though, I don't think that some of these people should have any say in this world because so many people are so greedy, and this is why Hoodie Allen said, "No Avicii" because I am the one with the final say in what goes on in this world.

Sports makes people happy, and that is fine by me, but there are other reasons why we are alive right now, and this does mean faith and finding a solution that can make the mainstream population happy, not just the people that are getting paid for what they are doing. It is what it is, but Hollywood puts out these songs so that I will listen to them, and in Atmosphere's song, "Hope," he says that "I hope that you are hearing this and this has solved more problems than most people know." I do know, however, that some people have picked up on this, including athletes, and it all stems from that drive I made to Hollywood because I was connected to my phone, and that is what led me to make those decisions that I made that day.

Additionally, he says, "Clear your mantel." They started at the end, and this also means that somehow, someway, I will be playing sports in front of people and making money doing it. If this is on the national stage, then this is why people are slowly and sometimes quickly training me to talk in front of people. I was never really a good public speaker, but actions speak louder than words, so maybe this will work itself out. I need my skills to come back, which they do sometimes, but I can be the best person in the world if my supporting cast was there for me more often. I answer people's requests all the time, so that's why Jessie J said that every second is a highlight.

I just need to start putting myself first so that I am not so miserable all the time. Regardless, I am ready for the full potential and perfection to start. The next part of the song, he says, "You know my name, it makes me better" because people are dying all over the world that don't know my name, and this is part of the fact that we are killing the flesh so that the people that are doing work in this world can get more powerful. Everyone's lives are not as important as others and everyone is not equal, and there are a lot of people in this world that don't bring any worth to society. I just cannot believe that I have had it this hard, and every day is a f——king struggle because of the goddamn people around me. I just need to focus on the positive and work on becoming a better person, even if the people around me aren't.

The next part of the song, he says, "The balance that you are holding." I am accountable for a lot of people's lives that are alive right now, and since I am making that list of my favorite people, I can start living my life more now, and certain people have more say in the world so that this can become more of a group effort. The next part of the song, he says, "They cheer for me, wait a minute I don't know, but anyway." Because of the bullshit that I have gone through in my life and the path that was given to me and how I have made the world a better place because of it, people are happy and cheer for me when certain scripts were written or because of certain moves I made to make people more successful and things of that nature.

Barenaked Ladies, "It's All Been Done"—the Barenaked Ladies released this song around the year 2003. They released this song because they knew when the time was right, it would make sense to me. In the first part of this song, he goes, "I met you before the fall of those." He is talking about the fake empire, and this involves Adam and the corruptness that goes on with this evil empire. Nevertheless, somebody in my life met me before they were going to go down. They should have never done some of the things that they did to me, so f——k them. The next part of his song, he says, "I let you take me home." He was talking about when I took that trip to Pennsylvania to free myself from the wrath of society. I didn't see any of it coming, and I ran out of gas, and all the things that happened to me on that trip were pretty cool, a little bit scary, but also like a coming to Christ moment.

Somebody decided to get a group together to direct me to take me home from that incident. The next part of the song, he says, "You said 'Goodbye,' I said 'Goodnight'" so that we can eliminate some of the flesh and remove two people from society. It's a revolution, and the world is too overpopulated, so we can gain from these people's losses. The whole concept of this song is that he is saying that it's all been done before. What the Barenaked Ladies mean is that the world forming into one big family has all been done before, and Noah's ark and all that kind of thing has been done, so let's make this happen soon and quick, but I think we also need to take our time because of all the things I was going through, and people are trying to build a new world built around me, but not everyone is obviously invited because I just need to trust the process and let the people who are helping me out guide me into this process.

Carli Lloyd knew me before the West was won. This means that there will be no more wars in human history after we win this war overseas. These stupid historians say that World War II is the war to end all wars, but there have been other wars since then, so that doesn't make any sense. Since we will be here forever, we need to make sure that peace is attained and that a World War III doesn't happen, but anyway, Carli Lloyd helps me out a lot, and we need karma to catch up so that we can actually be here forever and make sure that we can win this war overseas without anybody getting in the way.

In the next part of the song, they say, "I heard you say the past was much more fun." He is talking about Demi Lovato. She released a song called "Heart Attack" so that some of these old folks can enter their graves and the young people can benefit from them dying. Young people have even died of heart attacks, but it's a revolution. Demi Lovato released that song so I can listen to it and put eleven people into their graves since the world is too overpopulated anyways. Even if they don't die from heart attacks, they still shouldn't be alive anymore because they don't add any value to the new society we are trying to build.

The next part of the song I wanted to mention was that he says, "Will I see you on the *Price is Right*?" He is talking about that *Happy Gilmore* scene where Bob Barker and Happy Gilmore get into a fight, and since they are saying that perfection is my direction and I am getting better at golf that I will be able to prove my abilities to the world someday and kill it with golf. He says, "Will I die?" talking about Adam because that motherf——ker tried to beat me in this stupid f——king game, and now he has nobody to talk to, so that developed slow, but it worked because he just doesn't belong with the people that I belong with. To go along with this *Happy Gilmore* theme, I wanted to mention that there was scene that I can relate to. When Happy Gilmore got into a fight with his nemesis, his nemesis said, "Meet me on the ninth hole, there is a good surprise I have for you at night."

There was nobody at the ninth hole, and the sprinkler system went off, and he was really mad and felt like hurting his nemesis, but instead, he ended up becoming the better man and beating him at his own game. He won the tournament and made the best out of a bad situation. Nevertheless, on the ninth hole at Oak Marr, the hole is 144 yards, and it's always the hole I play worse at. Four is Satan's number, which is Jeff, who is my nemesis, and every time I play at this ninth hole, I think of Jeff and how much he has damaged my life. They came out with this scene a long time ago, knowing that I was going to play a lot of golf at Oak Marr, and the ninth hole is 144 yards, which is Jeff's number.

Most people wouldn't understand, but this is just how Hollywood has made me and how the golf course was designed. There is also a hole that is 166 yards which stands for a god character, who is me, and I usually play pretty good at this hole. However, the last time I played, I was able to overcome my inner demons and play well at this ninth hole. It's crazy how a movie that was made so long ago can be related to something I am doing twenty years later. They keep their secrets to themselves, but whatever, they choose me, so I am just going to go along with the process, and I am sure they are filling in people with the gaps of the people that they trust.

Taylor Swift, "Wonderland"—I want to break down this song of how she is trying to relate it to the public in my own words. When she says, "Curious minds," I think she is talking about the facts and information that people want to know about the world, and I don't think that everyone gets the point that Hollywood is trying to get across to people and why we are all alive right now. However, I did gain a pretty good fan base, and sooner or later, karma will catch up with me, and we will finally be able to form into one big family.

When she says, "Curious minds," she means that people were curious about what the f——k I was going through and how it is all possible. I felt the devil's arms twisting around me, and Hollywood saved me from any further damage. The devil was actually Jeff, but I didn't know at the time, and nobody believed me, especially him. I hate that kid so much, and when the time is right, I will be able to defend myself. In the next part of her song, she says, "I should've slept with one eye open at night" because Adam had a gun in the room next to me when he was staying here, and in Hollywood, they don't allow guns, and the mainstream population doesn't allow guns, so therefore, people who own guns shouldn't be allowed in our inner circle anymore.

The next part of her song, she says, "We found Wonderland, you and I got lost in it." She is talking about Anna (Jeff's fiancé).

Anna would be the clever one who led me on the path to perfection, so I don't know why she wants to marry Jeff, but we'll see how that all plays out. This song is about Anna and obviously about me. The next part of this song, she says that life was never worse but never better. She is talking about my relationship with Amber. It just means that this world has been taken off God's hands and given to the people.

Praying doesn't work, and I don't even know if God exists, and I rarely ever pray. I do a lot of other things for other people, but she is just stating a fact that people need to shut the f——k up and stop thanking God so goddamn much and take responsibility for your own goddamn actions. Furthermore, she says, "All alone or so it seemed" because I really wasn't talking to any friends and was pretty much by myself because things never turned out the way I thought they were going to, so I am by myself a lot, and this leaves me very depressed and lonely, but I had Amber, who I had to break up with to figure out the world a little bit better.

I don't want to invite everyone to the main event at the end of my story, and I probably won't because they were never there for me. F——k all of them. I was never invited to their weddings and I wasn't in their wedding parties, but people want to be there for me when things are great again?

F——k that. One part that was going through my mind was that I was going to build a whole new world with just one girl and say, "F——k you" to everyone else. Go on an island somewhere with everything that we need for the rest of eternity and start a whole new society. I don't know. I never got the respect that I deserved from other people, and nobody has shown me the love that I need, and it will all come down to me fighting Jeff until one of us dies to show who deserves more respect in this world.

Next, she says but there were strangers watching, and whispers turned to talking, and talking turned to screams. Amber and I got into a lot of screaming matches, and I knew if I married this girl, it would be a disaster because she was so f——king unpredictable and treated me differently like I was an outcast compared to the way she was treating other people. I am not very happy writing this right now, but I am just very frustrated in the way things have turned out in my life. This path that I was given was bullshit, and I wish I could do it all over again. There were strangers watching, and whispers turned to talking because people started to understand that Hollywood was making this music for me to listen to and that I really did need people's help to get me out of this shithole of a situation I was in.

Additionally, she says, "It's all fun and games until someone loses their mind." Adam was playing tricks with my head at Meghan's thirtieth birthday party. This life is such bullshit, and I wish that people weren't such assholes and greedy. I don't like many people that want to be a part of this life in the future. I also really wish she never had that kid because I hate kids.

The next part of her song, she says, "I reached for you, but you were gone" and she was talking about when I went to New York to visit Angie and we had a great night together, and we kissed in the morning, then I ran to my car. I guess she had more to say, but she knew she had to go back home because her parents weren't doing great. I am sick of this bullshit and am looking forward for change. The best part of this song is that she says at the end of Wonderland, we both went bad. I cannot wait for all this shit to be over.

Kid Cudi, "Cudi Zone"—he starts with saying, "Sorry, is this allowed?" He says this because so many people in this world are walking on eggshells, and we don't know when we can act a certain way and when not to sometimes. Next he says, "Some figured I was Satan bound, then all of a sudden they are face-to-faces." It is really similar to the movie *Face/Off*. Jeff is Satan, and I am the good guy because I proved my worth in this world, and he is the one thing that keeps me from attaining the goals for society every day. In *Face/Off*, the good guy wins, and the good guys always win. He says, "Cause I know they are trading places," which is how they portrayed the Jesus and devil characters in the movie Face/Off. It is exactly how I feel and am sick of it.

In the next part of the song he says, "How many niggas hate it because I left, but how can you blame me with my plan of attack?" I missed out on a lot of things because of the demons I was dealing with and the problems of the world I had to solve. This was my choice to save the world and to think and be smarter than the people in it in terms of common sense and to act right and do the right things and give back to the community more than anyone else in the world. I think people were made a long time ago, but now it's time for all of us to reunite and take this in strides, but karma needs to catch up, and that is the biggest thing. I need all the fears and pains to go away one day, but people are taking it slow, so it is a process, just like everything else in life.

In the next part of the song, he says, "It doesn't matter where you're from, all that matters is where you're going, go." When he says "go," he means that an old person is going to die, and this is just a process of elimination, and whoever is up next will be the next old person to die. They started at the end, so when I become famous, I will be able to unite everyone into one big family. I'll be showing how I've been living, meaning that people from the outside world who want to judge me, they should walk in my footsteps if they still want to judge me because of the hell that I was going through before everything in the world comes together again.

The next part of the song, he says, "Homie," not even meaning that it seems like everything we were taught wasn't even true, but it is true, and this monster of a person needs to give up his worth in this world because he is really f——king things up for me. The next part of the song, he says, "Floating, floating," and they make these songs so that I will listen to them. People look to the sky for guidance every single day, and when they see bright things and change, they want to believe it is from some force above us, but it is really me doing what I was born to do. There used to be people that knew that, but I don't know because I don't think outsiders are watching me as much any-more, thank goodness. The next part of the song, he says some lyrics and mixes in two "whos" because it is a revolution, and we need to kill the flesh. He says, "I am feeling all right" because I am starting to feel a lot better about things in recent memory, considering all these hellish things I was going through.

Furthermore, he says, "I forget about it all". He says that because the people outside my life wouldn't understand, so I don't get mad when people don't understand the things I am saying, so I forget about the things I know about the world and the things I have discovered because the average person wouldn't understand. Next, he says, "I'm balling, is this allowed?" He says this because society and what we are supposed to be doing right now is working until we turn sixty-two or sixty-three or sixty-five, then die later on in life. I am a rebel to the system, so when karma catches up, we won't have to worry about growing old because we will be young forever.

It is taking a really long time, but it will work. We are not supposed to be doing some of the things that I have been doing because that is not what the norm for society tells us to do. I don't care. I never chose this path, but I am happy with where I am at right now. He says in the next part, "But I am feeling like Shallow Hal." He says this because I really don't like ugly people that much, and it is part of the script that was written for all of us to enjoy. Then he mentions something about Jesus because creation needs a devil's advocate for everything in this world to remain equal. He says, "These are the things that make me smile" because I do a lot of good things, and they are constantly monitoring my progress in Hollywood, so when I do certain things that I do, Kid Cudi laughs.

Next, he says, "I am accustomed to new heights" because one of my fears is heights, and that phobia will go away once I stop living in so much f——king fear.

In the next part of his song, he says, "Though they think it's worthless." He is talking about the empires and how they think that I am not benefitting myself, but the good things I do for other people every day, they used to think it was worthless until recent memory, and now I will stop living behind closed doors and show my face. Additionally, he says they will love it. He is talking about my direction. The athletes will love it if I can actually achieve this high standard that the world has set for me. We are getting older, but like I said, karma will catch up, and we will need science and faith to pull this off, but they will have a field day with me if I can actually achieve perfection. He says, "Most likely, I am a faded man." He means that Jeff won't be talking to me or hanging out with my friends anymore, but we'll see.

In this song, he also mentions that I will find some peace "up there, up there." So he is talking about in the heavens, and even though I remain on the ground, I am still doing work in the skies as well. This is crazy because I have found peace with myself when I am by myself or when people don't do stupid shit to disrupt my peace. Then he goes back to saying "who" twice to kill the flesh, so he says "who" four times in this song to kill the flesh. He says "who" two more times to make it six total to kill the flesh.

Miley Cyrus, "Liberty Walk"—she talks about this song as a redemption song for me to get back at the people who put me in these terrible situations where it seemed like there was no way out. She starts out with this song as "Don't live a lie, this is your one life." She says this because too many people are living lies in their own delusional lives, and she wants people to step up to the table and start making their actions speak louder than their words. When she says, "This is your one life," this makes me think about "The Hell Song" by Sum 41. Everybody's got their problems, everybody says the same thing to you, and it doesn't matter how you solve them.

In the next part of the song, she says, "You won't get lost" because I have been lost so many times when I have left my house, even before I took that trip to Pennsylvania. The trip to Pennsylvania was in the same year the Mayans said the world was going to end, so I don't think that happened by accident. Nevertheless, she says, "You won't get lost" because people are helping me out to save the world and fix it as best as we can, so they started at the end, and I won't get lost when I leave my house anymore. Next, she says, "Just walk, just walk," meaning two people will start walking, wherever they are, and it will make an impact on the world.

She says it's a liberty walk because Hollywood and the professional athletes put me back into this hellish game that got me in trouble in the first place, so when I start walking and talking like I used to, and the fears go away, I will finally be able to do what I was destined to do. I am doing my work from home, which they used to think was useless, but my liberty walk will take me to my destiny, which is still yet to be determined. Maybe perfection. Maybe I will be talking on national television. I don't know yet.

In the next part of her song, she says, "Here are the boys that are trying to make you feel like less than that but really just try to put your dreams on track." She says this because there have been so many f——king guys that made me feel out of place, and I didn't fit in because of their own insecurities and jealousy. I think it is pretty boring when people talk a lot of times, so I don't try to fit in in certain situations since they are just wasting their breath, but she says try to put your dreams on track because we are not getting any younger, and I need to start focusing on myself instead of what other people want all the f——king time.

I need to make this clear-cut and put Romy and Ray and myself in the right direction to make our millions and billions of dollars. I am putting away people to their deathbeds who are getting in the way, and a lot of it is a process, and I need to be patient. This process is taking forever, and I am being really patient and am actually doing what I was born to do at my home every day.

She says in the end, "You know that it will be okay" because all that matters are the steps you take. She is trying to be reassuring in telling me to stop stressing, and every move I make has a positive impact on the world. When it's all said and done, everything will work itself out for me, and I just need to listen to the people around me and the advice of the people outside of my life to put the world and everything in the direction like us humans intended.

She says, "And everything else falls into place" because it will. I just need to be patient. She says, "Say goodbye to the people who tied you up." This is how they came out with the Bourne movies. Jason Bourne, as in Will Coakley, but I have been taking out the people who have been making our lives a living hell, and everything else that I have said in this book just makes sense to me, and it is all real, despite what other people might think. I have taken out members of the CIA, the Mafia, and pretty much other people who have gotten in the way of me achieving my destiny. She says that I will start feeling my heart again. I pretty much took over on the case of who lives and who dies, so once people stop dying, I will start to feel my heart again. I know the world is still too overpopulated, and this is why not everybody's lives are equally important. She says, "Breathing new oxygen" because I have cut back on smoking, but maybe I will quit altogether.

I need to achieve perfection, and anything less than that is a failure. I need to work hard to achieve my goals and the people who are still alive because I deleted some of those songs will help me achieve my mark. I know that people are still testing me, so I will continue to kill the flesh until my goals are attained. She also says in this verse that nobody breathes anymore because we are created new oxygen, and a new atmosphere and people just don't breathe the same air that they used to.

In the next part of her song, she says, "Don't stop keep on walking, don't stop, keep on talking," and this speaks to two people in the world that are together, and their moves have an impact on the world. The next part of the song is important. She says, "You just do what you were born to do" and everything just works our way. This benefits Hollywood, and it benefits me because every move I make is magic, and it will benefit the world and the people in it. She says, "Don't listen to all the people who hate because all they are going to do is make your mistakes for you." This is pretty much what has been happening. Whether it has been to my face or behind my back, everyone who has disrespected me has faced karma, and I don't give a f——k because I have had it several times worse than anyone else in this f——king world, so stop disrespecting me, and you will pay whether it's something little or something major.

Additionally, she says, "But they don't own you, I just told you" because people are giving me bad advice and f——king things up that I am trying to make positive, so f——k them too. I try not to hate, but sometimes the people around me make it hard, and I know it's because of the devil, Veltri, and it is so out of my control. I cannot let him and the devilish games he plays with me win. She says, "Don't like what you do, don't take the abuse." This is because of the abuse of people that put me in these terrible situations and f——ked my world up.

He scares me when he gets into certain mindsets. In one of their movies, they said the one thing that scares me is the devil inside of people. I don't disagree with that statement because that is when I have always gotten into trouble. I hate these games, and don't put the blame on me because of what you guys have done to yourselves. She says, "Move to the truth, people, c'mon." That means you because I have been very lonely and isolated, and it will all change, but I pretty much don't log on to Facebook anymore because so many people get so many likes on their posts and Facebook birthdays when I was hardly getting any. It is such bullshit, and most of these people are living lies as their lives, so it's whatever in the grand scheme of things.

Katy Perry, "ET Futuristic Lover, feat. Kanye West"—they start out with this song, saying, "I got a dirty mind, I got filthy ways." They say this because certain things I do inside my house are pretty dirty and filthy, even though I like to stay clean, but the dirty mind part kind of explains itself. Next, Kanye West says welcome to the danger zone because I am stuck deep, and it is a box full of tricks, but it is pretty dangerous to get too close to me because of all the elements and other things in the atmosphere, and the people that cross my paths enter the danger zone. I don't know what the fears are for sure, so they called this the "danger zone."

He says you are not invited to the other side of sanity. He was pretty much joking, but yeah, I have been diagnosed with mental illnesses since my early twenties, and they put this into scripts, and I am okay with that as long as people stop quizzing me. It was cool before because I was minding my own business, but a big part of me wishes I wasn't on that stupid Invega pill because of those back-to-back hospital visits that I had. It was such bullshit that I was paying a price for things that weren't even my fault. People are dying each year and each day, but that's their own problem. I wish I was never sent to the hospital those two times.

Katy Perry next says, "You're so hypnotizing, could you be the devil? Could you be an angel?" They only pray for more ends while I hope for the best, so they don't care what they put in some of these lyrics, but if you are going to disrespect me in your lyrics, then I don't want anything to do with you. She says this because they poisoned me in such a way that everything I do is special, and everyone doesn't have to understand, but in terms of the world, it does seem like everything we were taught when we were younger wasn't even true. I don't think a lot of people deal with any demon problems, but they still think it's the devil's fault. Put your own blame on what you are doing wrong in your own lives. I am the best person in the world since I am the most talented and have been through the worst.

Sometimes things seem to be getting better, and sometimes they seem to be getting worse.

Next, she says, "Your touch magnetizing." What she means by this is that my touch is strong and powerful. Additionally, she says, "They say be afraid." She is talking about the empire or the Mafia. They put me through some of these terrible tests that make my life a living hell. I never really believed in a god, and I know a lot of people around the world never really believed in a god either, so that is part of the reason why they came out with this song. However, they are ignorant and don't have any useful things in my life. Instead, they were causing me issues with my friends and family.

She says, "You are not like the others, futuristic lover, different DNA." What she means by this is that I am not like any other guy in this world because of my unique personality. In my opinion, there are so many people that are very similar, and I am just a different person than everyone else, and there will never be someone like me to ever exist on this world again. We need to make this life everlasting so that nothing is incomplete, and by doing this, we need all these steps and tests to work to perfection. She points me out separately from everyone else because I understand things at different levels than other people do and do not fit into the norm of society.

In the next part of her song, she says, "They don't understand you." It goes along with what she says in the previous part. I have a one-of-a-kind personality, and even though people think they are different from others, most people are pretty f——king similar with their fake laughs and smiles. In the next part of her song, she says, "You're from a whole other world, a different dimension." It wasn't from my genes, but it was how I was born and that I am from outer space, like a different planet. It is similar to the movie *E.T.*, and she started off building her song off this movie.

This part is crucial. She says, "And letting it go." This means that God is giving up his powers to me because we are giving power back to people and not by some invisible force. I know that a lot of people think that karma needs to catch up with me, but that's not what Katy Perry means in this song. God is giving up his powers cause there is no more time to waste, and we need to rely on someone we can see instead of some fictional thing that is in the sky. Furthermore, she says, "Kiss me, kiss me," because a lot of these Hollywood girls are obsessed with me, and even Selena Gomez before she released one of her songs, she says, "Every love thought's already been song," so I guess here's another one. She has a fiancé now, so obviously, I am not going to kiss her, but it's a good feeling that she feels this way about me. "Infect me with your love and fill me with your poison" is what she says next. This is just another part of the love song that she put in this part.

She says, "Boy, you're an alien, your touch so foreign." Another reason why she says this is because we are dealing with a lot of apocalyptic things, and God doesn't deserve to have this power anymore since he put a lot of people through hell since they were born. She says, "I am an alien" because that was just part of the script for *E.T.* The next part of her song, she says it's supernatural, and they came out with a script with the title called *Supernatural.* I haven't seen this show yet, but I will at some point. My powers are supernatural. It is pretty ironic because the pastor that I follow on Twitter says that our God is a supernatural God, and this is pretty much true. I don't know if I am God or not, but my powers are definitely supernatural, and I don't think a lot of people would understand because they don't understand life as well as I do.

My supernatural powers are part of the reason why this world is even going to be saved in the first place. The sky changes colors and does crazy things up there, and that is all because of me. The weather changes that are going to be positive in the future are all going to be because of me. I am sick of God getting credit for the things that I do. It is very annoying, so I don't think people can fully grasp that idea. I think a lot of these people are very f——king stupid. "You're so supersonic" is what she says next. It's like my powers are bouncing off the walls, even though I don't use my powers as much as I used to because once I step inside the line again and form into people's lines, that's when karma will catch up. However, the things I have done in the past were supersonic. "I wanna feel your powers, feel me with your lasers" is what she says next. This is what it used to be like, and people were hearing voices and crazy things because of me. This is what was happening before Peyton Manning said he was going to put me into that same game again. Now I am absorbing powers instead of dictating them.

Hoodie Allen says, "No Avicii" in one of his songs because Jeff and other people in this world don't deserve to have the say that I get in this world since they didn't do anything to deserve it.

Next, she says, "Every move is magic." It's true. They poisoned me in a certain way that every move I make is magic, and it only matters what steps I take. When I play bowling or play softball, it's all magic and benefits people from all over the globe. When I am watching TV shows, it benefits people around the world and globe. When I am working out, it benefits people in my life and around the globe.

In the next part of her song, she says, "On another level." I need people to calm me down at night because I live throughout the day on another level, and that is just how I was born. The meds put me on another level, and the coffee does too, and I get adrenaline rushes just from things I do within the confines of my house. Next, she says, "Boy, you're my lucky star." She is talking about the north star or the death star. However, as I said in the previous paragraph, it seems like everything we were told doesn't even seem like it was true.

Think twice before you make up your mind between Jeff and I. His heart is going to blow, and I am a way better person than he is, so I don't think it's hard to pick. She says, "For you I would risk it all." She proved this to me when she entered ESPN for one of their shows and acted disrespectfully toward the analysts just to prove that it's our time to break the rules and proves it to me in other ways too. She is a very good person and is another person whose life I saved.

Kanye West enters the next verse and says, "Getting stupid" because I don't say things like other people do and say dumb things sometimes because I don't take myself seriously sometimes, and I don't think other people should either.

Flobots, "Same Thing"—"Somewhere between prayer and revolution, between Jesus and Hughey P. Newton" is how he begins this song. I didn't see any of this coming, but after Sum 41 came out with the song, it makes no difference to me the Flobots came out with this song, "Same Thing." The revolution part stands for the part where we break free from the wrath of society and put the world on our own shoulders. I don't want to give Jeff say in the world because he doesn't deserve it, and neither do other people as well. They didn't go through the apocalyptic things I was going through, so it is so unfair if other people get the credit for saving the world when I am doing all the work and actually went through all of this bullshit. I answer prayers every day and all day long, whether I am Jesus or God.

Jeff is the devil, so he has no right to say some of the bullshit that he says, and I am very sick and tired of that asshole. The revolution part stands for the part where we say, "F——k you" to the people who think they run the world and we say that everything must remain balanced. It is unfair that a lot of people are going through these tragedies and that people are still homeless, and I don't trust half of the things that Trump says because he has had a very easy life and doesn't understand the struggles that some of us go through.

He says, "I am rooting for the other team in the culture wars." What he means by this is that I am not about the White pride bullshit and that I love Black people and Hispanic people and Indian people and other races just as much as I like White people. I think that to be that person, to be the go-to person, you need to branch out to people outside your country and be *real* with them. Not like fake-ass Jeff, but be a person of the people. Rely on those who are in your inner circle but also branch out to other people to create a unified front.

Next, he says, "Each day is the same, just the names keep changing." What he means by this is people who believe in a higher deity and Jesus want to see change, but these changes just haven't happened yet. We want to see a better world and an equal world instead of the people who run it, running it into the ground. We want to see peace in the world, and I know that Trump had it planned that way, but they weren't ready for the world to end till someone acted out and killed innocent civilians to keep the war overseas going. My prediction is that it ends sometime between 2020 and 2021. I never experienced any demon problems until 2010. Fort Minor said, "Eight years in the making as of 2012," so sometime in 2020, hopefully, this all goes away.

Next he says, "We've been all over the globe, but our government funds leaving our man, woman, and child dead, bloody, and numb." I think what he means is that our government funds aren't being used for the right causes, and it is leaving too many people dead because of the way the government is controlling us. This is also what he meant by revolution because we don't want to be controlled in the ways they are controlling us. Next he says, "People say slogans we don't know where we've been." This is another song saying that it doesn't matter where you've been and where you're going because what matters if what we're going to build as a big happy family in the future. When he says, "Numb," it means that people are oblivious to their surroundings and don't understand the pain that other people are going through and need to get out of their own ways to help out people in need. Stop walking in straight lines and start going outside of your comfort zones and be real with people and help them out.

Next, he says, "We've been overthrowing leaders with legitimate views, democratically elected, but we didn't approve." This is very true because there have been very smart and good people that never had a chance to show what they can do for us as a united people and voted for the wrong people. However, he says "democratically elected" because despite what people think, Trump was elected by 63 percent of the American people because of Mac Miller's song, "Donald Trump." I used to listen to that song all the time to get Trump to beat Hillary. The people voted him in, and that is how it should have remained instead of people wasting two valuable years in trying to find out that Russians interfered with our election. That was such a waste of precious time that could have been wasted on something else.

The next part of his song, he says, "With the blood on the streets while the people die." When he says this, he is talking about the gangs cleaning up the streets and the gun violence within cities. It is all going to end, but I just don't know when. When he says, "While the people die," he is talking about people that have died overseas in other countries because of poverty and hunger. This is going to end at some point as well, but I just don't know when. There have been way too many innocent lives lost and have died because of all of this apocalyptic stuff. And, again, when I say apocalyptic, I mean that. Stop playing *me*. It is getting really f——king annoying. You all weren't going through the bullshit I was going through, so you don't know what it's f——king like. If you would like to meet face-to-face somewhere, then make sure you bring a gun because I am bullet-proof, motherf——kers.

Furthermore, he says, "And its multiplying and why not?" The people who used to hate on me, even if they don't remember, like people that were dying from gun violence or other means, was for a reason, but it wasn't because they didn't deserve it because they did. A lot of people used to hate on me, so I started taking them out of society. In the next part of the song, he says, "The process of healing will take some time." This is what I was just talking to about with my therapist. I will be fully healed, and this is when the "fun" games begin. I am not talking about the apocalyptic things but the fun games like two-on-two basketball tournaments and everyone will get healed up as well.

If you can't get what you want, well, it's all because of me. I am willing to take on this responsibility and make all your best wishes come true! Next he says to "see the pain in your face is the same as mine." I have been through a lot of pain, and our faces are all unique, but my pain is far different from yours, so I don't want to hear about it and I will probably tell you that I simply just don't give a f——k.

"We're tired of the same thing and we are ready to make change" is what he says in the next verse. This is what I was saying in the above section is that we are ready to make change, and we want to bring heaven on earth and feel limitless throughout the day. Whoever is running these tests on me needs to bring that shit to life. Here is the list that he goes through in this song: "We want money for health care, public welfare, human needs, not corporate greed, drop the debt and legalize weed. Bring the troops back to the USA and shut down Guantanamo Bay."

In the next part of the song, he's talking about some of the people in Hollywood that were assassinated or overthrown. They actually came out with a TV script for these people that we are going to bring back to life. My mom is watching it right now. These are actually human beings that are brought back to life. I haven't watched the TV show yet, but I am curious to know exactly how the script goes. He mentioned seven names of people who were assassinated or overthrown, then he says, "Don't let them assassinate two more people." I don't know exactly who he is talking about, but I am sure that we want to keep them alive. Next he says, "Bring back eight people," who I am assuming are from Hollywood or from my life. For all the people who love me and have one-upped me to show their appreciation for all the things I have been doing, I say we bring back exactly forty people. There are still people dying every day, so when it is all said and done, there will be forty people that we will bring back to life.

Carbon Leaf, "What about Everything"—he starts out with this song, saying, "Holiday quiet on these streets, except for some starving leaves that didn't quite fall with the fall." I think what he means by this is that there is peace during the holidays when family get together, and during other parts of the year, things are chaotic and messy. When he says, "Some leaves didn't fall with the fall," he is saying that the changes of the seasons are different than they used to be, and because it is fall outside, it doesn't necessarily mean that the weather will be very cold or that changes in the atmosphere are a little different than they used to be.

The next part of the song is very important because this is when karma starts to catch up with me. He says, "In search of some rest, in search of a break, from a life full of test, where something's always at stake. I have been testing throughout my entire life and every stage of my life, pretty much. I know other people have been tested, too, but people are not dying or losing jobs or getting promotions and getting paid and making it to the professional ranks because of your tests. My tests are more valuable because I hold the future of the world in my hands, and all the answers we seek depend on how free or fake, so since nobody in the world has been as free as I have been, I have found answers that only the people that are helping out understand.

I don't think a lot of people in this life understand the meaning of it, and I am so sick of these bullshit tests, many of which many people have died from, especially in recent memory. I really never chose this path but am making the most of it. I have met and want to meet more people that are very interesting, down to earth, and naturally good people. Amber said she thinks my tests started later on in life. But that's not true, and it's not some bullshit God tests. These are tests that are killing the flesh every day so that we can build a new world without the weirdos and crazy people in it. I have the feelings in my system still that hold the key to the future of the world, and I don't think most people would understand unless they were actually walking in my shoes or helping me out on the regular.

In the next part of the song, he says, "When something's always so far, what about my broken car, what about my life so far?" I am going to interpret this part as when he says something's always so far, it means that we are always so close from making my pains and my fears go away, but then things always get in the way. This is why Danny Elfman came out with the "Little Things" song, and they came out with the script for that one TV show called *A Million Little Things*. It always seems so close, but then when something actually does happen, sometimes it seems like it is actually further away than it actually is.

I thought I was going to achieve perfection sooner, but it is taking forever, and I am never going to give up on my dreams. It is very important than karma catches up or this will never work the way that we all intended when I started realizing exactly what the f——k was going on with the world. When he says, "What about my broken car?" he is talking about the scenes in these TV shows and movies saying that I am in this movie that is a million lines long and the parts where they put in the car, such as the *Fast and the Furious* movies, these are scenes involving my life. Adam is buster (Paul Walker), and that is part of the reason why they sent him home. He is supposed to be my partner in crime but is a loner and is probably fighting for his life every day. When he says, "What about my life so far?" he is talking about the good and bad memories that I have developed over the years, including when I was younger and didn't know the things about the world that I do know now.

The CIA ran a shitload of tests through me in order to find a solution for the human race. We are closer than we have ever been before, but this isn't over yet. I am still living in fear, and the pains that I have been feeling since I was living with Eric and Sean in Centreville still haven't gone away yet. We are working on a solution every single day, and everything I do is important, and most people don't f——king matter. I don't care about your stupid bullshit issues when I am dealing with some serious real world things. F——k your baby and your weekend plans when I am trying to save the world every day.

In the next part of the song, he says "What about my dream?" He is talking about me being selfish and my own aspirations, which are how everyone else thinks anyway, and about the big picture. My dream is perfection in every sense of the word *perfection*. I don't have to have the perfect personality, but I need to dream big and make it on the big stage with perfection inside my head. My dream is also my vision, in which Hendersin put into his song with all the details of my vision in this book. The athletes will love if I can achieve perfection because I was just this low-life middle-class guy without a care in the world before this burden came to me. I dealt with it, and once Peyton Manning said he was going to put me into that same exact game again, my senses got stronger, and I learned how to become a better person and I learned much, much more about the world. I was actually able to write this book because of how hard Hollywood and the professional athletes made this for me.

In the next part of the song, he says, "What about airplanes?" and he means the airplanes that have crashed with casualties over the years. This is just like the movie *King Kong* where he swats out the airplanes that were attacking him in the sky and killing people. I was killing people because of this revolution that I was given. It was people who were attacking me, and the world is too overpopulated anyway, so why not f——king put them into the ground if they are not going to bring value to the world and to my life?

This also means the military and how they used this tactic to kill terrorists. I play this one Nelly song to try to end the war overseas with the song "Boom." Every time I play that song and the word *boom* comes up, some terrorist from Afghanistan dies. Next, and this goes along with airplanes, but he says, "What about ships that drain the seas?" Again, as a part of this revolution, some people on boats and ships out in the wilderness have died because they just don't belong into this new society we are building. The world is too f——king overpopulated, so why not kill a few of these motherf——kers and save the sky because these assholes are polluting areas with their existence on this planet? This also means the military because the ships were a part of the military's strategy to keep America safe. All the wars are going to end, and we will bring peace to the world. It is just a matter of when and how long it is going to take for both sides to form a treaty.

Furthermore, he says, "What about the moon and stars?" When he says this, he is taking about the universe and how we all came here through evolution. There are a lot of people that say that humans aren't supposed to be here right now. I totally disagree with that, and I believe that because through me, we are here for a bigger reason than others might think. We are here to create this world in which we are living in peace forever, and I don't need any help from the skies, and I am actually so goddamn sick of people pointing to the sky for guidance when we can just save lives because we are humans, and that's what humans do. I don't need God's goddamn help. I can just do this on my own, and f——k all that Jesus bullshit. I think people are crazy that go to church every day and that all gays go to hell and actually believe in all that craziness. The moon and stars are important, and they can tell a story in each person's life.

In my life, I am able to connect the dots in society and in the world to attribute to the people who will live through all this and their success in the past, present, and future. When people like Jeff tell me there are certain things they don't f——k with and they say the devil is one of them, I feel so f——king sorry for you because you don't know shit about anything. You don't know anything about this goddamn world, and I will f——king put you in my grave with my own two hands if you still think that the devil is at fault. On a lighter note, he says, "What about soldier battles?" I took this into my own life to try to help America win this war overseas and help them out in Afghanistan every single day. My dad and Gino told me that the war overseas is over, but they were wrong. The war in Iraq is over, but the war in Afghanistan isn't over, so I suggest they keep their f——king mouths shut and let me handle this kind of shit.

Anyway, Hollywood laid the lice in me without me even knowing that the war in Iraq was going to end, so my technology that I have been using actually ended the war in Iraq, and it is a matter of time before the war in Afghanistan ends as well. We still have a few soldiers dying over there, but I think by the end of 2020 or 2021, the wars will be completely over.

In addition, he says, "What about all the anger?" And he is taking about all the domestic violence and people hating on people for no reason. This is a very important part of the song and tells a good meaning because I have felt disrespected by a lot of people because of their beliefs in god (with a lower case G) and for other reasons when I wasn't doing shit to them. I still know how to fight, and I still have leverage over all of them in the future. Domestic violence was never an issue growing up, and we used to do bad things and never get in trouble for them. Everyone in this goddamn world is getting so sensitive to so much annoying bullshit. We are all alive right now for a reason, and it is our time to break the goddamn rules.

I am walking on so many goddamn eggshells because of these rules, and it's our time to f——king break them. When the *4400* episode came out when all the guys had extra testosterone in their system, this is why they came out with that episode. I have hit girls in the past but never will again. Professional athletes are getting in trouble, and people all over the place are getting into trouble for hitting women or for being too aggressive in public places. I guess it depends on what level you are actually breaking these rules. However, I don't think that some of these rules are necessary. At the same time, I do think that people need to calm the f——k down and embrace the changing culture and understand why certain people are the way they are and not judge others because you're not walking in their goddamn shoes.

In the next part of his song, he says, "I am not in need." What he means by this is patience is very important, and I don't need all these things I say I need right now, but I do need them soon. People are trying to calm me down every day and say just trust the process. I am trusting the process, but this is just taking so goddamn long, and because of certain goddamn *people* in this world, I am sick and tired of their bullshit reasoning and viewpoints on things.

My suggestion to you is, "Shut the f——k up before I shut you the f——k up." I am not in need. I have everything I need within my grasp, and I am living my life the way I want to. I don't care about my f——king salary and moving up in the ranks because I am not in need. I am just going to take my time and let these idiots make the mistakes for me while I win the world each day.

In the next part of the song, he says, "It's school, work, and then just life that just sharpens the blade." This is reality, and we can change this reality if we work together. We go to school, we go to work then we retire and die. I don't want to die. I am so f——king scared of the afterlife. I want to live here forever. For this to happen, karma needs to catch up with me, I need to step back into the line, or Jesus "*me*" needs to save us all. It is tougher now that I am older, but we need to keep pushing for this forever young movement. *We* can find a solution and take our mature minds and move them into our twenty-five-year-old bodies with some Will Coakley experimentation. Karma will catch up or else Hollywood wouldn't have released so many songs about it.

I am having a great time playing softball, fantasy sports, golf, and bowling and understanding more about life by reading, watching TV, and listening to what people tell me and dissecting these songs. I can't work because I am still living with too much pain and fear, but this gives me more time to save the world and do exactly what I was destined to do.

In the next part of the song, he says, "I think about time for fun, I think about time for play, and then I think about being done with no resume." I just covered the fun and play stuff in the last paragraph. It seems like I am living a life of leisure, but it's really not that simple. I couldn't work because I didn't have any ADD medication, and that is what got me through school and my work in my twenties. When he says, "I think about being done with no resume," he means that I won't have to apply to any jobs because I will just get rich starting up my own business. TI even wrote that in one of his songs, saying, "I got rich and I am a believer."

I believe sometimes, but with people like Jeff saying some of the things he said to me and when people are too fake sometimes, it makes it hard for me to believe. I am going to get to the youth movement and make all these things happen. I just need more time and I need to be patient, as I mentioned earlier with this topic. This is the most important part of the song, in my opinion. "With no one left to blame, what about fortune and fame?" This whole song he left for me to listen to and dissect like this. This means no terrorists left to blame, no more old people, no more people dealing with me, no more people making me fake on events, and nobody that is wasting my precious free time. I will become famous once all these things happen, but I need to be patient. This is everything I am going to talk about this song, and it is a lot to take in, but it is as real as it gets. If I can thank everyone in the future, I would do that now. If you haven't been part of it, at least you got to witness history.

Vanilla Ice, "Ice Ice Baby"—collaborate and listen. The word *collaborate* means that people are working jointly on an activity, especially to produce or create something. This is what my therapist and I have been talking about in our therapy sessions. There are too many individuals in this world, and we need to start working in groups. I play certain songs to make sure this is possible, such as Nicki Minaj's song when she says "I" on repeat so that people get out of their own worlds and start helping others. I'm talking about working in groups in the first section of my book, but this is the first part of the song. When he says, "Listen," he is talking about Adam (Jesus) who needs to start listening to people instead of saying, "What?" which happens too often. They put that part in Sum 41's song and Spose's song.

This Vanilla Ice song was an intro to Hollywood for future performers, so when I explain what I think the meaning of these songs are and how they relate to me, this song started off a lot of future singers who all sang about my life. In the next part of the song, he says, "Daily and nightly" because Kid Cudi came out with the song "Day and Night," as if I was God and Adam was Jesus and he was the lonely stoner or lonely boy in *Gossip Girl*, and I was conquering everything and saving the world as the God character.

The next part of the song, he says "Will it ever stop? Yo, I don't know." He is talking about this life. For instance, will it be everlasting? And when I come up with the response, I am like, "Yo, I don't know." It all seemed very simple a long time ago, and sometimes I want it to be everlasting and sometimes I don't. The biggest part of me wants it to be everlasting so that everything we have started with these transgressions and transformations will be complete. The age is just a number thing started with me, and it will end with me because we need karma to catch up with me.

The next part of the song, he says, "Turn off the lights, and I glow." What he means by this is that people are training me to talk in public spaces and to perform in front of large crowds. They are still quizzing me, but the tests aren't as hard, thank goodness, because I am removing people from the equation who don't belong in our society anymore. These people were holding us back and weren't bringing anything to the table, like I demanded.

We are all getting older, but the impossible has been done before, so why not have it done again? He was also setting this precedent for future performers in large crowds for Hollywood. In the next part of the song, he says, "I'll kill it in your brain like a poisonous mushroom." When he was talking about this, it meant that I was taking over the world, and whoever dies was my doing, but I wouldn't take the blame because nobody would really know what the cause was. For instance, the war overseas started because of me, and now Hollywood and myself are trying to correct it.

Xzibit came out with his song, "X," in 2000, and the war started in 2001. The whole world is being run by technology, especially mine, so this pretty much was what started the war overseas. I wouldn't have known in 2001 because I was just a freshman in high school or a sophomore. I didn't know the things about the world that I know now. The revolution part in terms of people dying in the US and in other countries is just population shrinkage. At some point, people will stop having kids. Sometime after karma catches up with me, we won't have to worry about overpopulation. I mean, people are dying every day, and that kind of takes care of itself.

In the next part of the song, he says, "Anything less than the best is a felony." He is talking about after karma catches up with me, and we are focused on the full potential theory again and when we actually do play pickup games of basketball of two-on-two and three-on-three and bowling tournaments and basketball in the pool and volleyball. If I am not the best, then this is all a waste because I am the best person on the planet, and I have had the toughest life. When they put up that one commercial, "The best or nothing," they were talking to me.

I was making this list of the best people in the world, but then I stopped because it was just wasting my time. I have my favorites, and everyone else that I run into after I stopped making this list is just another number of who is the best in the world and who has had it the hardest. I am also talking about golf and tackle football. The athletes work their asses off every day to get to where they are, but we can do the exact same, and I will be trained by professionals to compete at their level.

I don't f——king care. I can be as good as they are or else Hollywood wouldn't have come up with so many songs that I am the best person in the world. Furthermore, he says, "You better hit bull's-eye, the kid don't play." He is talking about one person dying, whether they were dealing with me for their own gains or because it is a population shrinkage. Then he says, "If there was a problem, yo, I'll solve it." When he says this, it reminds me of the global warming problems and the problems that I bring up in this book. Whether that means no more injuries or perfect weather throughout our entire lives, I can solve these problems because I have the power to. The weather is so hot in October, but it's better than it being so cold. I hope it remains this way through November and December as well.

Other problems are problems like overpopulation or the sun hitting the earth 10,000 years from now or California having too many earthquakes that it's going to separate from the US. Big problems and even little problems such as people not having friends or bullies picking on losers. Things of this nature and other things that I have and will solve every day until the world is as perfect as it should be.

In the next part of his song, he says, "Now that the party is jumping." I think he is talking big picture and the final festivities as if I am the last call for sin and we are all one united family. I might be God or Jesus, but in the Killers song, I am the last call for sin, so people will find their matches, and I will be with my soul mate. He is also talking about the parties all over the world but mainly the last call for sin part. Additionally, he says, "No faking" because I have been faking a lot because of my depression issues and the demon problems I have been dealing with.

Avril Lavigne came out with her song, "Complicated," to kill the flesh as a part of this revolution, and in this song, she says, "Honestly, I wouldn't see you faking" and then a bunch of nos because those people are just more casualties of society. I need to be a better friend, especially to those who have been loyal to me over the years. I never was asking for any of this, but this burden came to me, so I have dealt with it. I will be a better friend, and they started at the end, so this is our time to make a change in history, not the old f——ks or the young people but people of my generation to make a change. The more people that help me out every day is a bonus, but we need to keep things moving forward, and the people who are holding us back need to be eliminated. I see the big picture, and that is sort of how I am able to write this book because I bring up topics that cover a broad range of topics, and I can dive deeper into these topics once I start to think more clearly.

The next part of the song is pretty important. He says, "I go crazy when I hear a cymbal." They put this part in *Transformers*, and this is real life with me. My mind and my body go somewhere in the mix of the elements whenever something is going wrong in my life. I don't know who put this test on me, but it is what it is. I am okay with it because I am trying to make this life perfect. There has to be more to everything I thought exists, like heaven and earth combining into one magical force. I hold the key to the future of the world, and when I see these symbols and signs, I need to make it perfect and make everything connecting into the sky and into one big family.

The next part of the song is pretty funny. He says, "The girls on standby, waiting just to say hi. Did you stop? No, I just drove by." He is talking about this brunette girl who obviously knew who I was, and she was walking down my street one day when I was going through all of my transgressions. She was probably the hottest girl that I have ever seen that was ever interested in me. I nodded my head, and she nodded her head back at me. I have had plenty of other opportunities to get with many other girls in this world, but nothing has worked out yet. I can be patient on this matter, but the girl I saw that day seemed really down-to-earth, very, very cute, and someone who I'd would like to be friends with in the future. I was still trying to figure out who I was back then, so being in a relationship isn't really in my mind right now. Amber and I were lovers in a dangerous and hopeless time, but I will want to be friends with her again in the future and with whoever else passes my tests since I am taking over this goddamn world.

Next, he says, "Jealous, 'cause I am out getting mine." When he says, "Jealous," he is talking about my behaviors of the past when I used to be jealous of what other people were receiving in life and things I wasn't. I am still jealous because I deserve to be as happy as other people in the world, but I am still dealing with demon problems that most people would have killed themselves by now if they were dealing with the same things. I will be patient when it comes to getting in a relationship, and maybe I have already met that girl, but I will just be patient and let things develop as fate dictates.

Next, he says, "Falling on the ground real fast." He is talking about when I started playing that "X" song that I realized was actually killing people and that I won't see double vision anymore. When I was at a Halloween party, I fell on the ground, and this happens sometimes when things don't go my way, but I was so drunk and didn't know what I was doing, so I laid on the ground. I need to get back to the person I used to be, and that includes not being too crazy but also being myself in social situations and calm, like I used to be. I think I finally know who I am now and won't let anything or anyone stop me from reaching my goals in the future and bringing the world to the heights that it needs to be in the future.

Next, he says, "Bumper to bumper, the avenue's packed." He is talking about traffic, and this is another thing that I will fix for everyone. I just need more time. People are still training me to be the person I need to be in the future, and I will stop losing my mind so much when the fears start to go away, but traffic is one thing that I am destined to fix, and it also goes along with the lines of killing the flesh. This process seems like it is taking forever, but good days are ahead of us, so we will make this happen for everyone.

In the next part of the song, he says, "Police are on the scene, you know what I mean?" He is talking about my hospital visits and the asshole police officers that came to my house. My dad called the cops on me twice in a span of three weeks, which really was bullshit. It was just like when I was working at Comtek, and I was just working there for three months before all this conspiracy bullshit was run on me. The one cop touched my dick, and that was part of sexual harassment which I couldn't have reported. I am pretty mad that some of this bullshit happened to me, but if people can really save me, then f——king save me, and I will help you guys out in return. However, it seems like I am helping people out with nobody fixing my issues. Maybe I should just trust the process, but this goddamn process is taking forever, and we need to speed it up. This is all I want to say about this song for the time being.

Imagine Dragons, "Whatever It Takes"—he starts off the song with saying, "Falling too fast to prepare for this." What he means by this is that I am falling every single day, and it is hard to prepare for it because I never know when it is going to happen. I have been falling a lot ever since I was getting stuck too deep when I was twenty-six. I thought it was because I was just tired all the time and the things inside of me were making me fall. Then I realized that it was demons and side effects from all the drugs and things that I was going through. I started to realize recently that ever since the athletes said they were going to put me through the same game again and said it to my face and when Fergie came clean in one of her songs that it was all for a reason, and it wasn't anything I was doing bad. It was just the fact that we were following the devil's plan, and people in this world were following the devil's plan, which was making me self-destruct.

For instance, when they came out with the show *Grey's Anatomy*, they came out with this show as a sign of respect to save people's lives across the world with every positive step that I was taking.

In the next part of the song, he says, "Everyone is waiting for the fall of man." He is talking about Adam in this part. There are a lot of atheists that think that the apocalypse is a lie, and if I am God and Adam is Jesus, then they are pretty much following the devil's plan. When I say the devil, I mean Jeff. There a lot of people that started to realize that *F——k, maybe we are all actually going through apocalyptic things and that someone is trying to destroy our lives.* I am just human, after all, so I don't want people to put the blame on God. I want them to realize that Jeff is the devil and, of course, I have never been disrespected as much as that kid has, and nobody in the past had ever disrespected me as badly as this guy did, so I do want him to pay the ultimate price.

There are a lot of songs they put out that say that Adam should self-destruct, but every time he does, it seems like I do too. The next part of the song, he says everyone is praying for the end of times. A lot of the Mayans and Amazons were praying for the end of time. They wanted God to destroy the planet and end life as we know it on the earth. I have dealt with a lot of false prayers and people with not-so-good intentions for the planet, and this even means miscarriages. Overpopulation means overpopulation. These people, who I think are evil, were trying to make the devil more powerful than God.

Jeff deserves no more say in the world because that kid totally f——ked up mine a long time ago, and he is just a burden to what I am trying to do for the world. Then there are other people who are intentionally doing things to me who are going to hell and making my life worse. Those people are essentially following the devil's plan.

Furthermore, he says, "Everyone was hoping they could be the one." This means the chosen one. I was the one who actually went through all of that apocalyptic stuff on this planet, so I deserve to get that credit in the future. I might not be the one, it might be Adam, but nobody actually went through all of these hellish things and demon problems that I went through. When Eminem came out with the "Monster" song, he mentions Jeff's name because he was practically throwing me all over my house, and I do think he did that indecent exposure to me, but for myself, I don't have any evidence yet. A lot of people in this world think he needs to pay. Most likely, he will fade away from my life, then if Anna wants to be with me, then she needs to make that decision. Nobody can make that decision for her, but she is a precious person who is dating the wrong person. Many people in Hollywood think that Jeff needs to pay the ultimate price.

In the next part of the song, he says, "I love the adrenaline in my veins." He says this because when I am up and walking and talking, I love how that feeling is, and it also has to do with the certain medications that are finally working for me. I am not bipolar or schizophrenic, but I am just a guy who is praying a price for living now and conquering everything. I am the best person in the world, and everything will change for me one day as long as I remain patient. I love the adrenaline in my veins when I work out and when I am playing sports. I love when my heart is pumping in fresh oxygen into my system because it makes me feel high on life.

The next part of the song, he says, "Because I love how it feels when I break the chains." This is insane and I didn't know this was a part of my tests, but one of the hospital visits I took earlier on when I was about twenty-five years old and not aware of all these tests that I received in the past and the tests I was going to receive in the future, I was essentially breaking invisible chains. I started self-destructing after that, and they kept on apologizing and saying that it was malfunctions. People thought I was crazy, but if it was just malfunctions, then why is all of this crap going on with North Korea happening now? It wasn't just malfunctions. Everything I was going through was real, and I didn't know at the time that those were chains I was breaking. It means that I am free from death because I am sin, and God doesn't allow sin into heaven.

This is also how they came out with the show *Lucifer*. He is the devil and is free from death because he is immortal. Lecrae came out with that song, first saying that I am free from death, then he said, "Who is to say what truth is that people put themselves before Jesus, now we have to live forever until Satan's reach?" One day, Hollywood painted a six-pack on me as if I am the Jesus character that is going to save us all from Satan's wrath and save the world as Jesus.

I used to love how it felt when I broke the chains, but now I just want everything to go back to normal again, and sometimes I want to forget that all this has ever happened to me. I want it all to go away so I can start living a normal life again. It is pretty crazy that they can relate to breaking the chains to my hospital visit I had when I was like twenty-four or twenty-five years old. I have been on heaven on earth, and I want others to experience what I have experienced, but it is going to take some type of special pill for all of us to be on for this to happen.

In the next part of the song, he says, "I want to be invisible." He is talking about Adam because he is so isolated from the world and only pretty much cares about his wife and me. I am trying to not get him so isolated when he is more key in my life and get him acclimated into how we live our lives, but it's going to take some time. I still need to figure some more stuff out on my own and hope that everything still works out for me, but he needs to come out and act normal around the people I hang out with.

The next part of the song, he says, "Everyone needs to be part of them." He is talking about the 1 percent, pretty much the guys who run the world. They are working on the solution for the human race every day and pretty much remain in the background. They poisoned me in a certain way that only the right people who pass these tests will be a part of our future, but we have to be more inclusive, and this is why they picked me, an average guy who was just living his life to become bigger than life itself and run the world with real connections and with all different kinds of people.

In the next part of the song, he says, "I was born to run, I was born for this." What he means by this is that I was born to run from the police, I was born to run from the FBI, I was born to run from my haters and build this new world that we have been trying to build through all the tests that have been run through me. The cops have been acting weird around me, and the FBI are corrupt, too, and have been surveying my house and the people that I hang out with, just to make sure we aren't doing anything illegal.

The skits for *Prison Break* and the *Blacklist*, the corrupt CIA and FBI were involved. Some of them that did bad things to me in the past have died, but it's all about building a better future for us and for the people that have done good in this world. This also includes the poor and the middle class. Some of these assholes think it's okay to not include everyone, and I somewhat agree. There are a lot of losers and weirdos in this world, but we have to learn how to become more inclusive.

The next part of the song, he says, "Hypocritical," talking about me. I am the happy hypocrite as they relayed to the public in *Silver Linings Playbook.* Next he says, "Working on something that I am proud of." I think he is talking about my book because I was working from the ground up to build this book on everything that I have been through, including the positive and negative parts. Additionally, he says, "The vision we've lost." I don't think a lot of people understand, but the vision he is talking about is our belief systems, and who is the person who went through this hell to build the world that we are trying to build in the future? Why were all of these tests run on this particular person while everyone is living what Will calls "boring lives"? You go to school, you work, you retire, and then you die.

I see this as completely different. I say that karma catches up with me and we build heaven on earth here instead of following what society says we should do. People like Jeff could never understand this because they don't know what these feelings are like.

Third Eye Blind, "Jumper"—He starts out with this song says, "I wish you would step back from that ledge, my friend." He is talking about all my depression and anxiety and panic attacks. I have these reoccurring thoughts because people made my life so f——king difficult for me. Now Jeff wants to get some of the credit when I deserve all the credit because of how hard I have had it. It was all so f——king simple since 2012, but since people made this so hard for me, I am understanding the meaning of life a lot better than a lot of these nobody's in the world, and the people who do understand things a little bit better than the others, then more power to them. The next part of the song, he says, "You can cut ties with all the lies that you've been living in" because just like what Katy Perry said in her song, I fell for everything because of all the tests God put on me, and then I went from being a zero into being a hero for the world. I am talking about when my dad was making examples of me with the 1 percent, but I can't really hold grudges against them because they are steadily fixing me every single day, and I am going to get rich one day as long as I just stay the course and trust the process.

The CIA is the part of the government that keeps America and the world safe every day. They don't mind if outsiders die, but the bulk of the population pretty much remain safe every day. They used to send me on terrible missions at night and during the day when I was working and put me through some terrible tests, even when I was in high school, when I had no idea what the f——k was going on. People laid the lice in me so that I could figure this shit out and get fixed over time, but the CIA did do some terrible things to me, and some of them have died because of it. People are hoping that karma catches up with me soon because of some of the bad things that have happened to me in the past, and they don't want to be caught up in the middle of this anymore. Unfortunately, I am stuck pretty deep, so we all just have to trust the process and make sure things just go efficiently from here on out.

The empires or Mafia laid some bad tests on me as well with the *Star Wars* and the conspiracy theory when I was just at work for three months at Comtek. I ended up working there for two years, but still, some of the tests they laid on me were terrible. Also, when I was working at Comtek, the Amatse, the people who control who live and who die, laid some terrible tests on me as well. Luckily, I have taken that into my own hands now, and they don't say who live and who die unless it goes through me first. I think that it has always gone through me, so we'll see when Karma starts creeping up on me and things become more real in this world and people's problems start to get fixed quicker and more effectively if less people are dying and less children are being born into this world.

The next part of the song, he says this several times in this song that Anna would understand if we weren't destined to be with each other and I took on another soul mate. If I am going to be honest, I didn't know what love at first sight was before I met her when I was dating Amber. I have never told this to Jeff, obviously, but I thought her personality was perfect and her looks were perfect. I was dating Amber, so I didn't put much thought into it, but looking back at it now, yeah, I thought she was perfect. The next part of the song, he says, "The angry boy a bit too insane." I was always a crazy kid, and when I was drinking, my craziness would show a lot more. When I was playing soccer when I was younger, I was always getting into fights, and my insecurities wouldn't allow me to excel in other sports, but with soccer and with other people picking fights with me, I was always winning those fights. But, yeah, I had a pretty bad history of being angry all the time.

However, during the past ten to fifteen years, a lot of people have disrespected me behind my back. I would love for some of them so show their faces to me and we can meet outside my house anytime they want when it gets dark outside, and let's battle it out and see who becomes victorious. I don't want to put up with people's bullshit and all they have done and will continue to make my mistakes for me unless they really do want to fight me. And trust me, it won't end well for them. I know a lot of the athletes are fed up with the way things have been, just like I have, but at least they have a lot of money. I don't hold grudges against them because I know one day, I will get rich.

Jeff was the first person who really disrespected me to my face since grade school, but that's not entirely true either. There were a lot of fraternity brothers who used to think I was very stupid and that I didn't belong into the fraternity. Well, f——k them, too, because look at how far I have gotten when I was working with nothing in the past. If I am looking for a war, then I better realize what I am fighting for was what they put in another song. Believe me, I don't disrespect people that much, but if you are a coward and want to talk shit behind my back, then let's meet in my court any time after ten o'clock on the weekdays, and we'll see who is soft and who is hard then.

In the next part of the song, he says, "You know you don't belong." He is talking about Adam. I feel bad for Adam because he is the lonely stoner who doesn't trust many people, except for my parents, his wife, and me. He'll get back into the swing of things and start hanging out and talking to the people I talk to, but he really needs to develop more common sense and more social skills so that people don't judge him. I feel for him, though, because I have been judged for those same things in the past.

When Third Eye Blind says that Adam doesn't belong, it reminds me of that one *Seinfeld* episode when Jerry was dating that good-looking chick, and all of his friends were like, "Why are you dating that girl? She is a nerd and doesn't belong to someone as cool as you are." This is pretty much how they got this episode because of me being best friends with someone like Adam. He is pretty much the definition of eighteen, cool because his best years in terms of popularity were in high school when I was gaining popularity after high school. He is still my best friend and will be my best man at my wedding.

In the next part of the song, he says, "You're the first to fight, you're way too loud." For example, you can tell when I was talking about the people who used to talk trash about me and still might be, that we can meet outside my house any time after ten o'clock. I was always a lover and a fighter but more of a fighter. I am trying to be calmer these days and give love a chance when the timing is right instead of always being so goddamn angry all the time. People like to come around and pick dumbass fights with me and f——k with my mind, and that's all going to end because I am developing more and more connections with the environment and the world and with people every single day. Adam will always be my best friend as long as he is there for me, just like I was always there for him. I need everything from here on out to be run perfectly so that the excess fat can be eliminated and we can make sure things run smoothly with no stupid-ass interference from idiots and retards along the way.

The next part of the song, he says, "I do not think anyone knows what they are doing here." This goes along with Fort Minor saying in his song that "all the answers to life that we seek depend on how free or fake." In one of Sum 41's songs, he says, "Some say we are better not knowing what life is all about." Unfortunately, I know a lot more things than most people know, so I don't like it when people act stupid because I know that is the devil's interference in my life, and it is really f——king starting to piss me off. I know in the past all the bad shit that happened to me and how simple it seems now, but I am sick of people saying "What?" and "Huh?" It is so immature and just plain f——king goddamn annoying. Spose and Atmosphere both disrespected me in two of their songs, so they both wonder why they aren't as famous as some of the other artists in Hollywood. They did it to themselves, so I don't feel sorry for them. However, like I said, if anyone wants to pick a fight with me, then feel free to join me outside my house at 10:00 anytime, Monday through Friday.

I started to understand very clearly why I am here and why we are all on planet earth right now because of how hard life was made for me. It had nothing to do with God like a bunch of these dumbass Jesus freaks think it does. It has everything to do with people cleaning up this mess. There is no need to look to the f——king sky when we can just solve these goddamn problems ourselves. It is a lot simpler than it looks, and by the time I turn thirty-six, people will really see the benefits of society and see how precious life can really be.

I can't stand when people say life is too short. Karma will catch up with me, and we will be forever young, only if you want to be, of course. I would rather live here forever, then disappear and be a ghost for the rest of eternity. I don't think a lot of these annoying ass Jesus freaks understand that, though. I go through most of my days not believing that a god exists unless someone brings it to my attention. I just don't f——king care, but like I said, Spose and Atmosphere wonder why they aren't as well-known as some of the other artists in Hollywood because those other guys and girls didn't disrespect me like they did and a few others too.

The next part of the song, he says, "You've been dismissed." He is talking about an old person or a sick person. It is just a part of this revolution to kill the flesh and let the right people to continue to live on. What a lot of these morons don't understand is that the world is overpopulated, so people need to die every day. More importantly, people need to stop having kids. I don't think a lot of people get it. *The world is overcrowded. Stop having kids.* It's not f——king rocket science.

The next part of the song, he says, "Everyone's got to face down two demons." When he says this, he says that alcoholics have to deal with inner demons every day. People with mental illness have to deal with inner demons every day. There are other examples. I just can't come up with them off the top of my head. If people have lost their parents or siblings, then nothing is going to bring them back to life. I made promises to ten or forty people, depending on how this goes, that I would bring them back to life once karma catches up with me, but until then, more people will continue to die, and I am not making promises to any of them. You should have thought of this before life threw you too many curveballs when people started dying around you.

My demon issues have been way more severe than everyone else's, and this is part of the reason why I am the best person in the world. It's about time I start to show my face, just like Batman was going to in those movies. I can't keep on doing things behind closed doors. I am more active on Twitter and making more of an impact with people noticing besides the invisible cameras that are set up inside my house and in certain places I go.

Katy Perry, "Firework"—she starts off this song, saying, "Do you ever feel like a plastic bag drifting through the wind?" I think this is a metaphor for something, but I am not sure. Next she says, "Wanted to start again." Because of all these tests that I have been through and because I am pretty much alone by myself all the f——king time, I have a chance to rebuild my connections and start again in a whole new world. I gained many friends and didn't really lose any, and we have seen a lot of positive progress in the world. Even though I am depressed and lonely a lot in terms of the world perspective, there have been many advances, and the world has been benefitting, even if I have been suffering because of it. I had that indecent exposure, and Taylor Swift and Halsey both put in their songs, "Look at what you made me do" and "You don't have to say what you did, I had to go and find out from them." I still think Jeff was a part of this, and there are many songs that say the devil has a price to pay, and they are talking about Jeff when they say this.

I don't know all the facts because I got blindsided by it all until Peyton Manning said he was going to put me back into this devilish game again. That was the first person to say that to my face, and ever since then, the only person to really disrespect me to my face was Jeff.

I needed to start again, and this is also part of the healing process for me and for the world. The world will be right where it needs to be in the next two to three years as long as the people who are helping me out play their roles as needed and f——king help me the f——k out every single day. My parents are weird sometimes, and they bring me down, but I know the grass is greener on the other side, so I should be thankful that my parents are there for me. But, seriously, I took that trip to Pennsylvania in 2012 when I really thought things were going to change, and there were a lot of heaven and hell experiences on that trip, and I am still f——king living at goddamn home. So when she says, "Wanted to start again," it means that maybe my old friends who used to disrespect me will come back into my life and be nice. For the most part, they always were nice to me, but back in college and high school, we were all immature, but I had so many self-esteem issues that I couldn't really act like myself. Now I feel like I am walking on so many goddamn eggshells that I have no idea who the f——k I am sometimes.

In the next part of her song, she says, "Do you ever feel so paper thin, like a house of cards?" They came out with the script called *House of Cards* based on this Katy Perry song. I never really saw the show, but my parents watched it, and I heard it was good. I know they cancelled the show because of all the allegations against Kevin Spacey, but they made these songs and these scripts for me, and people love them and probably don't understand the meanings behind them unless they are directly affected. When she says, "Paper thin," I think she meant that because of my exercising and pooping and peeing that I am losing weight, and then the script is based on the government and other things in this world, so maybe it also applies to some of that bullshit that's going on in the world.

The next part of the song, she says, "Do you ever feel already very deep, six feet under, screams but nobody seems to hear a thing?" When Sum 41 came out with the songs "Some Say We Are Never Meant to Grow Up" and "Think Twice Before You Make Up Your Minds," it seems like everything we were told in the Bible weren't even true. Katy Perry took this to heart. She wrote these two songs about, "Could you be the devil or an angel?" and "Six feet under"

189

because she knew all the benefits it would land her in the real world and in her life if she chose to be on my side instead of the losing side.

I made so many people, including famous people, believe in my product because I was stuck so deep before Peyton Manning and the athletes actually did put me in this game again, and a lot of people could hear my thoughts and shit, even if they were private. They weren't talking to me about it, but publicly, a lot of people actually were. All the answers we seek in life depend on how free or fake, and I have learned so much since I broke up with Amber. I used to talk to her telekinetically all the time, and she would always laugh. It was pretty funny, and she was probably the best girl I have dated up to date. I know I have to work on my anger issues, and the real world has really been terrible to me, but things will change, and the people who were really and nice to me will see their benefits and have already seen their benefits as long as you don't break any of society's rules that have a lot of walking on so many goddamn eggshells.

The next part of her song, she says, "Do you know that there's still a chance for you?" because I am thirty-three now, and I still think I can achieve perfection as long as this all works out perfectly. Every single day, people are working on a solution for the human race, and I still feel forever young inside my mind. As I told my therapist in my last session, my thirty-fourth year will overcome all the fours in the world; my thirty-fifth year will overcome all the fives in the world, and thirty-six and sixty-six are golden because everything in the world is equal that year. I need to keep my goals focused and make sure that this all works according to the plan and that nobody f——ks it up. Everything in the sports world, homeless people will not be homeless anymore, middle class will get paid accordingly, and I will be rich. There will be no more wars, and peace will be attained in the world. We will find cures for illnesses and make sure that people stop having so many goddamn kids.

The next part of her song, she says, "There's a spark in you, you just got to ignite the light and let it shine." When she says this she means the light inside of me because I am the best and nicest person in the world, and I am proving it every single day and letting all my demons and emotions out so that I can be normal again. The spark inside of me is my emotions and how I express myself to others. Most people were starting to love me in the world, whether they were strangers or people in my immediate circle. Hollywood started at the end ever since I was three years old, so I am not too worried about what's going on with my loneliness.

Jeff is mean whether he likes it or not, so Hollywood is intentionally making it harder for him now so that I can be happier. You have to take your wins with your losses. When she says, "Let it shine," she is talking about the world around us. Let the world shine, let your spirit shine, and remove any doubt in your mind that you don't belong in this world. I was never one for pretenders and fake people, and when people start acting fake around me, I don't how to respond because fake people are the worst. They make everything in life worse. I know that I am trying to make Adam sound like he is my best friend, but I cannot rely on that motherf——ker. He is way too inconsistent and wouldn't be there for me in a time of crises. He is there for me, then he disappears, which is bullshit because I am always there for people, even when I am feeling down.

The next part of her song, she says, "Just own the night like the Fourth of July." *Own the Night* was another movie they came out with a while ago. I know people that were on the wrong side of things back then died because of the script that was written. Some of them were bad and some of them were wasting their time on this planet. The Fourth of July is the nation's holiday, so she put that part in this song because a seven-nation army couldn't hold me back, so they are intentionally making it worse for America's God, who is me.

The next part of her song, she says, "Come out and show what your worth." I need to prove to the people who run the world and the athletes who said I couldn't make it in the big screen that I am worthy of people paying closer attention to what I can do for the world. The next part of her song, she says, "Make them go uh, uh, uh." When I play this song, three more couples in this world find their soul mates and get engaged and get married. On this front, for myself, I need to be patient, and it's more of a wait and see approach. I know that I am good luck Chuck, which was another movie they came out with, and a lot of girls were masturbating to me to find their soul mates and whatnot. It works, and a lot of them are embarrassed to cross paths with me because it is a little bit disgusting, but f—k it, it is our time to break all the goddamn rules.

The next part of her song, she says, "You don't have to feel like a wasted space, you're original, cannot be replaced." I don't feel like a wasted space, but apparently, some people in this world thought I was because of the 666 in my phone number. I was so scared when I started living in fear and pain, but then they were like, maybe karma will catch up with him, so I am not even sure if I am the devil anymore. She made this song pretty simple, but if people were hating on it, then f——k them because honestly, most people don't deal with any demon problems throughout their entire lives, and I am the one who had to earn my stripes to get to where I am going to be at in the next couple of years.

The next part of her song, she says, if you only knew what the future holds, after a hurricane comes a rainbow. This means when I am all healed up, when I step back into the line and when karma catches up with me, people will be going to look for someone for answers, and that somebody is going to be me. Maybe I am God or Jesus, but for this song, I am the devil, and f——k it because like I said earlier, most people don't deal with any demon problems throughout their entire lives, and they still blame everything on the devil. They are useless to me and go around spreading the Word of Christ when everything in the Bible is a f——king lie.

The next part of her song, she says, "Maybe there's a reason why all the doors are closed so you can lead yourself to the perfect road." This is what I am doing on a daily basis. I am making progress in the world, and when I think of this, I think about all the people in the world I have been able to connect with and the progress we have made as a society to form into one big family. Nobody in the world compares to me, and nobody has done as much for the world as I have. The perfect road will be determined in the next few years, but for now, I will continue to do what I need to do every day and make sure that all the ducks are in a row so that we can execute our plans the right way.

Furthermore, she says, "Jeff's heart will blow." Everyone who dies in this world is because of me, and Jeff's heart will blow because in the Bible, it says, "Thou shall not kill." Well, the world is too overpopulated, and too many people are having kids, so people need to continue to die every day, and kids need to die to because there are too many f——king kids in the world. She says that Jeff's heart's going to blow, and when it's time, we will know. I need to start feeling my heart first before that happens.

Atmosphere, "The Best Day"—he starts off with this song, saying, "I had a rough day, but that's life, it happens." He is talking about the general population, and every day cannot be a great day for everyone. Every single person in this world goes through highs and lows, whether you have a mental illness or anything else that you are going through. Every day at work isn't going to be a great day because you might get into a fight with your boss, you might have to work extra hours and not get paid for it, or for any other reason. You might have a rough day because you're losing with your gambling and in a fantasy. Another reason you might have a rough day is because you're recovering from an injury if you're an athlete or even if you're in the middle class. Maybe you just lost a loved one, and that would make you have a rough day as well. He is talking about it in general when he writes this song.

The next part of the song, he says, "I woke up on the dark side of my mattress." When he says this, he is talking about depression and if people quit their jobs and they don't feel like going to work anymore. This can even be applied to grade school and college students when they don't feel like going to class and feel a little bit down, whether they just drank the night before or whatever the case might be. The next part of his song, he said, "I guess I forgot to set my clock, overslept, almost lost a job." This all goes in hand with saying that kids don't want to go to school anymore, but this is big picture, so he is talking about middle-class people who don't want to go to work anymore and are sick of the way they are being treated at work. Also, people might be tired of their job and just simply don't want to be a part of that company anymore.

Personally, I don't want to work for someone who gets all the benefits of my hard work when I am making shit money, so that's why I wanted to start my own business. I don't want to take orders from people in the business world, and I would rather venture off and do my own thing. Of course, I never chose this path, and because I was taking chances with the system, and the CIA and KGB are the main reasons why I am not working right now, but f——k it. I'll make my millions and be able to afford more things than a $50,000 or $100,000 paycheck can do for you. There are so many people across the world that hate their jobs, and I don't want to be one of those people. I would rather enjoy what I am doing and work with people who I trust instead of taking orders from people when the head of the company gets all the credit for the work I am doing. I would rather manage my own company and not be that lonely accountant who hates their job day in and day out.

The next part of his song, he says, "And to top it off, I'm kinda hungry." He is saying this for homeless people and for people who can't afford to spend a lot of money on meals and are working minimum wage jobs. In one of his songs, he says, "Lately the meal got tasty for me and only me in particular." Eating breakfast in the morning is very important, so Hoodie Allen even put that in his song that "I have to eat breakfast to get a well-balanced diet." I think it's important to realize that not everybody in the world is going to pass all these tests, and there is no cure for cancer, so not everyone is going to make out of this alive, but for those who need to eat, they need to take time out of their day to eat good healthy meals.

The next part of the song, he says, "Can't eat till I find my money." Again, he is talking about those who don't have that much money in the world, not about these greedy assholes that don't give back to world like they should. He is talking about middle-class and lower middle-class people who are living paycheck to paycheck and can't afford to go to a Morton Steakhouse or even lonely people in the world who don't have that many people in their lives like some of us do. This is part of the reason why I want to make as much money as I want to make. I want enough so I am not worrying about money anymore and so that I can give back to the community like any world leader would do. There are so many selfish assholes in the world, and I will never be like them. I barely have any money right now, and I still help people out with the power of prayer and when I started to finally show my face and help people out with generous gifts.

The next part of his song, he says, "They don't want me in a bad mood, afraid that it will spread and everyone will catch an attitude." He says this because he is talking about the CIA, and when Offspring said in his song that "if you can't get what you want," well, it's all because of me. They want me to be happy, but it is kind of hard when there are so many fake assholes in this world that do their fake laughs and smiles, and frankly, sometimes, I am straight sick of it. G-Eazy wrote in one of his songs, "What if the fakes would die and only the real survived? Take a look around and you might be surprised." This applies to so many goddamn people in this world who just seem very fake to me, and I hate going to parties or hanging out in big groups of people. Sometimes it is kind of good because then you can really tell who is real and who is fake in this world. I go in and out of happiness, and a lot of that is because of the people around me.

This is part of the reason why I didn't want to go to Jeff's wedding because I know how people get nervous in social situations or whatever the case is with what I talk about with my therapist that people just start acting differently. I used to be like that, but because I have been real with all the tests I have been given, I can really tell who is fake and who is real. Hollywood can tell too because I don't think a lot of people understand life as well as they should, and all the answers we seek depend on how free or fake. I know way more than most people do because of how real I am. There are certain other people in this world who I am not going to mention that aren't quite as real as I am, and I think they are very stupid for not picking up on some of the signals that I can pick up on in this world.

The next part of the song, he says, "Coworkers make me sick, and a manager really ain't shit, but I can't quit, so I am holding onto my face like f——k this place." This part of the song goes along with everything else I was saying about workplace misfortunes and even things that I have dealt with in the past that I don't plan on dealing with anymore. When he is talking about managers really ain't being shit, he is talking about what I was saying in the previous paragraph that many managers thinking they are smarter than they really are, but in reality, the people who are working for them are actually smarter. There are flaws in my code, and one of those is that there are people who are better and have had tougher lives than certain other people who are on my list. I guess I stopped making that list, and everyone else that runs into my life just falls in line.

The next part of the song, he says, "Hell no, I ain't going to school, the teacher's a jerk, he must think I am a fool." Like I have mentioned in other sections of my book, I think big picture, and this song is big picture, so he is trying to include more portions of the population and starts off with how work sucks and about broke people trying to make more money to eat, and now he is talking about grade school students not going to school. Teachers are another way to make the mass control of the population on all of us angry. There are a lot of rebels in the world, but none as severe as me because I am the biggest rebel to society, and I will prove that to everybody who thought I couldn't pull this off a long time ago.

When he says, "He must think I am a fool," maybe he is talking about people in classes who don't show themselves as being smart but actually could be a lot smarter than people give them credit for. There are a lot of shitty teachers in this world, and I especially noticed that in college when I was diagnosed with all those bipolar meds that were f——king with my mind and actually making me bipolar when I wasn't bipolar at all before I took any of those meds. There was this one Russian teacher who wasn't explaining the things that we were supposed to be learning very well, and a lot of people were failing in his class because of the teacher and the information he was feeding us when it was so much different from the tests he was giving us. There were also a lot of very good teachers. I had this one English teacher that would always call on me because he knew I was smart and would get the answers right. This was before I was on any of those bipolar meds that f——ked with my head.

I would run into him at the gym, and we would always talk about life and about the classes. I had this other accounting teacher who would also always call on me because he knew I would get the answers right and trusted that I would get great grades. I ended up with a C in that class because I stopped trying, and maybe I got bored and didn't care as much as I should. However, he was a great teacher as well. You have to take in the bad with the good in this world, and throughout my time in school, I had a lot of shitty teachers and a lot of great ones.

In the next part of the song, he says, "All the kids mess with each other always and all day." He is talking about kids bullying on nerds and even kids f——king around with each other and misbehaving in school. I was a bad student when I was in elementary school, and then, when I was a junior and senior in high school, when I started gaining my self-esteem that I lost because of bullies and the "cool" kids who peaked in society at the age of eighteen. The next part of the song, he says, "Class warfare up and down the hallways." He is talking about the same thing in that complete sentence. For my personal experience, I was only a bully when I lived in New York and was hanging out with the "cool" kids and would think I was the shit. When I moved here, people made fun of me because I was from New York, and I looked out of place since these kids were making fun of me, and I just didn't feel like I belonged in a place as real as New York compared to a place as fake as Virginia.

I started gaining self-esteem when I was a junior and senior in high school and sort of created my own groups of people I wanted to hang out with. Most of them weren't too popular. It was just a bunch of cool kids who I liked, and we all got along with each other. Of course, we would fight just like every other group of people do in this world, but we were the group of people that were more like rebels to the system compared to the popular people who would only let certain people hang out with them. Some of the parties I threw and my friends threw, they would show up, but I never really hung out with them in school. Some of them I did because of sports, but mostly, I stayed within my group.

The next part of the song, he says, "And if you ain't popular, nobody talks to you unless they mocking you, not even the hall monitor or the bull driver." I experienced a lot of this from sixth grade to ninth grade. Once the 9/11 attacks happened, I started to get more popular for some reason. Maybe it was because we knew we were going to win this war and it had something to do with ISIS. It definitely had to with that. I dealt with a lot of bullying and things that I shouldn't have dealt with because I wasn't as cool as other people in the school. I never hung out with the popular group in school, except in elementary school. In ninth grade, my dad got a job offer to move back to New York, but more upstate. I wanted my dad to take that offer because I was sick of all the fakeness and unnecessary bullshit in Virginia.

Right now, I am happy that we still live where we do because now I relate to a lot of people in the world and I am right where I am supposed to be. Even when I was one of the best players on my freshman football team, I never got any playing time because the whole system was political. I grabbed one fifteen-yard catch in one of the preseason games and never saw the field again because the "popular" kids were the ones getting the playing time, and the kids whose parents gave more to the community were the ones getting playing time. When I was a senior in high school, I was playing soccer, and again, I wasn't getting that much playing time because it was the "popular" kids and kids who were playing with Oakton soccer for a longer period of time that were getting the playing time. I was better than half of the kids that started over me, but I just wasn't getting the attention that I deserved back then.

However, when I was playing on my club team with people who I saw eye-to-eye with, then I was getting noticed, and because of my trainers advice, I couldn't made it on the college level if I kept on playing. Hollywood put in a lot of their songs that I am the best person on the planet, and sooner or later, I am going to show off my skills to the world instead of doing everything in private. There were a lot of people all over the globe who started taking recognition in everything I was doing for people, and I want to keep that trend going forward, but I need to do it in the national spotlight. I know I will be able to at some point, but I want whoever reads this part of my document to realize that the benefits that I have given to the world outweigh the negatives by a landslide, and because of certain people in this world, I am finally starting to think about myself a little bit more.

Knowing the new Will, I see the big picture and how all of this impacts the world. I started making my favorites list, and I am the best person on that list, and I stopped making it after about forty-five thousand people. The rest of the world just follows down, depending on when I run into you and recognize your name and your face.

The next part of the song, he says, "It's a bad day, bad week, and a bad month, but nobody wants to trade with my bag lunch. Someday, I am going to be so cool. For now, I got cheap shoes, so I keep losing." Again, he is talking about big picture, and when Halsey says she thinks that there's a flaw in my code, she is talking about things like this. Many people have had very, very bad days, and other people on my list really haven't dealt with shit throughout their entire lives.

I know that I earned my stripes and everyone in Hollywood and the pros know about my direction, so I can just not say, "F——k you" to the people I haven't seen in a long time but embrace them back into my life. I think we are just one big family waiting to connect with each other on levels never seen before in humanity. This is also why Facebook, Twitter, and Instagram were invented. This is a way to connect all of us through the sky, through the Internet, and through this one person named Will Coakley. Many people have a lot of bad days, and maybe it's because they don't feel like they belong or they made stupid errors at work. However, you are not alone. Hollywood knows at some point, there is nothing left to fix in the world, and I will be speaking in front of everyone and showing everyone my work, which includes things that I put in this book. I will need people to look at it and revise it, but for the most part, I am getting smarter and more knowledgeable and try not to hate on people so much. It is kind of hard when people bring in so much bullshit and nonsense into my life.

The next part of the song, he says, "Girls give no love to a poor man." He is right about this on so many levels. I am sick of lying to girls, saying that I work right now. I am the most important rebel to the system that is alive right now, so there is a reason why I am not working right now and worrying about other things in the world. I want my perfection and my path to perfection to be achieved sooner rather than later, so I need the people in the world who know what they are doing to help me out on a daily basis and make sure there are no more flaws in our code and in the new society we are trying to build. I have been poor pretty much my entire life, and my dad is finally able to pay off the house, but there are people in the world who are way more poor than I am, and they also have trouble getting girls.

I think a lot of guys try too hard, and a lot of guys are living in their parents' houses. When you're in high school and college, you don't really know what you want in life. You are pretty lost, and unless you are smarter than me, which I doubt, then you don't understand why the gods put us on the planet right now. If you have met your soul mate in high school or college and continue to spend that time with them for the rest of eternity, then good for you, but most people find their unique somebody after school and after you know what path society has put you under.

The next part of the song, he says, "It's a prison, the clock is warden, and it don't get no better when I get home so I listen to the voice in my headphones." When he says this part, he is talking about lonely people in this world who have nobody to turn to. However, they have music, and they are still alive, and somehow they can connect with me, and in the future, they won't be as lonely as they were in the past. Most of these assholes and selfish people in the world don't quite understand this as well as some of us do, but those people are just as equally important to society as Lebron James and Stephen Curry are.

There are no cures to diseases yet, but we will come up with a solution to these types of problems. When he says, "It's a prison, the clock is a warden," he is talking about these kids in school who are suffering through some useless bullshit that doesn't mean shit in the real world. A lot of people that reach millionaire and billionaire status don't even go to college. They learn these things from their parents, and when you're someone like me who holds the future of the world in our hands, then you just start to understand and justify the meaning of life to others. School teachers don't get paid as well as they should, and other people in the world don't get paid as well as they should. Well, I am here to solve your problems.

By the time I turn thirty-six, everything in the world will have changed by then, and we are all invited to the final party. There are many bullshit rules and regulations that we all have to follow. However, this will all change, and at some point, people will stop having kids, and all the old people who will be dying in the next three years will be stopped, and we will be living in this new beautiful world that the rulers of society have planned for us, and our existence on this planet through me will benefit everybody on the planet.

The next part of the song, he says, "Can't dance with an upset stomach." He is saying that people need to eat and stay healthy, and I will have the entire world jumping like a house of pain, and this includes in clubs and maybe even as they have shown in some movies on the streets as well. We need to find cures for the hunger and diseases, but this line is pretty simple. The main word in this line is *dance*. We all need to find our soul mates, and then we can go on from there.

The next part of the song, he says, "The overdraft notices just kept on coming." He came out with this line because before, when I was working and spending money that I didn't have, I would get a lot of overdraft notices from the bank. This also applies to other people who get overdraft notices. Of course, in the next three years, this won't be an issue because I will be rich, and other people will benefit from the positive changes in society. Furthermore, in the next part of the song, he says, "Top of your head stops growing hair." This has to do with karma catching up with me and a solution to our age problems.

Karma will catch up, and we will be forever young, and he came out with this part because I used to always go to therapy and was scared about the hair loss on my body, but it was just another way to get a solution for the world problems, and this means that everything is run through me, and we will be forever young. The athletes knew exactly what they were doing when they said they were going to put me through this exact same game again. I could also be Jesus, and once I am healed up, then let the games begin! Somebody in the world has been feeling these pains since 1966, which also proves to me that everything happens for a reason, but I must have also put these pains on that special person from heaven somehow and some way.

When Portugal. The Man came out with this song, he says, "Is it coming? Is it coming? Is it coming?" He is talking about karma catching up with me. Somebody was born in the year of the razor blade, which was 1901, and they have been feeling these pains since 1966. This makes everything pretty simple, which probably means that I am God, and they came out with some songs saying that I am only human after all, and I have made mistakes, but don't put the blame on me.

The next part of the song, he says, "Broken glass, computer crash." He is talking about when I was hanging out with Shaker and Allyn and we were all shitfaced one New Year's, and Allyn threw me into a glass that shattered in a hotel room, and we each had to pay like $300 for that. This is how he came out with this part of the song. When he is talking about a computer crash, he is talking about the entire conspiracy theory that was run on me, and when I was in my basement and my work computer kept on crashing on me, it was just a stupid-ass test run probably by the CIA to put the fear of death in me. It could have also been the amatse who are the guys who make us live in fear.

Whatever the case, this is how Atmosphere came out with this part of the song. Furthermore, he says, "Car won't start and the tires went flat." When he says this, it reminds me of all the times I have had car problems and all the car problems that exist in our society with all the many people that are living in it. I have run out of gas in my car many times in the past and crossing my fingers that will never happen ever again. I know many people go to the shop to fix their car problems whether they are rich or poor or somewhere in the middle. The most important thing to remember is that these problems are fixable, and at one point or another, there will be nothing left to fix in the world. At that point, people will be going to someone for answers that that person is going to be me.

The next part of the song, he says, "Plus you haven't had sex in how long, afraid to admit that the fire's all gone." He is talking about age again and how age will just be a number if we execute these plans as perfectly as we expect. I have trouble getting up sometimes, and the Austin Powers movie when he said, "I need to get my mojo back,"

I sort of need to before I get another girlfriend. It was because I was self-destructing, and Hollywood resurrecting me from the dead to understand all these things that I understand now.

The next part of the song, he says, "Better half is talking about separating, you wish you can take it back to yesterday." He is talking about how hard relationships are and how high the divorce rate is. All people in relationships need to see eye-to-eye, and you need to find the right person who will always be there for you in sickness and in health, even though our health problems won't be an issue in the future. They came up with this rule, last call for sin, because everybody in my generation and even people in the younger and older generation have already found their soul mates, and we are all invited to the final party. This will be great because it means that I have finally reached my goal in uniting everyone, and we are all as happy as the people who started these tests intended. I know some of them have died, but most of them are still alive, so congratulations to all the people who made it to the final test.

The most important part of the song, he says, "You not alone, its hard as hell, but waste no time feeling sorry for self, we'll be right here with your war because you're the one we make this music for." This is just a very large amount of people who can help me out every day and put the good into the lives of all the people who have passed the final test. They like to love me in Hollywood, so I am happy that I can help them out as well.

Because of my communication and connections with people in Hollywood, Jennifer Lopez wore earrings from Kohl's instead of that fancy jewelry that people in Hollywood are told to buy to show off to the world. This didn't happen by coincidence because I was watching a little bit of her new show, *Shades of Blue*, and sometimes I can read the dialect that other people cannot see, and I saw that she said, "Well, I can do better than him as a boyfriend." The next thing I know, she dated Alex Rodriguez and was wearing earrings from Kohl's instead of the expensive jewelry that people in Hollywood are taught to wear.

I have also taught Selena Gomez about how to represent her in different ways and to protect her from the paparazzi and other people's viewpoints on what she does with her life. She wrote a song about me because of everything I have done for her. And why have I? Simply because she is a cool person and because I have the ability to. I also have taught other people in Hollywood such as Justin Bieber on how to behave around the paparazzi so that they do not get in trouble with the paparazzi as much and on how to stop caring about what other people think after a certain point. How would these judgmental people handle your situations differently? My guess would be way worse and with more issues.

Women's USA Soccer team victories in 1999 World Cup and in 2015 World Cup. The way I move and the miracle child I was born to be has turned me into saving women's soccer in 1999 and 2015 in the World Cup. In 1999, I was in North Carolina with my friend, Ryan Bullock, and we were watching the 1999 World Cup. People later proved the theory that it was his family and me who saved the championship for the women that year. Ryan had banged his head on the ceiling by jumping off the stairs, and I believe in the theory that what doesn't kill you makes you stronger, so I believe this had something to do with this.

In 2015, when I was gaining my powers, there was nothing that was going to stop me to aid the women's national team this year to win it all as well. I was at a bar with my boy, Andy Lee, and we were watching the game, but like any other event, I planned for these things in advance. Carly Lloyd had a first half that can never be matched in history with four f——king goals. The whole place thanked me for their championship, but their play in the tournament can go unprecedented to many things I have seen as a fan watching these sports.

I was watching the USA soccer game after all the girls on the team thanked me for their 2015 World Cup Victory, and Carly Lloyd had just fallen on the ground while I was listening to Asher Roth, who is a pretty big dickhead out in Hollywood, and the message that was being sent to me was that she was going to hell for the way she was acting and for the ways that she thanked me (thank you, sin). It just seemed pretty hateful to me, and it's not our fault that we were born this way and the for how I go out of my way to help others. I know it was whoever Jesus is, and it's something that a lot of us refuse to believe in. So I reversed that curse and put it on some of them assholes. That shit pisses me off just thinking about it. I know it was just in my head, but it was still so disrespectful.

C. C. Sabathia announced that there are sixty-two black players in baseball. Be careful when you go to Boston. This just reminds me that the whole Jackie Robinson thing could actually happen again. There are still a lot of people that are pretty racist in this world and wouldn't oppose of what happened. But with me alive, there's no way in hell that this would happen. I knew it was coming at some point, but I didn't think it would happen so soon and that it would, in fact, be in Boston, the town that took all those championships from teams that probably deserved them more. As I am writing this, the fans in Boston give Adam Jones a standing ovation.

Syncing up the lower, middle, and upper classes together, we will do this by everything I talk about in this document and by my weaponry. My weaponry includes my personal songs, my phone usage, my computer and all of its documents inside, and my TV and all the TV shows, and movies that are relevant. The books I read, the everyday activities I perform, the places I travel to, and the words coming out of my favorite lists. This list includes about 2,200 people right now. This has been a work in process, and one of the first keys to this was to help the upper class understand what the middle class was going through in terms of living from paycheck to paycheck. Also, it was very important for all of us to contribute to help out the lower classes whenever we can and however we can. This has been going great as I mentioned earlier that the homeless rate went down 47 percent in the past few years, thanks to people caring and a little bit of Will power.

Another big breakthrough was that a new treatment for patients with a form of congenital retinal blindness has shown success in improving vision, according to results posted by *Nature Medicine*. When I was at Becka's wedding, I smoked weed with my cousin, and it sort of cured my vision since everything my dad put me through, I was able to overcome that adversity. I wanted to add this section for blind people because I have had experiences with being blind and not being able to see straight since I was born to conquer everything.

The Adam LaRoche incident arose from the movie *A League of Their Own* that was made in the '90s. I know the movie is based on the women's teams that were playing baseball in the time of World War II, but this particular incident they put in the movie because of the future that was being seen from people in Hollywood. The bottom line of the story is that Adam LaRoche had his little boy in the clubhouse and the people that ran the team didn't like it, so conflict arose, and it forced Adam LaRoche to quit baseball.

In the movie, the scene includes a little rowdy kid who is a little bit of a troublemaker, and the coach was very adamant about the kid leaving the clubhouse since he wasn't supposed to be there in the first place. The coach is being played by Tom Hanks, and this part of Adam's LaRoche's life was deemed to be inevitable. At the time, I did not think it was fair to cast judgment on Adam LaRoche and what he thought was best for his son, but I can kind of see both sides of the equation. If Adam LaRoche was to play baseball again, then I think this scenario would play out differently.

In the TV series *Friday Night Lights*, the starting quarterback in the first season was hurt really badly and was pretty much paralyzed. He was forced to quit football and lost many friends and was in the Special Olympics and things of that nature. In real life, there is a guy that is a couple of years younger than I am who was an athlete, a very good student, and I think they monitored this character from what was going to happen to him in real life. He ended up getting into a terrible car accident that left him paralyzed from the neck down. I did not really know him that well, but a few of my friends who were in the fraternity knew him well.

I feel bad for the kid, but if that's what fate intended for him, then it's f——ked up. I wish him the best and don't really want to think that his life could have gone so great to a terrible accident in a matter of a weekend. One of the reasons why I bring this up is to point out that there are differences between real life and what you see on TV, but there are also many similarities that exist between the two.

When I was watching the TV series *Episodes*, starring Matt Leblanc, I found a lot of similarities between the show and probably his life and a little bit of mine as well. There was one scene that stood out to me in particular. The director of NBC is seeing a shrink and thinks things are talking to him, and a writer thinks his show is going to be a disaster because he keeps on hearing Matt LeBlanc's voice, saying he won't do the starring role. I think this might have actually happened in the show *Friends* in terms of Matt Leblanc saying that he wouldn't do the starring role but ending up doing it anyway, and the show stood for what a lot of us are in terms of our personalities in America. This also goes in line, in terms of myself, of the conspiracy theory with aliens and the CIA. They would like to hack into my computer and my phone and try to take away the information I was learning in the real world and on why they were attacking me, and because of this, it forced me to alienate myself from the population and quit the day jobs I had.

Now I am much more focused, have my goals in line, and see the big picture. I have the ability and power to help people out on a daily basis, but I can also help people when I start making my millions and give back to the community. I can share this story and let people know why the world is a better place now than it was ten years ago, and a lot of that is because of the way we have revolutionized over this time.

On Sunday, June 18, 2017, there was a random kid who was dealing with some heart transplant problems, but as of this date, he is okay. His favorite player in the major leagues is Xander Bogaerts of the Boston Red Sox. On this date, when the announcers announced this to the general public, Bogaerts hit two home runs. It was really exciting for the people who were watching this game, and to top all of it off, the Red Sox won this game. Maybe it was fate and destiny coming together for this little kid.

I bring this up in this section because in the movie, *BASEketball*, there were parts in this movie when the main character promised a little kid who was having a heart transplant that he would hit three home runs for the little kid. He ended up hitting two, and the little kid either survived or died. I can't remember, but hopefully, in the real world, this scene has a happy ending. I think if you can really relate to these movies, you would get life better and maybe enjoy them to their fullest extent. It is also relevant to this whole idea of becoming one because this entire movie is based off three regular guys who became famous off an idea that you can mix baseball and basketball together to create a new game that became famous worldwide.

This is very similar to what I am trying to do by hopefully creating games that can help all of us form one, whether this is three-on-three basketball, pool basketball, whiffle ball, or anything else that people would enjoy playing and watching. I would really like to see us all get more involved instead of the pros playing and everyone else just sitting at home and watching these games on TV or in the stands.

This year's Milwaukee Brewers team, and I am assuming in the years going forward, reminds me of the team that was displayed by Hollywood in the movie Mr. 3000. I was watching the Yankees versus Brewers game, and the way the team is constructed is similar to the roster that was comprised in that movie. The young star, Domingo Santana, is very similar to the young confident star that was displayed in the movie, and he is only twenty-four years old. We will all see where his career takes off from here, but from the looks of it, he could be a key contributor to the Milwaukee Brewers in the upcoming years. These are just my observations, but I think it is a good comparison.

Forgetting Sarah Marshall—Matt Ryan is dating or married to a girl named Sarah Marshall, and I have him in a fantasy football league that I have been trying to prosper in, and it's stupid, but I think because of this movie being on TV often (like what people call the TV gods), I think this is part of the reason why I can't catch a break in this league. I don't know what Hollywood has against Sarah Marshall, but it's affecting my performance in this league, so I hope this curse ends soon. I am going to keep Matt Ryan again, and I hope that Hollywood doesn't interfere with my fantasy league and that he performs the way that he was destined to perform. I am really hoping to finally make the championship one of these years, and hopefully, this luck comes to me next year.

Charlie's Angel's—I picked up on this sign from this movie when I was watching it about a month ago on TV and because Jeff keeps saying I remind him of Charlie from *It's Always Sunny*. Anyways I had dealt with demon problems throughout the last eight years, since I was pretty much twenty-four years old. There are three girls that helped me with this curse. Jamie Hoang was there pretty much from the beginning, so she resembles the Asian women in the movie. The other two girls are Angie and Amber, my two exes. They helped protect me from the wrath of the devil, and it worked out pretty well. Because of these three women, I have been able to get past this curse and move on with my life.

It's funny because my imagination, especially when I was at home, is priceless and very crazy. These three girls are perfect to fit into this role. Hopefully, in terms of this aspect of this part of my movie, it gets better and they can actually help push the world in the right direction as well because I always got along well with these three ladies, and whether I see them on a regular basis or in my dreams, they are still my girls and always will be.

Transformers, Revenge of the Fallen—the main concept behind this movie is a kid who was displayed by Shia Labeouf who goes crazy because he is looking for signs and connections that can save the human race from the evil aliens. I found relevance to this movie because some days from around the time I was twenty-five to around the time I was twenty-nine, I would bug out when I would think of signs and connections. I started writing all these thoughts down on notes and in this document to refresh my mind. This reminded of a scene in this movie when he would write down all this Japanese language on a chalkboard, and he would start talking really fast which reminded me of when I was scared like a motherf——ker, thinking of all these conspiracy theories that I was involved in and I was talking really fast in therapy.

Another point that I wanted to bring across in this paragraph was that Shia LeBeouf's sidekick in this movie was a Spanish guy. I was practically best friends with a Spanish guy named Rico in college, and I feel, like, somehow and someway, we are going to connect in the future. I mean, I figured out a while ago that I was born for a reason, and once I figured out the meanings behind everything I was going through that we would all become who we were destined to be. I don't think that aliens are ever going to attack us in way that some people would have thought of, but I do also think there are friendly aliens in the universe.

There was an episode of *It's Always Sunny in Philadelphia* where the gang helps out a terrorist group in Africa by giving them funds to support their operation. This episode reminded me of the crisis with ISIS in Africa now. I know they were making jokes on the show, but it actually kind of is a real-life crisis now, and I think these groups started forming in Africa a few years ago, but as Americans, we have the tools to defeat these evil criminals. I am eager to see how we can stop these terrorists in the next few years with Trump at the helm.

Gossip Girl—the characters in this TV show remind me of the people in my life, and I wanted to explain how in this section. Chuck Bass reminds me of myself. He is a character who realizes at some point in his life that college and the nine-to-five weren't meant for him. So he started his own business and became a multimillionaire doing this and ended up with the girl of his dreams at the end of the TV series. Penn Badgley reminds me of Adam because they called him lonely boy in this series. Adam has been known to be lonely for a number of years now, and the character in this series has a lot of similarities to the Adam that I know in real life. Jenny Humphrey reminds me of my sister, Meghan. She is someone who tries to fit in with the "cool group," and one day, it hits her that she is actually cool herself. I loved how they displayed this character in this series.

The character Nate Archibald reminds me of my friend, Jeff. He is well-disciplined and is always willing to help others. He has his whole life planned out pretty well and has a great family life. Furthermore, the character Blair Waldorf reminds me of Jeff's girlfriend, Anna. She is a little bit rebellious, and he is happy when she meets new people, and her personality matches up pretty well with Anna's. Lastly, the character Rufus Humphrey reminds me of my father. The character on the show is always thinking of family first and has a reputation for putting his kids' lives ahead of himself. He is very selfless and provides well for his family.

Collateral Beauty—I ran through this script in my house when my parents were here but even outside of my house somctimes. The prime basis of this movie was that Will Smith was crazy because he had three elements—love, time, and death—that were make-believe characters, but he could actually see them. The friends in his life pretended that they weren't there because of their own greed. He had lost his child and ended up with his wife at the end of the movie.

So, in real life, the CIA or other people spoke me to across the world, and people thought I was crazy. It was sort of what Einstein went through or Abraham Lincoln. I was never crazy. I fell into this rut by mistake because I am battling demons every day, and this was only to make me stronger in the future. I am still aiming to achieve perfection, and this is part of why I am working out every day and am still playing basketball, bowling, and playing golf with my dad. I was talking to nobody, but I wanted to make the world a better place, but now we are all getting older too.

It's stupid to still be playing these games. It's time to buckle down and focus on the future. We are building up a new world, and I am trying to get as many people from the outside world involved as possible. I displayed craziness throughout pretty myself my entire life, but nowadays, I mostly stay evened out and try to do the right thing for this new society we are building.

Just like I've mentioned in parts of this book, I have been victimized by conspiracy theories and such. I have gotten in trouble with the law in the past, but now I am trying to be a law-abiding citizen in recent memory. I just wanted to bring up a few points here with a few judges that could have been wishing for the worst for me. I am pretty much coming back down to earth now and becoming normalized again, but in the movie, *Law-Abiding Citizen*, Gerald Butler goes after a judge for not handing his case the right way, and I always wanted to know how deep this conspiracy really went.

Nevertheless, if there are judges involved, then I want to know exactly who so I know how to handle it the right way. Also, in the *Dark Knight*, the Joker goes after a judge who he thinks is conspiring against him. So maybe there are two judges that are on the wrong side of the new world and new society we are trying to build, and if that's the case, then they will be taken care of accordingly.

I was watching track and field on August 7, 2017, and this part of the story definitely goes under this title. The movie *Mr. Deeds*, starring Adam Sandler, is a movie based off a low to middle-class man taking over his uncle's company after he had passed away. The uncle had passed on his entire billion-dollar company to his nephew, and the uncle's name was Blake Prescott. I was watching the track and field on this Saturday and noticed something that stuck into my mind. The first and second place finishes of one of the matches had the last names of Blake and Prescod. A few years back, I opened up my eyes to witness history as we see fit, and this just made sense, and it is entertaining and funny to me that the first and second places were Blake and Prescod, and the uncle's name in the movie was Blake Prescott.

So I have been observing the mixed signs from *Happy Gilmore*. One of the signs I wanted to discuss, and I had no idea this was a problem at the time, is the homeless rates in Portland, Oregon. I recognized it in Watsky's song, "Cardboard Castles," but I first knew about the problem when my ex-girlfriend's friend told me about this problem. My therapist has also told me that is has been a recurring issue in Portland for years. I have solutions inside my creative mind, but some people would have to leave planet earth for that to happen. We could also ask people from Hollywood and the professional leagues to donate some charity money toward these people so they could live in the same place peacefully and not have to navigate south to San Diego every winter just to live another year. We can make this happen!

Also, they depicted Happy Gilmore as a crazy boy who brings in crowds of all kinds to the venues, and he ends up making the cocky leading winner of the previous tournaments to look foolish as Happy Gilmore creates havoc for this loser. Picture me as Happy Gilmore and picture some douchebag 1 percent clown as the guy that I make look foolish. We'll just go with someone who everyone seems to like but is definitely a douchebag. For shits and giggles, I'll say Warren Buffet.

Jennifer Lawrence just came out with a new movie called *Mother*. It is a scary movie, but I think the point that the director is trying to reach out to people is that Mother Nature is actually pretty f——king scary, and because of all these deaths because of Mother Nature, this movie was necessary. There is only one person who knows how to control Mother Nature (me), so I can take care of this problem; it is just taking some time. Jennifer Lawrence is going to chill for the next few years until a new role comes up, but until then, I assume she is relying on my mother and myself to help her out.

I started analyzing the movies they produce and how they relate to me. So, in Offspring's song, they said that if you can't get what you want, well, it's all because of me. In *Hunger Games*, they provide the people in the game with supplies and goods they need to survive in the games. So, in my house, and even when I'm hanging out with friends and pretty much wherever I am, I can provide people with what they need. It's been progress every day in my life because of everything I have been doing for other people.

The girl in this movie is actually Halsey. I figured that out by just doing some simple math in my home. This was her ticket into Hollywood, and she has become very successful because of it. People that were haters and abused this power have died because they were too weak to be alive right now. It's pretty cool, and I can't wait for more people to enter my life.

They created the script *Deadpool* based on a character that had found the cure to everything in the world, and he was a victim of bad people doing bad things to him, so he decided to go on a revenge battle and kill them all. They came out with this script with Adrian Hernandez being the bad guy. The guy that killed two people who was a Patriots player, and apparently, he was a coward, according to one of Flo Rida's songs. He must have been a person who did bad things to me because they base all there shit off the things that go on in my life. So he ends up saving the world and is a bad guy that just gets paid to kill worse people than he is.

See, I was never a good person, but I am more mature now, and I am still doing what I was born to do every day. I was a shitty person for the longest time and I was going through hell, and I believe Adrian Hernandez was part of the reason. Therefore, he committed suicide in prison because he was f——king with my dog with technology with who knows what. I am trying to get to the bottom of it, but more importantly, I need to start seeing eye-to-eye with the people in my life and just follow the script to my life. A lot of people have made a lot of money due to the misery that I have gone through in real life, but soon enough, I will clearly see that this will pay me dividends, and I will overcome all this bullshit adversity and be famous one day.

The movie *Taken* came out because they came out with a plan for the world that I was the "last call for sin," and I needed direction to perfection. I am also Mr. Magic in the good old days, which means that every girl in the world that is still alive is taken, and there is one more girl left, and that is the one that I am meant to be with. This needs to happen quickly because we aren't getting any younger. However, if karma catches up with me, then we can take our time finding our soul mates.

It is hard to keep a relationship with someone who doesn't see eye-to-eye with you or if you are in a wrong situation, so I can try to guide people to find their soul mates, and I am working on all my bad things that have caused me to break up with girls in the past. I still feel like everything we have been planning can work, but it is just taking more time than I would have expected. The movie *Taken* also has parts where a bad group of guys takes girls and uses them for money for profit. I know that girls have used me in the past few years or longer than that to find their soul mates, but I don't care. I just want people to help me speed up the process so that we can actually be here forever and not be destined to live in an afterlife that no one is certain of.

Kesha and Macklemore came out with that song "Good Old Days." Nevertheless, I watched this movie to find signs and symbols to see what they are trying to say in this movie. From the bottom of my heart, I know they are saying taken because there is one girl left in the universe that is for me, and that is the girl that I will be with forever.

The script for *Equalizer*, featuring Denzel Washington, was created because everything in this world was created to be equal. So people who don't belong in this new society that we are trying to create and people who are doing wrong for society we eliminate so that everything becomes equal at some point. Hollywood wrote this script, knowing that this would benefit me and benefit the athletes that work hard to make this world an entertaining world. Of course, I think outside the box and believe that instead of everyone just being fans that we should create leagues for the middle class and lower class and that literally everything in this world is equal.

Jeff needs to give it up because he can't see the world the way that I do, and he is part of the problem, not the solution. If people wanted to pick him, then they would have, but they picked me. Furthermore, for the script of equalizer, I kill the flesh so that the people who are actually doing work in this world can benefit from it. I can't stop and I won't stop and if you don't add value to this world, then you probably need to leave because the world is too overpopulated, and we don't need you anymore.

Denzel Washington is the perfect character for this movie, but I can be pretty scary when I want to be, and in my solution pit, this will benefit many people who do fantasy and other things in life that deserve to be happy.

The script for *Wanted* was written when I was hanging out with Seaman a lot. There was a lot of talk in this movie about assassins training a kid to be the person he was born to be and conquer the world and run shit in the world when the time was right. He was just a regular billing accountant that was sick of the same boring shit in his life and then ran into a few bad people that had terrible intentions for him. This person just happened to me. I was just minding my own business, and all this trouble found me, and here I am now, understanding why I am alive right now. These people happened to be the Illuminati, KGB, and the CIA. They wanted to train me to rule the world one day.

Katy Perry said in one of her songs that "I fell for everything and I went from zero to hero." In the movie, he decided to kill them all and let fate sort out the mess. I took the deaths in this world into my own hands, and less people are dying every day now. I did this because I didn't trust anything invisible or anyone else to take this job seriously. Then I was hoping that karma could pick up on me and we would all be forever young. Now if things aren't going right in my world, then I'll pick off some additional pieces just for the hell of it. I know that the Mafia was involved in this shit as well.

Katy Perry laid it out pretty well in her song that I went from zero to hero because there were a lot of factors in play in my life, and I don't know who was doing what to me. So then will.i.am said to forget about all the evil they feed you, and we should all just be one happy family. The 1 percent is trying to use me to cure time so that we can be forever young. This process is taking forever, and they are going to train me how to run a business and be successful and how to talk in front of a big audience, which I'll need in the future. They have trained me how to fight since I was about eighteen years old, but guns are terrible, so I will never touch one.

I have learned a lot from so many different people in the world, but Danny Elfman said that at one point, it will all come down to me when there is nothing left to fix. Nothing has ever been perfect on this planet, but we can try our hardest to make the world the best and safest place to live. There is a lot more I can say about this script, but I'll just leave it like this at the moment.

The Bye Bye Man—this script was written based off N'Syncs song, "Bye Bye Bye." We used this song to kill the flesh and for me to pick off the pieces of this population that didn't belong anymore. I couldn't believe it when they made a scary movie out of this. I never saw it because I am scared of scary movies, but it is still pretty cool that they built their society around what was going on in my life. I know there was a lot of people worried about what was going on in the news and people missing people that were gone too soon, but the world is simply overpopulated, so this song was too necessary.

It started when I was going to perform in the fraternity games, and we were going to dance to "Bye Bye Bye." Ever since then, I was picking off pieces of the population with this song. I eventually deleted this song when I figured out that we probably took it far enough. After that, N'Sync came out with a song, saying that everyone knows about my transgressions and about my direction. I was clueless until I took that trip to Pennsylvania. Then my eyes started opening up, and I started seeing the world the way it was intended to be seen. However, what was going on with me before and even after that trip with all those demon problems was unacceptable. I am still battling demon issues, but it's getting better, and Hollywood started at the end, so I know I should be good as long as I can rely on them on the regular basis whenever they are available to help me out.

The script for *Pitch Perfect* was written with certain characters in mind, and let's just say that they came out with my personality with the main guy character. Well, I believe that I have talked to two girls that they cast in the girls group on Tinder. The one girl, "Fat Amy," I went on a date with. I have never dated an ugly girl who didn't have a good personality, so I knew going into this that this date wasn't going to work out, but she will meet someone one day that will be her perfect soul mate.

There was another girl that seemed pretty crazy and judgmental that I was talking to on Tinder. I just talked to her one night, and that was the end of that. She is crazy and has an outgoing personality but probably wasn't my type either, so this didn't work out. Hollywood is corrupt, but they have built this world surrounding me in the future, which hopefully is coming on soon, and they put these different people into this script, and the people that don't fit into our future plans we have been eliminating.

The script for *The Mechanic 2* was written when he fell in love with an Asian girl who I am thinking they named as Jamie, but he has built up enemies as he is transporting goods of all kinds. Maybe this could be in the future when I am working and meeting new people and delivering goods to people of all different races and genders and different types of people.

There are two scripts written when the love of his life is an Asian. The other is *Mission Impossible 2*. In *Mission Impossible 2*, the guy is working for the CIA and is given orders that are practically impossible for them to complete, so they give it to one person who has the ability to save the world in ways that the CIA cannot. In *The Mechanic*, the script is written for a person who delivers goods, no questions asked.

When people were counting on me to deliver their products and what they needed to complete their tasks in their own lives, I would help them out, without asking why or how. I would just get it done. This included when people wanted me to kill someone for them or if someone needed progress in the world. I would get it done without asking second questions. It is what it is, but I stopped working and went through all these tests to make the world the best place it can possibly be to live in. Inside my solution pit, I have been working with different tools to help people out and make the world progress. Whether it was Hollywood giving me orders, the CIA, or the 1 percent, I would get these jobs done because they just couldn't do it themselves.

This is part of what I have been doing during my free time, and I thought that *The Mechanic 2* and *Mission Impossible 2* were written for this purpose. The girl he falls in love with is Jamie in both these scripts, but we'll see. She is difficult to read, and whatever is intended for me in the future will determine who I am 100 percent surefire meant to be with.

When they released the script for *A Star Is Born*, they were trying to cater to the group of the population that was dealing with mental illnesses. I told Hollywood I would hook them up if they help me out every day and into the future and bring me to the destiny that I deserve. When Jeff was acting like an asshole toward me, he played the Spose song "Gee Willikers" and "Adam's Song." When he played those songs, he asked me if I liked them, and I said no. When he mentioned "Adam's Song," he said, "Yeah, it is about suicide." Therefore, they released this script with the guy dying at the end with suicide. They were talking about me. I am not going to die and will never die, but that was just how this particular story ended.

When Lady Gaga was speaking after she won this award, she was saying that she hopes that everyone with mental illnesses start to feel better and look forward to a better world. Jeff was being such an asshole to me, and I think when people describe the person that was driving him to commit suicide, like the bad character in this movie, was Jeff. I have been depressed for a long time with the way that people have treated me in the past, and it is getting better now but still has not been okay. I am never going to stop, and if I can thank everyone who is helping me out behind the scenes now, I would. This movie is called *A Star is Born*, and if perfection is really my direction, then maybe there were indirect meanings toward my direction in this movie.

Lady Gaga and Bradley Cooper deserve major props in this movie, and it makes me think that I am not supposed to be in this bullshit two-star town and that I should actually be in Hollywood right now. This is all I want to be right about this script at the current time.

I was thinking about the movie *Transformers* and how his car was like an "alien" from outer space in the first and second movies, and Will Smith said that the scripts were written based off my life. When I was sixteen and taking my driving test, my car that I was training with sort of took on a life of its own and was controlling me instead of me controlling it. It was sort of like an alien was taking over the car, and I wasn't driving it. After this, they created the script based off the conspiracy theories that the CIA threw into my life and how it relates to me driving my cars that I have driven since I was sixteen. They replaced Shia La Beouf with Mark Wahlberg as I was getting older.

The CIA did some bad things to me, and I forgive them, but a lot of it had to do when I was driving my car. The *Transformers* script was written based off the car that turned into an alien. Blink 182 released a song saying, "We all know conspiracies are dumb," but maybe this fear was supposed to make me stronger in the future and create perfection out of a nobody that was living a boring middle-class lifestyle. Now we need the signs and symbols to connect so that we can show the world what we have been trying to develop and create this new world, and we can remain forever young. I had this image running through my mind about my car and how they created this script because they started at the end but have been tracking my life ever since I was very young.

The script for *Blue Bloods* was written about blue bloods and the NYPD and how they are doing so many "good things" for the world. It's hard to discriminate against any group because of a few people acting disrespectful. However, there have been many NYPD officers that have committed suicide in the past few years, and I think it was part of the unwritten script for *Blue Bloods* with relevance to the NYPD. The writers and actors on this show are instrumental to helping me fix global warming, mainly because of Donnie Wahlberg and the guy that was dating Monica in friends. The other characters are just as important, but Donnie Wahlberg appears in New York City every New Years and keeps on complaining about the weather when he knows in the next year or two, with a lot of effort from several people, the weather will get better.

I think it's funny because they filled me in on their secrets, and I don't really talk about it except to my mom and my therapist. Moreover, they foresaw the NYPD officers committing suicide, and I follow this one girl, Erin, who knows a lot about the news on Twitter, and so that is part of the reason why I know about this.

They created the script for the *Last Ship* based on Kid Cudi's song "Alive." Every time I listen to that song, four people die. They were people or families of people that had issues with me. They either disrespected me in the past or in the present. In this song, he says that "there is a sexy lady who is pure she has the cure." In the script for the *Last Ship*, the role of the girl who they killed off the show was the woman with the solution to our issues for the world. The main guy is very smart and is very strong and knows how to defend himself, and whenever confronted with an issue, he always has a backup plan.

This script was also written for our troops overseas. We need to end all wars and find peace within the world. People are bringing this on upon themselves because of their own actions. If people cannot unite with each other and agree on basic shit, then what I am trying to accomplish for the world can never be attained. There are people in this world that purposely do shit to get me annoyed and frustrated, and I wish they would just stop. Anyway, this is the basics for the script for the *Last Ship*.

Taylor Swift released her song, "Blank Space," after I was going through all those apocalyptic things that Hollywood and the professional athletes were going through to make this way too hard for me. I still don't understand why because I've been going through hell, and it was totally out of my control. In "Blank Space," she mentions *The Perfect Storm*, and the script for this movie was written in 2000. I took into my hands who lives and who dies and because of how hard people made this for me, the perfect storm hit Puerto Rio and Texas a few years back, and several people died because of it. This was the script for *The Perfect Storm*, even though it was based on a true story.

I saw this movie once or twice a long time ago, but I don't really care. I knew that the world was too overcrowded and that all these people were just casualties of society, just like I was when I was lost and didn't know I was lost until I started figuring out some of these answers. I can relate to most of the music they put out and even the ones where they hate on me. It is too unacceptable at this point and pretty immature to release songs that hate on me when I never did anything to you.

Taylor Swift is really creative, but people really put me through hell, and at some point, I won't care. But for a little while there, I was wondering why I was stuck so deep. All of my fears will go away. However, there would still be a lot more people that would be alive today if they didn't make it so hard for me. Also, maybe we wouldn't have aged so much if people didn't make this so hard for me.

Now Jeff wants the credit that I deserve for the good things I was doing for the world. Just like my therapist and I talked about how Trump has had it so easy, so has Jeff. I have had it a million times harder than that kid has, so if he gets that credit, it would be so unacceptable. I am the one who went through all of these hellish things, and nobody else besides me deserves this credit when the world is perfectly fixed.

The script for the latest *Robin Hood* was based on my latest interaction with this girl named Robin, who I met on Twitter. She was sending me on all these missions to give her money so that she can recharge her phone and keep on texting with me. After this, I started to get fed up because it wasn't going anywhere, and I was wasting too much money, so then I starting killing haters in this world and pretty much excess fat from this world until she stopped talking to me. It worked because eventually, I stopped responding to her, and she stopped texting me. These people, whoever they are, have trained me to be the person I am today, and I am very different from everyone else in the world. I believe and I think Hollywood believes that all these people were people that hated on me either presently or in the past, so they died for a reason. Every single person they had die in this script were the people I was killing from inside my home.

I was playing "Bye Bye Bye," "X," and complicated songs to make this happen. I've had enough, and now I am more under control, and I think this is all I have to say about this subject for the time being. However, I do need people to train me to play sports and to do business and how to be a better person, amongst other things which I am trying to work on every day.

There is a lot I can write about the script for *Prison Break* and how they came up with the characters and the names of the characters for *Prison Break*. I just wanted to talk about this one scene first. All of my enemies are either dead or in prison, so there was a riot in, I think, Brazil where around fifty-two inmates were killed. In one of the episodes for *Prison Break*, it is about a riot and prisoners trying to escape, and they were all terrible people. Nevertheless, in real life, fifty-two prisoners ended up dying because of this prison break.

The next part I will mention is about the character T-Bag. The character is Ryan Bullock, my longtime best friend from soccer in middle school and high school. He is very creepy around girls and is really funny, and the moves that the character in the show made reminds me of Bullock a lot and the signs that connect would make T-Bag to equal Ryan Bullock.

The two main characters from the show are Adam and I. The two masterminds that save the world and do a lot of harm to it, but anyway, we are the tag team that sort of f——ks up the world, but also, people love us because we have better personalities than most people in it. Most people are boring and useless, but not Adam and me when we were having good times back in the day. I think a lot of people are just going through the motions, but Adam and I were having so much fun when we were living with no cares in the world.

The script for *Shooter* was written because Mark Wahlberg is kind of a rebel to the system, and there were a few people who went behind his back to try to set him up. Well, there is probably a lot I can write about this movie, but the one scene I wanted to talk about was when he cornered the guy at his house to try to get some truth to why they wanted beef with Mark Wahlberg, and the guy ended up killing himself. When I heard the news that Islamic State leader Abu Bakr al-Baghdadi killed himself and his three children, this scene kind of reminded me of that part of that movie. The troops were closing in, and he found no way out but to kill himself.

I thought it was the writer of the "Seven-Nation Army" that was blocking my vision and holding me back one day, but it was actually the Islamic State leader, and now he is dead. Congratulations to our troops and the corrupt Hollywood, but especially congratulations to me!

20 Percent Concentrated Power of Will Coakley

Will power, motherf——kers!

I started taking over the world in a productive manner when I was twenty-five years old. Here are a few things that come to mind right now. When I was dating Amber, we took a visit to the Martin Luther King museum to celebrate his history and all the precious moments for the Black community in today's world. I then went into therapy and told her that it is important to remember that he had his support system with him and it was much more than a one-man operation. A lot of his praise and what he means to the world comes from the people that he surrounded himself with, not by just his thoughts and smarts.

When I listened to the *Today Show* on NBC a week later, Common, the rapper, said the same thing that I had told her on the *Today Show*, not verbatim, but it was very similar. This also can fall under the "Endless Connections/Signs," but I thought I would put it in the will power section.

Around one or two years ago, when I was twenty-nine or thirty years old, I started thinking of ideas of how to clean out my closet and the best ways to go about this process. Within a week, Hoda Kotb and Kathie Lee had a ten-minute clip on the exact same things I was doing in my closet, except obviously, it had to be more professional since I was just in my room and they were on TV. I was like, "Wow, this is crazy." I guess I do know what's right sometimes, and they came up with a lot of unique ways with guest appearances of people on how to keep the clothes that you need and give the rest to people that actually need them.

I found this very interesting because I have been tested so much because of the fact that people were actually going to have to rely on me in the future. Well, that future is coming on quick, and I feel like I am pretty prepared for it. I just wanted to say real quick that it is up to people to keep up the pace and not fall behind the master plan.

Hollywood came out with the movie called *Hidden Figures*. There is a reason why they came out with a movie with this title. The reason is because we have a pattern in history to not recognize all the instrumental players that have led the world to get this far in its history, and we should start appreciating these people a little bit more. I think the Martin Luther King example is just one example. Here is a question: what about all the people that explored foreign land way back in the day? Did all of them get the proper credit? I know the Bible, which so many people don't even bother reading anymore, gives people credit, but I highly doubt it was the powers of just one man that had healing powers. I also do not think that Noah's ark ever happened and that we were destined to come ever before in history before this assignment was given to me. I think those are all lies so that when I was born, people would be like, "Well, this has already happened before." In my opinion, my job has been way too hard that I cannot fathom the idea of trying to do this twice.

When I was around twenty-seven years old, I used to make fun of Kesha's songs as a joke when I was by myself. Within a year, Anna Kendrick appeared on *Saturday Night Live* and played out a skit where she was doing the exact same thing, except she was on TV doing it. I guess this is a part of my takeover, but it was pretty cool seeing it. She killed it on *Saturday Night Live*, and I guess they all kind of do to a certain extent. I am getting annoyed with them ragging on Donald Trump all the time, though.

When I was hanging out with my close friends, my friend, Romy, and I were talking about ideas how to create a $15 minimum wage for people that work hard and do not see the rewards. Well, the federal government started to try to figure out ways to increase the minimum wage to $15 an hour, which I thought was pretty cool. Also, I listen to a Flobots song called "Same Thing," and in the song, it states that we should not use our greed and focus on people instead. So, in nine states of the United States, companies will require five days of sick leave a year. Also, for Walmart, the hourly wage will increase from nine to eleven. To go along with the same concept as the $15 minimum wage that Romy and I were talking about, DC Voters backed initiative to raise tipped workers' wages to $15. The primary election voters in the district have approved Initiative 77, which includes what I have just said, and it had to be Initiative 77 because my cousin Ray is 77 to connect the dots with me, Will, at 66.

To add to the above section, Maryland has now become the sixth state to adopt a $15 minimum wage. I had a conversation with my friend, Romy, when Trump was first elected president that the minimum wage should be $15 an hour all across the board, and now it's real, and six states have come to the realization that this is necessary. I am a big believer that everyone should get treated equally, besides the fact that we are killing the flesh, but the world is overpopulated. For the people that are still alive, we need to come toward equal rights. Even though I have had it the hardest in the world and am the best person in the world, everything in this world should be equal.

Judge Blocks Medicaid Work Requirements in Kentucky and Arkansas

A federal judge in Washington threw a significant roadblock into the Trump administration's efforts to compel poor people on Medicaid to work in exchange for health benefits, rejecting a Kentucky program for a second time while saying that rules are in effect in Arkansas can't stand. The twinned opinions Wednesday afternoon, in a pair of states that have been national leaders in the move toward Medicaid work requirements, cast doubt on the Trump's administration's

approvals of effort to revision the public insur-
ance program. The opinions undo the permis-
sions that the US Health and Human Services
Department gave those two states, telling the
agency it must reconsider the applications with
an eye on the effect on poor people who depend
on the coverage.

This is huge because it's some of those asshole Republications that
are not narrow-minded that they cannot possibly see the big picture
and how their actions affect others who are less fortunate. I give money
to the homeless all the time, and I am constantly helping out those
who are less fortunate by answering their prayers and trying to get the
people off the streets, and f——k Jeff for thinking the way he does.

The FDA approved a novel antidepressant
for people with depression that does not respond
to other treatments, the first in decades to work
in a completely new way in the brain. The drug,
a nasal spray called Esketamine, has been eagerly
anticipated by psychiatrists and patient groups as
a powerful new tool to fight intractable depression. The spray acts within hours, rather than
weeks or months as is typical for current anti-
depressants, and could offer a lifeline to about 5
million people in the United States with major
depressive disorder who haven't been helped by
current treatments. That accounts for about one
in three people with depression.

When Sum 41 came out with "The Hell Song," he said I would
answer people's requests that were most important. Well, this seems
pretty f——king important to me, and I am so happy that the scientists were able to come up with this idea to help out people with
depression.

"Self-professed Neo-Nazi Who Drove into Charlottesville Crowd Pleads Guilty to Federal Hate Crimes"—James A. Fields rammed his car into counter protestors at a 2017 White-supremacist rally, killing Heather Heyer and injuring thirty-five others. Hollywood is trying to hang out to what's golden, and that's me. When I went to GNC, there was the number 35, which stands for my thirty-fifth birthday when karma or the US officially win the war overseas. I am not sure which one will happen.

Miley Cyrus said that "all that matters is the steps you take and everything else falls into place." So by making these steps to GNC, I was able to take down this hater and throw him behind bars. Fields was convicted late last year in state court of first-degree murder and other charges in the ramming and was sentenced by a jury to life in prison.

F——k these low-life assholes that don't see others people's pain as seriously as they should. There are a lot of people that are doing a lot of good in this world, and this James Fields guy was not one of them. He was one of Trump's supporters, and there are a lot of people that believe in my products, not in the bullshit that Trump is doing. He is now not helping out the Special Olympics. Like, what the f—k is that crap? People need to get their priorities straight and understand that there is more to life than your own personal bullshit issues and greed.

When I was around twenty-nine to thirty years old, I started drinking coffee and throwing this into the solution pit as a way to heal ourselves, instead of it being connected to negativity and having positive results on our bodies. Then, all of a sudden, a report came out that drinking a certain amount of coffee each day could help you lead longer lives. I think life will become simpler when people feel more protected and have a sense of worth. I bring this up because my friend, Andrew Micik, was freaking out one day and came across this article on the Internet. All I said was that I drink that much coffee each day because I didn't know what else to say. After all is said and done, we need to turn these things into positives in people's lives instead of all this negativity that flows across our society.

There is a new news report that came out on July 11, 2017, that drinking coffee can help people live longer lives. I think that scientists had proven this theory over the past year and a half and have more conclusive evidence that this theory is actually correct. They are even saying that drinking coffee with sugar and other sweets that people like to put in it also can lead to people living longer lives. This is great news because I know a lot of people around the globe, especially in the United States, are addicted to drinking coffee. If we want to look at this from a signs point of view, Ray and I are destined to get our products into 7-Elevens across the globe in our business. This report came out on 7/11 in 2017, and this could just mean even bigger things for Ray and myself for the future.

When I was thirty-one years old, I had an instantaneous moment when all of a sudden, all of the toxins in my body were going through detox. I was just sitting on my couch and trusting the people that know what they are doing, and all of a sudden, my body started going through detox. I feel a lot better since that day, and it has been an ongoing process ever since then. I advise that other people do the exact same thing and that we make this more of a group effort, based on the results that I have produced in this world.

I went to New York one weekend to visit my ex-girlfriend, Angie, and this was around the time when I was finding myself again and figuring out the world. She had lit me up just like Fall Out Boy says in his song called "My Songs Know What You Did in the Dark." So I have had people lighting me up with their eyes for years to turn this solution thing into a group effort. Anyway, she lit me up, then I starting driving and acting exactly how I did when we were dating. I met up with her when I was around twenty-seven or twenty-eight. Back at that point, I was changing all the time, and my mind was a complete mess. I was starting to drive like I used to because I had to stop driving for a little bit with that entire alien and conspiracy shit going on.

This trip to New York to visit her had actually helped us both out. For me, I was starting to realize who I was again and becoming the Will Coakley of the past and present. I had cut off communication from everyone, but now that I am older and wiser, I plan to make a killing in this new world we are building.

When I was driving in the car with my dad, I was listening to Train's song, "Mermaid," and simultaneously, the part of the song that said, "Heaven's gates came on," a guy opened up the door to a gas station in Fair Lakes shopping center. I thought this was interesting because it was somehow connected to the music we were listening to in my dad's car. I am very interested in signs and connections in this world; I thought this was a great first step to realizing these connections.

During this past all-star game, telepathically, I had told certain people that were betting on the all-star festivities to put money on Devin Booker for him to twin the three-point contest. First off, he had to overcome the adversity that had Klay Thompson winning the entire three-point contest. However, Devin Booker was able to overcome those odds, and he ended up winning the contest, and those people have a little more money in their wallet now. Also, when I had helped Philadelphia Eagles win the Super Bowl, my dad told me of reports where big sports gamblers were putting money on this game for the Eagles. Nevertheless, I had this on my mind during the game, and I was able to deliver for these folks as well.

Okay, so let's say the CIA is not behind these conspiracies and it is in fact other people across the globe. Again, this was when I was around twenty-seven years old, but I started noticing that there are people in the world that can control the weather. I started to feel it out when I went on a cruise about an hour away to more southern Virginia. Sometimes the sky gets pretty crazy, and you can see pink and blue and in more recent memory, there are clouds covering the sky when it is like a hundred degrees outside. In the Killers song, "Spaceman," it talks about how the storm makers say that it isn't so bad. However, it's pretty scary knowing that we have people in the world that can control this shit.

Anyway, when I took this road trip, I stopped at, like, a Walmart and was just smoking cigarettes in the parking lot when in a span of three minutes, it was raining, and very dark clouds were overcoming the sky. Furthermore, in a matter of fifteen minutes, all the clouds began to disappear, and it was sunny and seventy degrees outside where I was. Everyone talks about how great the weather is in Southern California. I think it would be amazing if we, as a society, can make that great weather exist all across the globe.

To go along with these past thoughts, I know how to change and fix the weather, and I am getting better at it every day. My Uncle Ray once told me that there was a hurricane coming to Louisiana in excess of sixty miles per hour, and I somehow was able to break it up overnight. There was another instance when the weather guys said a storm was coming toward the DC area, and I was somehow able to avert the storm into the Pennsylvania/Pittsburgh area. It is pretty crazy, but since I was destined to save the world, I think this is pretty cool that I am able to do these things for society.

To add to this section, I was with Allyn one day, and this came to my mind as we were having a conversation. The weather in Chicago and the northern states needed to be addressed. I know that on the news one day, people were complaining about the weather in Chicago and maybe the unpredictable weather had something to do with what we were doing on planet earth. Mother nature has not been kind to many people over the last few years, so this wasn't a surprise, but I believe it is a problem that we can fix over the next year or so.

Another example is when I started to really dive into if it's possible that we could all stay forever young. I was just speaking my mind when I was by myself and had some free time when I was twenty-seven years old. Thanks to the Offspring song called "You're Gonna Go Far, Kid," it had mentioned to trust the band N'Sync. So, throughout my rumbling to myself that night, when I was on another level, I had said, "Age is just a number" countless times. The whole revelation started with me in real life, and then within a week, I was watching a member of the N'Sync band on the *Access Hollywood* show on NBC, and he had mentioned that age is just a number to him on his fortieth birthday. However, many other people in the world talk about age just being a number to strive to be the best until they die, which I learned in therapy, but the members of N'Sync are on the same page as me as if we will stay forever young. This is how this eye-opener started.

I started having experiences with ghosts when I was nineteen years old, when I was living in my fraternity house in Centreville, Virginia. I used to be scared and defenseless when ghosts would enter into my life, and they were all over the fraternity house. I have been dealing with this issue ever since then. However, I thought of using some common sense and using this as value for the world. I have the power, so I thought, *What the hell, I will start using this power to make people's lives better.* This is only for people that believe in things like this.

One of my personal trial and error experiences was to put them in athlete's bodies, manly professional football players, in order for them to excel throughout certain times of the game. This theory is still a work in progress, but it has been beneficial. Another example of this is when a player's father passed away on the Butler College basketball team. Their team was an eighth seed in 2016, barely making it into the tournament, and I helped the team win by having his everlasting spirit spark victory for the team. Now that particular spirit did not leave the team's house, and Butler ended up entering the NCAA tournament as a number four seed the following year, which was in 2017.

Another part of the solution is healing our bodies with drinks, food, water, etc. It was 2015, and Russell Wilson, the Seahawks NFL quarterback, claimed that water healed an injury he received in 2015. I believed him right away, but he had many doubters to his theory. I tested it out at home, and the way that many variations of foods and drinks made me feel after those who believe in miracles believed him, and everything I am trying to do, it works so well, and as of 2017, the theory, in my eyes, is fool-proof. If I can get this going on a worldwide basis, then we have something going with this part of the solution. I would drink water, and the way it was entered into my body felt like I just automatically got stronger, just like the scene in *Space Jam*. Not only that, but I also think we can use this to heal our injuries because I have felt different after putting certain things in my body and using it to heal injuries. I ate a yogurt on May 13, 2017, and all of a sudden, my back wasn't in the type of pain that it was before.

In the past year, ranging from football season in 2016 to baseball season in 2017, I have noticed an increase in the amount of injuries in pro sports. I think there are a few factors that could be behind this. Maybe guys' bodies aren't as hydrated as they should be, and maybe Mother Nature has taken a toll for the worst. Believe it or not,

Mother Nature can have a major impact on how we perform as athletes. For instance, I talk about this with my boy, Jeff, a lot, but the Nationals and the Yankees have been hit hard with the injury bug in 2017. But I am always a believer that things will get better, so let's be optimistic, and I feel like injuries in pro sports and rec sports will get better, let's say starting in football season in 2017. If not, then definitely, injuries will get better by the start of baseball season in 2018.

I'm looking at the current Nationals injury report on July 18, 2017, and some notable injuries, such as a free agent pickup in Adam Eaton who will be out for the entire season. Another player on their MLB roster, Jason Werth, will be out until at least July 28 with a toe injury. I know, personally, I have dealt with my share of injuries, but if we can make progress in this area, I know they would all be happy, and being healthy is one aspect of life that we all aim for every day. Michael Taylor, an outfielder for the Nationals, will be out until July 26 with an oblique area. I know if we can dig deep into the main atmospheric or inside our bodies to see what really causes these injuries, we can make significant progress.

Looking at the New York Yankees injury report, the details don't look too much better for these players. Michael Pineda just went down with a season-ending injury, due to an elbow injury, which I believe will require Tommy John surgery. Two of our main prospects, Dustin Fowler and Gleyber Torres, are out for the season with knee and elbow injuries. You never want to see the young guys with injuries like this because they are still trying to prove themselves. Aaron Hicks and Tyler Austin, two guys that are young enough to still make a big impact on the years going forward, are out with injuries until August because of oblique and hamstring injuries.

One guy I wanted to point out is Greg Bird. Going into spring training and after he made significant progress with his defense and offense, he has been dealing with injury problems all year. He is around twenty-four years old and has shown that he can make it in the big leagues. He is out until September with an ankle injury. Again, these injuries suck, and like I have said before, many people think this is just a part of life. I am kind of looking at this from a different perspective and want to find a solution for this ASAP.

There are many haters out there that thought Andrew Luck wouldn't play again or would never be the same player again. I answer prayers since I have the magic inside of me, and I can overcome anyone else's say in the world by my saying "actions speak louder than words." I hold key parts of the future in my hands, and one of these is making sure the players in professional sports are healthy every week and every day. I added this below the section above because I do believe that progress was made in the baseball season, and fewer injuries have occurred this year. I really wish the best for Andrew Luck and hope that he rebounds and proves all of his haters wrong.

In my opinion, everyone deserves silver linings, and for athletes, if they have no more injuries, then what's left for them to complain about in the professional ranks? Maybe they can still complain about the reporters and about the contracts, but unless you are an asshole or someone who is inconsiderate of other people's feelings, then you do not wish any ill intent on the athletes that make our days every day and every week, if we are talking about the NFL.

The same thing applied to Carston Wentz when he went down, but I do believe that Nike folk were the reason why they won the championship. Even still, people were probably hoping Wentz got hurt for their own self-gains so that their own personal teams were going to win that year. Looking forward, we will see how this NFL season plays out and wish teams will rise above adversity and win the NFL championship in 2019. It's all set up perfectly so far, and once we can figure out the signs and connections that connect, we will know which team will win next year.

Taking control over who has new little people enter the world. I gave this responsible to the people on my favorite list, which includes the people I am closest to. Like my therapist and I were talking about, people need to start seeing the big picture and realizing that everyone's actions have consequences on others. There is only a certain amount of people that can be on planet earth at one time, and when couples are having ten couples, that is pretty more unacceptable. So every time that certain people on my favorite list and myself go to the bathroom, there are new little people entering our world, but that also comes with consequences as people have to die for other people's greed. This will end when I say it's going to end so that people are not so goddamn selfish.

Vegas—there is a bunch of people with authority that wanted to make Vegas a better place to accommodate people with different needs for such a great place in the US. So now they have an NHL franchise and a NFL franchise. They needed my smarts and my mind to accomplish this. This all started when I went there to gamble on sports for my boy Allyn's bachelor party two years ago. I did a lot of sports gambling, and since everything I do has been deemed to be special, this new direction Vegas has taken is going to be successful and help out so many different people.

There are people that are not so happy about all the additions Vegas is making, saying that it doesn't make sense that Las Vegas now has sports teams, but again, look at the big picture and imagine how many people like to visit there every year. There are so many things that make perfect sense, and Vegas having sports franchises just makes a lot of sense to me.

I am acting as a god in this world since there really is no God. When I started gaining control over the world in the exact opposite ways as Hitler, I just randomly started answering people's prayers. For instance, Katy Perry needed help with something or other, and I heard her voice on a Wednesday. On Friday, I saw on the *Today Show* that she was really happy that her prayers were answered, whatever they were, and it was really only I. Another example is that Patrick Ewing, the ex-Knicks basketball player was looking for a head coaching gig for nobody knows how long, and I was able to answer his prayers within a three-year period. Nobody really knows how many other good deeds I was able to perform this way since I was gaining this power, and it feels good to make people happy in the ways I have been able to.

I have found out a way to reach out to people and answer their prayers while they are praying or before prayers are even being formed. I gave one example in the previous paragraph about Patrick Ewing seeking a coaching gig, and I was able to hand that to him. Now I am going to talk about John Lynch. I've been listening to him talk about the NFL for the last however many years, and now he finally wanted to be a GM in the NFL. I remember when I was younger, I would watch him play every single Sunday as a safety. He was one of the best White safeties to play in the NFL. I was able to grant his wish to be a GM in the NFL for the 49ers. It makes complete sense to me.

The 49ers have been on a slippery slope and sort of in freefall mode over the past few seasons. He could bring some real stability to this organization. Anyways, I listen to this one Timbaland song called "Throw It On Me." What this song means is that if you are in a pickle or you need something to happen for you, just throw it on me, and I will answer these requests ASAP. Furthermore, I can be there for anyone, whether it's science or faith, unless the requests are extraordinary and unrealistic.

In this part, I just wanted to explain people's successes with video games with people thinking outside the box and what it means with fear, anxiety, and hope, three things that I think and talk about a lot and what it means to be a minority in playing video games.

The outline of Davionne Gooden's new computer game may feel familiar. The main character must defeat villains to reach an ultimate goal. But woven in are elements that set the game apart. The main character is stuck in a coma, and the villains are nightmares. Players confront issues of anxiety and depression. And through an all-Black cast, Mr. Gooden deliberately features the experiences of people typically absent from mainstream games. "If you're a White creator, you rarely think about that," he said.

Gaming is a multibillion-dollar business and one that has remained largely white and largely male. Five years after "Gamergate" exposed the kind of toxicity that can lurk in a community where diverse perspectives are underrepresented, little seems to have changed for minorities and women in the industry. Today, people like Mr. Gooden still confront an industry that infrequently reflects who they are. Three out of four people working in the gaming industry are men. Almost the same proportion identifies as White. And those numbers have hardly budged since 2015, according to surveys conducted by the nonprofit International Game Developers Association. "If you're a young person of color playing games, you don't really see yourself represented," said Mitu Khandaker, a professor at New York University's game center. "That kind of instills in you this sense that maybe I don't really belong." That lack of diversity in mainstream gaming—games made by the handful of large development companies—can be cyclical, turning people away from the industry, said Dr. Khandaker, who is also the chief executive of Glow Up Games, a research and development studio focused on diversity. Women, for example, are rarely promoted to senior positions or made the heads of studios. Many gamers say toxic harassment online is still an everyday fear. Some like Mr. Gooden, 21, see signs of hope. He started making games shortly after he got his first laptop in the fifth grade and discovered a game-developing program online. He never stopped. In Mr. Gooden's roleplaying game, She Dreams Elsewhere, the main character, Thalia Sullivan, navigates her own mind, battling nightmares as she tries to eventually figure out how she fell into a coma. The most recent I.G.D.A. survey found that 81 percent of those in the industry feel that diversity in the workplace is either very important or somewhat important, up from 63 percent in 2015. And developers have more outlets to get their games in the hands of players, including online platforms like Steam and crowdfunding sites like Kickstarter, as well as gaming conferences and festivals. "I'm an optimist," Mr. Gooden said. "I hope that things will eventually be better as a whole."

When "Gamergate" unfolded in 2014, the world was exposed to the toxic side of gaming. Spurred by a misogynistic post online from a game developer's ex-boyfriend, mobs online publicly attacked female creators and players in a targeted harassment campaign. Women routinely received rape and death threats. Dietrich Squinkifer, better known as Squinky, knew many of the victims. Watching friends being targeted was scary, but not surprising for Squinky, who uses "they" and "them" pronouns. Squinky had tangled with the same culture before. They began making games in the early 2000s. Squinky's first job in the industry was with Telltale Games, a company based in San Rafael, Calif., known for The Walking Dead, a zombie apocalypse adventure game. Squinky, 33, said that as their career progressed, they increasingly tried to advocate a better understanding of race, gender and sexuality in the industry. Colleagues saw Squinky as a troublemaker, and bosses were quick to reprimand. They burned out of mainstream gaming. Now, Squinky pursues independent, artistic projects, like Robot Slow Dance. It's a game in which people use controllers to make two miniature foam and metal robots dance with each other. "I think that's part of the reason a lot of my focus in my work has gone more toward more experimentality, installation and performance art, following more of an art world tradition," Squinky said. "I am to some degree scared of creating something that will get popular enough within the video game world community that it does receive that kind of backlash." The game itself is a commentary on social gender norms, which are nonexistent for robots. "They won't make the same assumptions as humans," Squinky said.

Emma Kidwell's father is white. Her mother is Japanese. But growing up in the overwhelmingly white, rural suburb of Walkersville, Md., she felt detached from her Japanese identity. Making games would help her reconnect. She became interested in gaming as a child, watching her brothers play games on Xbox and PlayStation. About three years ago in college, Ms. Kidwell tried building games for a narrative design class. Through games, Ms. Kidwell, 25, found she could tell stories about her personal life. She made one about the awkwardness of buying condoms at a store; she made another about watching her grandmother grapple with dementia. In January, her grandfather in Japan died, rekindling Ms. Kidwell's childhood uneasiness about her biracial identity. So she made the interactive, web-based game Half. The narrative game takes the player through a series of Ms. Kidwell's memories. She wrote about feelings of wanting to look more Japanese, about how her mother stopped talking to her in Japanese and about how she was mistaken for being Chinese. "Since then, I haven't felt the same really weird self-consciousness," she said.

In Joyce Lin's new tabletop card game, players role-play as girls with crushes on each other. One might become Avery, who is Japanese and Scottish and pansexual, or Ioh, a Korean tomboy. Draw another card, and Avery and Ioh might meet at a gas station at 1 a.m., with one need-ing a ride. Together, players craft a date: Will Ioh give Avery a ride? What is the best way the early morning can unfold, based on each character's personality traits? Ms. Lin, 21, said the game, Queering Spacetime, is an attempt to put forth a positive representation of queer relationships, often overlooked in games and media. "Usually, in dating sims, you have to impress a character," she said, referring to simulation games. "It's sort of one-sided." Ms. Lin, who recently came out, said her game exemplified "the queer form of resistance"—building safe spaces together as a shield against all that is harmful in the world.

Julian Cordero, 22, loves soccer but hates its competitive culture. So, when he made a game about the sport, it wasn't about playing a match. The game, which he made with his develop-ment partner, Sebastián Valbuena, 28, is called Despelote and is set in their hometown, Quito, Ecuador. In first person, the player kicks a soc-cer ball around city parks, meeting people along the way. "Ultimately, the game for us is a game about soccer, but it's not about the competitive aspect," Mr. Cordero said. "It's quite the oppo-site. It's about the human aspect, and the relation-ships that sort of develop through kicking a ball around." With Despelote, Mr. Cordero is trying to use soccer to reject the competitiveness of gam-ing, which he believes engenders the misogyny and consumerism that have been endemic to the culture. Mr. Cordero wants people to know that he likes making and playing games, but he's not a gamer. "I wouldn't really call myself that," he said.

Aziza Brown is proud to call herself a gamer. Ms. Brown, the founder and chief executive of

Dynamik Focus, an e-sports and content creation team, said coverage of the industry erroneously dwelled on toxicity and "Gamergate" when discussing the lack of diversity. Other, less sinister reasons lurk behind the demographics, she said, and they can be fixed. Some people of color may be less likely to have access to the expensive, high-speed internet connections necessary to play at a competitive level, she said. There's also what Ms. Brown called an "information deficit"—not knowing which tournaments or clubs to go to or whom to meet in the community. Ms. Brown, 39, points to her own experience as representative of how things can change. Growing up in New York, she played many video games, particularly fighting games like Street Fighter. She played in some tournaments but then went to college at Stony Brook University and studied engineering. When she returned, she set out to find a robust gaming community: tournaments, clubs, friends. Through Dynamik Focus, she now tries to help others find their support groups. Ms. Brown was, for example, one of hundreds who attended an annual conference for developers of color in Harlem over the summer. "I had a talk with a woman in gaming, where I was like, please come to the offline communities, come to other places, because once the anonymous barrier is gone, you can see the person to their face, you can confront them, that behavior stops," she said.

When I heard that Taylor Swift was going to be in court for her ex-DJ groping her at a meet-and-greet, I knew that she would come to me for help. Nevertheless, I was able to get her the victory in court. Not only this, but I have also been able to get athletes and others off domestic violence charges and things of this nature. I know that everyone deserves a second chance in whatever they are trying to accomplish in life, and Taylor Swift is my girl, so once I saw this go public, I knew I would be able to get her a victory in court, and because of everything she stands for, I am on her side. I've seen a lot of pain in this lifetime, and frankly, I am sick of it. I wish everyone would just be appropriate and cooperate within the rules placed in society.

Derek Jeter has had plans to own a baseball franchise ever since he retired. I don't know how the f——k I am able to answer people's prayers, but I do because I am able to, and I have the free time to do this kind of work. Anyway, he is now a minority owner with the Marlins and will have something like a Magic Johnson type role with the team. Derek Jeter will run the business side and baseball side of the organization. This is a great first step for him after retirement, and I am glad I could help aid him with his post-retirement plans.

I am a big believer in Tim Tebow and what he is trying to do in baseball. Anyway, he prays a lot and believes in the kingdom come. The next thing I know is that he is on the all-star team in the double A league and is trying his hardest to make it to the majors. If this happens, this would be a blessing and a very great thing for the sport of baseball.

He wasn't quite able to make it as an NFL player, but maybe baseball can work out for him for the next four to five years or longer than that. If Tim Tebow proves to the world that he is worthy of being a major leaguer, than all I can say is, "F——k you" to all of his haters.

I just want to explain in this section how all of Trump's lovers need to shut the f——k up because of how bad of a president he is. I started following *New York Times* reports to see what good and bad things are happening in the world and see how they impact me. This is how I found out about the progress in video games. For Trump, the headline reads "ISIS Reaps Gains of US Pulling Out of Syria:"

> The troop withdrawal ends American operations against the terrorist group conducted jointly with a Kurdish-led militia. American forces and their Kurdish-led partners in Syria had been conducting as many as a dozen coun-

terterrorism missions a day against Islamic State militants, officials said. That has stopped. Those same partners, the Syrian Democratic Forces, had also been quietly releasing some Islamic State prisoners and incorporating them into their ranks, in part as a way to keep them under watch. That, too, is now in jeopardy. And across Syria's porous border with Iraq, Islamic State fighters are conducting a campaign of assassination against local village headmen, in part to intimidate government informants.

When President Trump announced this month that he would pull American troops out of northern Syria and make way for a Turkish attack on the Kurds, Washington's onetime allies, many warned that he was removing the spearhead of the campaign to defeat the Islamic State, also known as ISIS. Now, analysts say that Mr. Trump's pullout has handed the Islamic State its biggest win in more than four years and greatly improved its prospects. With American forces rushing for the exits, in fact, American officials said last week that they were already losing their ability to collect critical intelligence about the group's operations on the ground. "There is no question that ISIS is one of the big winners in what is happening in Syria," said Lina Khatib, director of the Middle East and North Africa Program at Chatham House, a research center in London.

Cutting support for the Syrian Democratic Forces has crippled the ability of the United States and its former partners to hunt down the group's remnants. News of the American withdrawal set off jubilation among Islamic State supporters on social media and encrypted chat networks. It has lifted the morale of fighters in affiliates as far away as Libya and Nigeria. And, by removing a critical counterforce, the pullout has eased the re-emergence of the Islamic State's core as a terrorist network or a more conventional, and potentially long—lasting, insurgency based in Syria and Iraq. Although Mr. Trump has repeatedly declared victory over the Islamic State—even boasting to congressional leaders last week that he had personally "captured ISIS"—it remains a threat. After the loss in March of the last patch of the territory it once held across Syria and Iraq, the Islamic State dispersed its supporters and fighters to blend in with the larger population or to hide out in remote deserts and mountains. The group retains as many as 18,000 "members" in Iraq and Syria, including up to 3,000 foreigners, according to estimates cited in a recent Pentagon report. Abu Bakr al-Baghdadi, the Islamic State's self-proclaimed caliph, is still at large.

"Our battle today is one of attrition and stretching the enemy," Mr. al-Baghdadi declared in a video message released in April. Looking comfortable and well fed, he sat on the floor of a bare room, surrounded by fighters, with an assault rifle by his side. "Jihad is ongoing until the day of judgment," he told his supporters, according to a transcript provided by SITE Intelligence Group. Against the benchmark of the Islamic State's former grip on a broad swath of geography, any possibility of a comeback to that extent remains highly remote. Changes in the political context in Syria and Iraq have diminished the Islamic State's ability to whip up sectarian animosity out of the frustrations of Sunni Muslims over the Shiite or Shiite-linked authorities in Syria and Iraq—the militants' trademark. The government in Baghdad has broadened its support among Sunni Iraqis. President Bashar al-Assad of Syria, by crushing the revolt against him, has left Sunni militants less space to mobilize. And many Syrians and Iraqis who lived under the harsh dominion of the Islamic State strongly oppose its return.

But as an underground insurgency, the Islamic State appears to be on the upswing. Militants have been carrying out "assassinations, suicide attacks, abductions, and arson of crops in both Iraq and Syria," according to a report this summer by the Pentagon inspector general for operations against the Islamic State. It is establishing "resurgent cells" in Syria, the report said, and "seeking to expand its command and control nodes in Iraq." The militants have been burning crops and emptying out whole villages. They have been raising money by carrying out kidnappings for ransom and extorting "taxes" from local officials, often skimming a cut of rebuilding contracts. Their attacks on village headmen—at least 30 were killed in Iraq in 2018, according to the Pentagon report—are an apparent attempt to scare others out of cooperating with Baghdad. "The high operational tempo with multiple attacks taking place over a wide area" may be intended to create the appearance that the Islamic State can strike anywhere with "impunity," the report said.

Mr. Trump first said last December that he intended to withdraw the last 2,000 American troops from Syria; the Pentagon scaled that back, pulling out about half of those troops. Military officials, though, say that helping the Syrian Democratic Forces hunt down underground cells and fugitive fighters required more training and intelligence support than an open battle for territory. Even the partial drawdown, the Pentagon inspector general's report found, could be "detrimental" to the American mission in Iraq and Syria. Last month, as if to prove its continued vitality, the Islamic State claimed responsibility for a minibus bombing that killed a dozen people near the entrance to a Shiite pilgrimage site in the Iraqi city of Karbala. It was its deadliest attack since the loss of its last territory. And within hours of Mr. Trump's announcement almost two weeks ago that American forces were moving away from the Syrian border with Turkey, two ISIS suicide bombers attacked a base of the Syrian Democratic Forces in the Syrian city of Raqqa.

"The crusaders have given up," Islamic State supporters crowed, according to Laith Alkhouri of the business risk consulting company Flashpoint Global Partners, who monitors the group's online messages. Other messages "urged ISIS 'soldiers' everywhere to double their efforts," Mr. Alkhouri said. The missions against the Islamic State conducted by the Syrian Democratic Forces—sometimes as many as two dozen a day—had included both counterterrorism patrols and raids on militant cells. Some were carried out jointly with American soldiers, others alone, according to United States officials. But the Kurds, an ethnic minority sometimes disparaged by Arab Syrians, faced resentment among the Arab residents of northeastern Syria. In part to try to win support from those communities, the Kurdish-led forces pardoned and released hundreds of detained ISIS fighters or supporters in so-called reconciliation deals, relying on informal relationships with community leaders to handle their reintegration. The Kurdish-led militia even incorporated some of the released Islamic State detainees into its own forces, said Dareen Khalifa, a researcher with the International Crisis Group who has traveled to the region extensively and documented the "reconciliation" pardons in a report last summer.

The Kurdish militia leaders said: "What do you want us to do, kill them all? Imprison them all? The best way forward is to keep a close eye on them by keeping them within the S.D.F.," Ms. Khalifa said in an interview. She said that those enlisted had not been Islamic State leaders and that so far there had been no recidivism. But now the American withdrawal and the Turkish incursion are threatening the informal supervision of those former prisoners, Ms. Khalifa said, creating a risk that some might gravitate back to fighting for the Islamic State. Turkey, which has battled Kurdish separatist militants at home for decades, launched the invasion primarily to push back the Kurdish-led forces in Syria. Without American protection, the Kurdish leaders are now switching sides to ally with Mr. al-Assad.

This is all I want to say about this subject for right now. What I am trying to say is that people are *wrong* if they want Trump to be reelected. I thought it would be a good change for America, but he is seriously f——king things up. I am looking for better things coming in the days ahead, and I know that I can do things behind the president's back, things that others cannot provide for other people. I will continue to do this unless things start to change and I get my back life in order. Even when I am hanging out with friends and family, I can still help out other people. Thanks for reading this.

"Microsoft Wins Pentagon's $10 billion JEDI Contract, thwarting Amazon."

In "The Hell Song," Sum 41 says I help out people's problems that are more urgent and what's most important, so I guess this was one of those things. Here is some of what the article said:

> The Department of Defense on Friday awarded a $10 billion technology contract to Microsoft over Amazon in a contest that was closely watched after President Trump ramped up his criticism of Amazon's founder, Jeff Bezos, and said he might intervene. The 10-year contract for the Joint Enterprise Defense Infrastructure, known as JEDI, had set off a showdown among Amazon, Microsoft, IBM, Oracle and Google for the right to transform the military's cloud computing systems. The acrimonious process involved intense lobbying efforts and legal challenges among the rivals. The contract has an outsize importance because it is central to the Pentagon's efforts to modernize its technology. Much of the military operates on 1980s and 1990s computer systems, and the Defense Department has spent billions of dollars trying to make them talk to one another.
>
> The decision was a surprise because Amazon had been considered the front-runner, in part because it had built cloud services for the Central Intelligence Agency. But that was before Mr. Trump became publicly hostile to Mr. Bezos, who also owns The Washington Post. The president often refers to the newspaper as the "Amazon Washington Post" and has accused it of spreading "fake news." In public, Mr. Trump said there were other "great companies" that should have a chance at the contract. But a speechwriter for former Defense Secretary Jim Mattis says in a book scheduled for publication next week that Mr.

Trump had wanted to foil Amazon and give the contract to another company. The issue quickly became radioactive at the Pentagon. The new defense secretary, Mark T. Esper, at first said he wanted to take several months to review the issue and then, a few days ago, recused himself from the bidding. He said he could not participate because his son worked for IBM, one of the competitors for the contract. As recently as this month, the betting was that Microsoft would, at most, get only part of the contract and that the Pentagon would use multiple suppliers for its cloud services, as do many private companies. Microsoft was considered in the lead for other government cloud programs, including an intelligence contract; only recently has Microsoft opened enough classified server facilities to be able to handle data on the scale of the Pentagon contract.

"The acquisition process was conducted in accordance with applicable laws and regulations," the Defense Department said in a statement on Friday. "All offerors were treated fairly and evaluated consistently with the solicitation's stated evaluation criteria." Microsoft did not immediately have a comment. Amazon, which calls its cloud platform Amazon Web Services, or AWS, said in a statement that it was surprised by the decision. "AWS is the clear leader in cloud computing, and a detailed assessment purely on the comparative offerings clearly led to a different conclusion," Drew Herdener, a spokesman for Amazon, said. "We remain deeply committed to continuing to innovate for the new digital battlefield where security, efficiency, resiliency and scalability of resources can be the difference between success and failure." The award to Microsoft is likely to fuel suspicions that Mr. Trump may have weighed in privately as well as publicly against Amazon. Experts on federal contracting said it would be highly improper for a president to intervene in the awarding of a contract. Price Floyd, a former head of public affairs at the Pentagon who consulted briefly for Amazon, said he thought Mr. Trump's vocal criticism of Amazon would give it ample grounds to protest the award to Microsoft. "He's the commander in chief, and he hasn't been subtle about his hostility toward Amazon," Mr. Floyd said.

Microsoft's win has implications for the cloud computing industry, in which businesses rent space on technology companies' server computers, giving them cheap and fast access to storage and processing. Amazon has long been the dominant player, with about 45 percent of the market, trailed by Microsoft with around 25 percent, said Daniel Ives, an analyst for Wedbush Securities who has closely followed the JEDI saga. Landing the JEDI contract puts Microsoft in a prime position to earn the roughly $40 billion that the federal government is expected to spend on cloud computing over the next several years, he said. Losing the bid is also a hit to the reputation of Amazon, which decided last year to open a large outpost in Northern Virginia that will eventually employ at least 25,000 people. Unifying information in the cloud has obvious benefits for the Pentagon as the military moves to greater use of remote sensors, semiautonomous weapons and, ultimately, artificial intelligence. It is particularly crucial now that United States Cyber Command has been elevated to the equivalent of Central Command, which runs operations in the

Middle East, or the Northern Command, which defends the continental United States. But some critics of the process argued that such a large contract should not be awarded to a single company, while proponents said using only one provider would eliminate glitches in military systems and streamline communications.

The initial reaction on Friday from some lawmakers was positive, mostly because the long-delayed contract had finally been issued. Representative Jim Langevin, a Rhode Island Democrat who has immersed himself in cyber issues, suggested the military was finally catching up with private industry. "Advanced general-purpose cloud is the industry norm, and it's past time the Department of Defense had access to these capabilities," said Mr. Langevin, the chairman of the Armed Services Subcommittee on Intelligence and Emerging Threats and Capabilities. "I look forward to continuing to use my position in Congress to increase access to next-generation technologies that support our war fighters." But Senator Mark Warner, a Democrat of Virginia, said on Twitter that it was "important that we maintain a fair & competitive process" and that "for the President to use the power of his office to punish critics in the media would be a complete abuse of power." Amazon, Microsoft, IBM, Oracle and Google began battling for the JEDI contract more than a year ago. Google dropped out last October without submitting a formal bid, saying the military work conflicted with its corporate principles, which preclude the use of artificial intelligence in weaponry. The Pentagon said in April that only Amazon and Microsoft met its technical requirements for fulfilling the contract. In an unsuccessful legal challenge, Oracle alleged that Amazon had biased the process in its favor by hiring Defense Department employees to work on the bidding process.

In August, the Defense Department's inspector general announced that it had assembled a team to review the JEDI process. But while that was underway, Mr. Trump raised his objections. The process froze, and Pentagon officials said time was being wasted—which would ultimately put the United States at a military disadvantage. "In 20 years of covering tech, I've never seen a battle for any type of contract reach this level of nastiness," Mr. Ives said. He said he saw the ferocity of the contest mainly as a response to Amazon's enormous success as the pioneer of cloud computing, which is now the foundation of much of the digital infrastructure of private industry. He said Amazon's revenue from federal government contracts, about $200 million in 2014, had reached $2 billion this year, much of it from the C.I.A. and other intelligence agencies.

I was on my porch, thinking that it would be great if the Lakers grabbed Lebron James instead of Philly. I thought this would be great for Magic Johnson and Kobe Bryant. Philly already won in baseball before, they've already won in football, and I thought there was no need for them to be great at basketball right now. If Los Angeles landed Lebron, then they would have a great opportunity to defeat Golden State next year. Golden State has already won three out of the last four years, so Lebron signed a four-year deal, and now they have the chance to build a great team around him. He is still arguably the best player in the NBA, and with the depth that Los Angeles is trying to build, they can defeat Golden State next year. Also, other teams are getting stronger and can beat Golden State. Chris Paul resigned with Houston, so that is optimistic for Houston fans, and we will see how the NBA develops next year.

Good things, I believe, are happening in fours as of the year 2018, and there were exactly four players that were elected to the Baseball Hall of Fame in this year. Those players are Chipper Jones, Vladimir Guerrero, Jim Thome, and Trevor Hoffman—four well-deserved hall of famers. Nevertheless, to talk about signs and connections a little bit more, Chipper Joneses last name ends in J, and Jim Thome's first name starts with J. Guerrero's last name starts with G and Trevor Hoffman's last name starts with H. G and H are back-to-back in the alphabet, which I thought would be noteworthy to point out here. So I figure in 2020, the figures will be good things happening in sixes and bad things happening in zeroes.

I wanted to mention that the baseball games ending in a particular result for a reason in this section. The Cubs and Brewers games both had back-to-back seven-run games. In Katy Perry's song, she says that it takes two to connect the dots. Well, the other person is my cousin, Ray, who stands for seven. The scores ended in seven because of whatever Ray and I were doing while these two teams were playing during their allotted slots. The Yankees lost to the Rays, 6–1, and this was because of the magic inside of me that is connected to my phone, so the Rays scored six runs.

In this world, I am all about progress and this was progress because now we have figured out the sports world, and it makes more sense now, at least to me, as to why players fluctuate more and why teams do better or worse throughout the season. We can even pick up on trends from day to day better because of the connections that are in the sky. In addition, the White Sox beat the Tigers, 6–5, on August 15. I was able to beat my dad in this score. The Twins beat the Pirates, 6–4, on August 15 as well. This was a victory for me because the score ended with a six, and again, I have been working with nothing, with no one's help, and I was able to deliver a 6–4 victory for the Twins.

Friday, August 17, I noticed that the Red Sox beat the Rays, 7–3, and this was because of whatever Ray and I were doing throughout this game that brought the Red Sox a 7–3 victory. For the games played on Saturday, August 19, there were two scores I wanted to mention. The Marlins beat the Nationals, 7–5. Since my dad stands for five and Ray and I connected the dots adds to seven, this is why the Marlins won this game. It would be nice to see the Nationals be good, but they just won in hockey, so the fans cannot be too greedy.

This year, I was hoping the Marlins would do well because of Derek Jeter and because I like good underdog stories. Nevertheless, the Marlins ended up winning this game, 7–5. The Tigers beat the Twins, 7–5. Again, same concept, since my dad stands for five and Ray and I stand for seven, this was another reason why the Tigers won this game. Another team that I find interesting is the Athletics, who have crept up on the Astros to tie them for the lead in the AL West standings. Boston is really killing it with eighty-eight wins, when the Yankees only have seventy-seven wins. As of right now, the Yankees would be the wild card team, but it's crazy that the Red Sox are playing so well. Their home and away splits are great with forty-four wins on the road and at home. Cleveland is killing it in the Central division in the East with a 70–52 record and are twelve games ahead of the twins.

To go along with this section, the Red Sox beat Cleveland with a 7–0 win. It takes two to connect the dots, so whatever Ray and I were doing during this time period, and Shaker, can help the Boston teams win as well. I really do not want to see Boston win another championship, but they are putting together a great season, so if they deserve to win, then that's what it's going to be. The signs added up to Boston winning this game, and good for them because they are just outplaying their opponents this year. Detroit beat Chicago White Sox, 7–2, on this Thursday, August 23, and this has to do with the signs connecting, just as I have mentioned in the previous two paragraphs.

Eminem can help Detroit win, and whatever Ray and I were doing during this time period helped Detroit win this game. It is what it is, but we'll see how the season ends up. Nobody really knows who's going to win the World Series, but Detroit put together a great game to enable them to win.

To go along with the previous paragraphs, the Chicago White Sox beat the Tigers, 7–2. It takes two to connect the dots, so this was Ray and my doing for the White Sox to conquer their demons today and win this game. It was the reverse of what happened in their previous matchup. Detroit had won that game, 7–2, and in this game, the White Sox won, 7–2. It's like reverse psychology or some shit, but the methods work.

The Rays swept the Red Sox over the weekend of August 25, and this was because whatever Ray and I were doing cursed the Red Sox for three straight games, and I was able to shake the shake a little bit better, so Shaker's say in the world went down, and Ray's went up, so both of us were able to break free a little bit better. It could work out for the Yankees in the standings if their momentum keeps up, but we'll see. Athletics beat the Twins 6–2, and the sixes stand for me, so I brought them this joy by them winning this game.

Fixing traffic patterns and car accidents—I started working on this assignment when I was twenty-seven years old. It started when I noticed I could fix traffic patterns that I saw on the news. I would also drive around the streets near my neighborhood and saw more traffic patterns that could be fixed. This might even go back to when I was twenty-five years old as a part of the solution for the human race. There is a road called West Ox that only had one lane for about three to four miles, which caused a lot of bad traffic patterns. They eventually extended it to two lanes and not much traffic patterns to complain about ever since then. This had to do with the hard work of the road workers, the money from the government, and my powerful mind to persist people to make these changes. Also, String Fellow Road in Chantilly, Virginia, decided to make the same calls and changed to two lanes to help with traffic changes.

With the same three things in play, the traffic changes all of a sudden changed, and not many people were complaining about the traffic patterns on this road anymore. Furthermore, I believe it is the same all across the nation and around the world.

Fixing air flight problems—this arose into my life around four years ago, when I was twenty-seven years old. I had all these crazy ideas in my head, and one was fixing the air flight problems that arose into our lives. I believe it's crazy how much security has bumped up, but for the actual air flights that have been saved because of that test I had to pass, it is astronomical. There is still a lot more work to do with this part, but overall, I feel like this section has been a success so far.

There was one instance, which has been well-documented, and it is in a movie called *Sully*. The air flight people saved the day, but it must have been one of my movements during this period that also helped save the day. There is a shopping center I go to regularly called Sully Shopping Center. Maybe one of my trips to this area helped save the flight and all the passengers on board.

A prime example of this was when I was coming home from a flight for my cousin Ray's wedding. On the way back, one of the flight attendants was giving me problems, so the other flight attendant starting giving her problems, and every passenger on the flight started clapping for me. I wasn't even doing anything, and the flight attendant that was giving me problems seemed to be on a power trip. I had just walked onto the flight with, like, twenty more passengers behind me, and she told me that there was no more room for the bag I was carrying onto the flight. The other flight attendant bumped into her with a bag in her hands so I could walk by. That is exactly how it went down.

There was a flight three months later in April 2017 when a passenger got removed from a flight because of a different flight attendant giving the passenger problems. Now United is reviewing their policies to make sure that they provide for their customers in a way that is suitable to their customers. It was like a scene from *Meet the Parents*, but I kept silent and was going to just go about my business. This was necessary if those of us that actually enjoy acting like ourselves want to be happy.

To add to this section, I was reading in the Yahoo News that a woman was kicked off a flight and arrested for giving her Business Class blanket to her son in need in economy. This incident occurred on Copa Airlines after a flight from Panama City to Lima, Peru, in June. She called this "abuse" from the plane people, and I can't say I don't blame her. We have rights as citizens, and this goes above and beyond the harsh realities that face our society. If people are going to be this strict about a goddamn stupid rule that probably shouldn't have existed in the first place, then what the hell are we living for?

Father Time—I figured I could put some significant dents into Father Time about three years ago. So far, a lot of success but a lot more needs to be accomplished. It is Morgan Freeman's eightieth birthday on June 1 of this year in 2017. I am going to start working out and lifting weights consistently on this day. It will be like my personal trial experiment, and whoever wants to help is welcome. We have to get down to the bottom of this soon, so I figured June 1 of this year was the perfect date to try this theory.

Many of us have been in and out of being convinced that we would remain forever young. I figured now better than ever was the time to make this real with the right combinations of faith and science. Another big jump with all the elements with society was when Dwayne Wade dunked a ball, just like he was twenty-six and in his prime again. This happened when I was in Florida with my family. The announcers were like, "And Dwayne Wade just put a dent into father time with that miraculous dunk." It was awesome, but it was also just part of this process.

Saving Facebook—Facebook has been in jeopardy of being closed down because of the users' inputs on what the primary use of Facebook has been for. Because of my dedication to this interface, this will no longer be an issue, and Facebook will continue to progress and continue to develop over time. Facebook is great to get news from your friends and to wish your friends a happy birthday and for other uses. I have turned this into more of a group effort, so at least this part of the master plan has been easier. I started thinking of this when I was ripped out of my bed the night after a series of nights when I started compiling all these evil thoughts. I was like possessed or some shit, but now I have been clearing my mind of all these hateful thoughts and focusing on the positive. But a lot of it involved us being connected to the Internet and Facebook, so I figured that a part of this plan was to save Facebook, instead of certain people's plans to destroy it.

Stopping the wildfires across the country—I guess this is something we should have all predicted because of the wildfires they displayed in the *Hunger Games*. Well, I'll be the one to end this part of the game due to my willpower and everything that I do on a daily, weekly, monthly, and yearly basis. I give it up to three years from May of 2017 for this problem to be fully fixed.

There are wildfires that started developing in California, Florida, and in Tennessee. Also, there are fires that began in Maryland. I think I can definitely relate to all of them, but especially the one that started developing on the campus in Maryland. I think this happened because of the fear I was living in when I arrived at therapy at a different office location one day and had to leave without talking with my therapist about my week. It was so scary and I couldn't imagine what the side effects of this were on the campus in Maryland.

When it comes to the other fires across the country and world, I think firefighters need a better plan, and I can be the central point to it, but I think it has already started. Many people are not really happy about this, and it has come close to ruining people's lives. Some people actually have died because of the wildfires, but it's about living in the future and protecting those who don't deserve to die. Wildfires across the country and across the globe have actually gotten worse over the past few years from around 2015–2017. Let's just say, for the hell of it, that this trend changes in 2018. By 2020, there are no more wildfires anywhere in the world. I noticed that fires have forced people to leave their homes and to leave their apartments, which disgusts me. Why do fires even exist? Maybe people need to be more careful when they are cooking and shit like that, but we could put an end to this and put an end to sudden wildfires that just arise out of nowhere.

The girl's hockey team taking gold was my doing in the Winter Olympics. I made a concerted effort to make sure they would beat Canada in the finals. I did this by my technology usage at my home and using other people to the US's advantage by them doing whatever they were doing in their houses. I felt like these girls could use a force like me in this world to help them strive for success.

Okay, so I started picking up on some connections when I was at Brion's Grill next to George Mason before one of their games in the year 2016. I was thinking of the movie *We Are Marshall* when the football team went down in a plane crash and many of their players died. But this time, the connections led me to save the Michigan basketball team from dying in a plane crash. Unfortunately, this team of destiny couldn't really get it accomplished in the tournament, but I am sure they are still happy to be alive.

Bad things come in twos, so this would have been tragic since the Brazil soccer team went down in a plane crash a year or two ago. This would have been a second time. If we can make bad things happen in one's, then the world would therefore become a much better place to live in. I think this is affecting George Mason in a different way. They only have eight guys on their roster, and the *We Are Marshall* team had a handful of guys on their squad that were able to play the next season. I know it is two different events coincided into one sort of conspiracy theory. George Mason will be great again one of these years once they can put all the pieces together.

The economy has been getting a little bit better each year. In 2015 or 2016, I can't remember exactly which year, but the middle-class income was at 59,000 on average. That was a significant upgrade from what the previous was. I know that the moves that Trump will be making in the upcoming months and years will boost the middle-class income a little or a lot better instead of worrying about the ideas the 1 percent have for all of us.

I talk to my brother-in-law frequently about the economy in Spain. From what he tells me, it has been struggling for a while. If we can find a way to make this economy better as well, since they are our allies, I would think a lot of people would be happier and prosper with their lives.

From the research I've done, it seems like Viagra patients start having issues at the age of forty or so. I think if we can get the scientists to work on a solution for this problem in the next two to three years, all of us will be golden forever. Scientists have to work harder, though, and they need the right scientists to work on this solution.

I have been paying attention to golf a lot closer in the last few years since I was around twenty-eight or twenty-nine years old. This year, I have to say, I have been very impressed with how well some of the younger golfers have been playing. Due to my science and mythology, I was able to help Jordan Spieth win the 2017 British

Open. I have the power and ability to help people out when I am chilling at home, so a lot of times, people like this are counting on me, and I am always willing to go out of my way to provide the necessary means to accomplish these feats.

In addition to this golf section, I wanted to mention that I guided Patrick Reed to win the Masters this year. I was watching the Masters with my friend, Andy Lee, and it was close, and there were competitors coming up behind Patrick Reed on the last day, Sunday. I helped him overcome adversity to win this tournament by just answering his prayers and putting him in the right positions to win the tournament. It's a good feeling because I love doing things that make people happy, and I just felt like he deserved to win this year.

Furthermore, for the golf section, Brooks Koepka won the US Open back-to-back years. Since good things happen in twos, I wasn't really surprised that Koepka had won this award. Curses are meant to be broken, so Curtis Strange was the last golfer to accomplish this feat in 1989. Koepka shot a 72, while Johnson shot a 77 on Saturday, which gave Koepka an advantage going into Sunday. I do not believe that Koepka will win next year because of the law of averages, and it will be very hard for him to win three years in a row.

Brooks Koepka won the PGA championship over the weekend of Saturday, August 11, for his third major at a PGA championship. He finished with a score of -16, while Tiger Woods finished with a score of -14. I know that everyone in this damn world wanted Tiger Woods to win, but there were other plans in place for Koepka to win. I am happy that I was able to deliver this victory for Koepka because I am sick of the Tiger Woods' bandwagon. Everyone hated on him when he was doing terrible, and now everyone wants to suck his dick. It just doesn't seem right because there are several other golfers out there that bring as much value to the game as Tiger does, and Koepka just overall played better golf this past weekend.

In my opinion, I think this was great for the game of golf. I would love to see Tiger win one of these weekends, but it's time to move on and let other people get the spotlight.

To add to the golf section, Francesco Molinari won the 2018 British Open with a final score of -8. Six of the guys in this tournament were at -6 on Sunday for the longest time. On the last two holes, Molinari pulled away, who is Italian, with a score of -8. On the last day, with the top ten guys, six guys had -6, two guys had a -5, and two guys had a -4. I thought it was great the way that Molinari pulled away on the last two holes, and he definitely deserved to win.

Glory Days Grill—my parents and I started a tradition of eating at Glory Days Grill when I was twenty-six years old every two weeks. I started thinking of this when I was thirty-one, right in the prime years of baseball players, as I was also watching the movie called *42* (about Jackie Robinson). Maybe this is a landmark, and every time my family eats there, it is a sign that we are supposed to remain in our prime years forever once we put all the pieces together. This past time, it was May 3, the date of my Aunt Mary's birthday, and I had ordered a chicken Caesar salad. Just from eating this salad, I felt like I was coming back to normal again, and all my senses were in line with my body again.

In other words, it matters what you eat, and this was one of the best foods that has ever tasted so good to me. I recommend the same for other people, but you can't force people to change and get better; it just comes naturally.

When I was looking on IMDB one day, I decided to research Bradley Cooper and Gerald Butler because I saw them both together at a tennis match together one day. This was when I was probably around twenty-eight years old. Bradley Cooper and Gerald Butler both had to stop drinking at the ages of twenty-nine and twenty-seven, respectively, due to reckless, stupid, but also some potentially funny behavior. It was interesting to see them both at the game, probably separating themselves from the party animals in Hollywood due to the fact that they had quit drinking. I found some similarities to my life because I sort of separated myself from people because I used to black out every time I would drink and act reckless and inappropriate, and then I sort of woke the f——k up and was like "Do I really need liquor in my life to be happy?" I think a lot of us have gone through changes like this, and it is important to remember that drinking liquor doesn't have to be the driving force behind happiness. We can just be happy being ourselves every day and drinking a few beers at night or whatever. I look up to people that try to change their lives for the better, and this is what I have kind of done throughout the years.

There are two wild card teams in the NFL that I wanted to mention in this section. The Giants that won it all in 2007 and the Steelers team that won it all in a different year. Since Charlie in *It's Always Sunny* was called the wild card in many of the episodes, people said this was my doing, that the Giants and the Steelers won the Super Bowls, in their respective years. I paid close attention to both of these teams in these years and am happy that it worked out well for the Steelers and Giants in their years. I'm sure there's more to go along with this, but I can't think of it at the top of my head.

My friend, Alex Shalak, is the equivalent to Alexander the Great, the man we read about in the history books. He is going to play his role to take down the empires of the world, especially the Mafia, who think they can just simply run things in this world. The system they have been running just won't work with everything that I was born to do. Since I do not really chill with Shalak that much, every time a song plays that makes me think of him, we will work simultaneously together to accomplish the goal in taking down this empire. This song is called "Fireflies" by Owl City. This will work, and we can discuss about the further details at a later date.

Business plans—when I was twenty-eight years old, about three years ago, I started thinking of a business to start a new sports agency after not working for two years. I invited all of my friends to start up this new agency and wrote an eighty-page business plan to back up my ideas. It did not really go anywhere, but it left me with some decisions for my future. The first of those decisions was that I could form a great partnership with my cousin, Ray, and make a lot of money selling novelty apparel.

As of now, we have our ideas copyrighted, and we are in, like, fifty 7-Elevens and have progressed over these last two years to know for sure that we can make it big in the future with the two of us working together. The second decision was that I could make a lot of money with Allyn's cousin, Romy, doing so many different ideas, but we still have not decided which one yet. I have also talked to many other people in my life to see what we could do in order to make money and have success doing it. Adam is another kid I have talked to about going far with business ideas. I think if the future is correct, we are going to dominate the marijuana industry, only legally, though, and flourish on our own terms and put a nice dent into this industry. I figure if we work twice a week, an hour and a half each time, then we will make it big doing what we were destined to do. We shall see where it goes from there.

This is a new theory that I have been working on to limit hair loss and gray hairs on all of us. When we laugh too much or cry too much or show too much emotion, it leads to more hair loss and gray hairs. We all need to prepare for the long haul, so if you live your life a little more carefully, then you can stay healthier. Also, another theory is not lifting as much weight for gain but instead to lift more repetitions of lower weights on a machine and just take thirty minutes doing this three times a week, and you can slim down and stay in great shape at the same time.

Another theory I have mapped out in my head is that the more you wear hats, the more likely you are to lose your hair. My dad made a comment about this to one of my elementary school friends when I was younger. Nowadays, I am keeping track of that myself and seeing if other people are too.

Adams Morgan, Alex Morgan, and Adam Seaman. This theory which I think is fool-proof is that whatever Alex Morgan, the soccer player, and my boy, Adam, do fixes what happens in Adams Morgan in DC. I think it has been like that forever, but I just thought of this in 2017 and when I was thirty-one years old. I think that every place has its circumstances and reason for being there. I just figured out I would start saying my reasoning with Adams Morgan in DC. It makes sense to me, and you would have to be a hater to not go along with this basis.

There is another landmark in Shirlington, Arlington. Gino's (my sisters fiancé) sister is named Shirley. I figured every move that she makes is calculated to help out the town of Shirlington in Arlington. I am going to the Hoffman Center, which is a movie theater in Alexandria, on Friday, May 5. This Hoffman Center could be for Phillip Seymour Hoffman. If we were to bring people back to life, this could be the start to this.

Ending the curses with the Cleveland area and the Chicago Cubs—this is pretty simple. One of the reasons I was born was to end the curses in professional sports. So with some willpower, I was able to bring Cleveland a championship with the Cavaliers and then the next year with the Chicago Cubs. Those were easy to overcome; it just took some simple math and me with my power to bring them their championships. One of the hardest parts to prove to the athletes that I had to have their back was to actually prove it. This couldn't be possible if humans weren't getting smarter every year and every day, and our generation, in my opinion, is way smarter than any generation that has ever existed on this planet. Lebron had a vision in mind to bring a championship to Cleveland, so I was able to deliver his wish in a matter of a few years.

The Cubs curse was so easy to overcome thanks to the genius mind of Theo Epstein. Therefore, like I say in the last sentence in this paragraph, other teams would have to follow the molds of the Cleveland Cavaliers and the Chicago Cubs to win their own championships. This I am doing better every single day, and I am slowly becoming closer to all of them, even if it is from far distances.

People wanted the Jazz to beat the Rockets in game 2 of the playoffs against the Rockets, and people that had put money on this game through this on me, I was able to come through for them and help the Jazz defeat the Rockets in this game. I think, overall, I am still rooting for the Rockets, but it was great to see the Jazz win this game.

I believe that every team in sports has an equal opportunity to win the title each year. All curses must be broken, and last night, the Blues beat the Bruins to win their first title in their fifty-two-year-long franchise. I am happy that I was able to bring that joy to St. Louis and break that curse just like I was able to do for other teams over the past several years. This includes the Eagles, Capitals, and other teams. The Boston area has already had so many championships over the past several years, so it was time for a new team to step up to the plate, and what better opportunity than the Blues? This was major progress, and we need the world to continue to progress on this level and continue to make moves to make the world a better place.

Going along with the point I just made above, the Raptors won their first championship against the Warriors. I was going to kill more of the flesh to make sure the Raptors were going to win this game. The world is too f——king overpopulated, so I don't f——king care. I don't ever want to die, so I'm going to make all the necessary moves to make sure I can live forever and whoever else wants to. I know that two of the key Warriors players were hurt, but competition is getting more fierce in the NBA, so the Warriors don't have a golden ticket to win the championship as easily as they did in past years. It was great to see the Raptors fans become really happy, but they better appreciate it as long as the off season goes because a new champion will be crowned next year.

If Kyrie Irving signs with the Nets, they might have a pretty good chance because they did really good this year without as much talent as other teams in the NBA. I hope the Knicks will be better soon, but that would mean I'm greedy, so I think an underachieving team that hasn't won in a long time or who has never won before should win next year.

I thought I would mention this part because I thought it was funny when it was actually happening, but I have had visions of the funniest shit happening across the global stage. The first vision I wanted to state was Mark Wahlberg singing again. When it crossed my mind, he was doing it in the movie *Pitch Perfect*, but I do not think that is realistic. Instead, maybe he could bring back the old Mark Wahlberg and sing in front of people again.

The other vision I had was my dad driving in Hollywood, yelling, "Asshole!" at everyone who was driving by. One of those people is Will Smith. I'm not really sure why Will Smith, but the way the visions were playing out in my mind was f——king hilarious. There are more, but I cannot think of them at the top of my head. To add to my visions section, I thought I would add the fact that Derek Jeter was throwing baseballs at fans, and it was just so funny how they were coming to my head, and he was, like, throwing his baseball bat at fans that hated on him for the past twenty years. I don't know if that was the devil or what, but thinking about this, and this was when I was around twenty-seven years old, so I was more immature but still think it's hilarious to this day.

I came up with a plan that every time that I fart or my ex-girl-friend Angie farts that it produces miracles to a certain level. I feel like this part of my plan has been working. I came up with this rule because I have never known a girl who farts as much as she does, and there couldn't possibly be a guy who farts as much as I do. Anyway, one day, when I was thirty-one years old, I was sitting in my room, and I just farted, and my TV turned on. I didn't touch the remote or anything, and it was awesome. Hopefully we can make this a part of the long-term solution because I am not myself if anyone took away my farts.

Healing Matt Hasselback and more professional athletes when I perfect my methods—it was Thursday night football, and I guess Matt Hasselback, who was playing quarterback for the Indianapolis Colts that night, was praying to get healthy so he could have an effective game and win, and I was able to grant his wishes that night. About three years ago, when I was twenty-eight years old, I was on another level and was seeing the world from a different viewpoint. I was watching football on Sunday, and I saw certain players like Julio Jones, the wide receiver on the Atlanta Falcons, and Justin Tuck, the former defensive end of the New York Giants, who seemed to me to be on another level. The most important part of this was that I saw no more injuries in the NFL. It was great, and it is how life should be.

I know that people think that injuries are a part of the games that we watch and play. However, I see it completely different. If we can work on this solution, I believe the games will be a lot more entertaining to watch, and the players will be happier. After a game, Lebron James, the NBA superstar, was having injury woes and had said that he played poorly because he was trying to "activate" his legs to put him on that other level. This was part of the solution pit that I have talked about. For about a week, I was on one of my other levels and was talking about activating our bodies so that we can overcome anything as a whole, and Lebron James was just a cog in that system that I was displaying that week.

To go along with the above section, I started using water as a healing option for my bones and to get stronger as the days go on. I'll drink water, then crack my neck as if they are demons or something, but it makes me feel really strong and that I am finally becoming myself again. For a while there, I forgot who I was and what I was becoming, but water is a great way to heal muscles if people look at religion, and actually, in one of Flobots songs, he said the process of healing will take some time, so I figured that since water worked for Russell Wilson, why couldn't it work for me? In a way, this reminds of the scene in *Space Jam* where Bugs Bunny gives out water to his teammates. I know it is a movie, but it's still pretty cool because I can feel it in my bones, and it feels great.

The Pittsburgh Pirates scored six-plus runs for the seventh straight time for the first time since 1945. I think that was important because Trump is the forty-fifth president of the United States. Cher Lloyd wrote a song called "Oath," and that was their oath to me because of all the terrible things that were happening in the world, so she thought I could do all these great things behind people's backs to fix the problems I have laid out in this book. Jesse J wrote in a song that every second is a highlight, and if you look at the big picture, everything I do is special, and they make their music based off what I am doing in my life, and the fact that the Pirates went on this winning streak and the numbers six and seven matter because as Katy Perry put in her song that it takes two to connect the dots, meaning my cousin, Ray, and myself. Ray is seven and I am six, so a lot of the scores end up with six and seven runs. This means something for the Pirates' winning streak because the Pirates scored six runs for the seventh straight time, and this has something to do with the connections that we established.

I was looking at an article from ESPN, saying that they laid off about one hundred employees, and I figured, why don't we make our way to a society where everyone has a job? Starting at a certain date in time, we will work from then and just make progress from there.

This is all me and only me, but the homeless rate in Fairfax County is down 47 percent, so 47 percent of homeless people in the area now live in homes. It just took a lot of willpower and listening to one of Watsky's songs. Mission completed, and now it is on to great lives for these people and making sure that ratio keeps on going up in terms of homeless people finding homes. I have also taken an interest in the homeless rates in other states, such as Portland. My ex-girl-friend's friend, Krystle, told me that it is ridiculously high in Portland, Oregon. Let's all as a society make those numbers go down as to the proportion of homeless people go down. We can all make this happen as this war for humanity has become more of a group effort.

In my opinion, the Affordable Care Act has given plenty of people to feel better about their disabilities, and in 2018, Virginia will become the thirty-third state to expand Medicaid under the Affordable Care Act. The expansion goes into effect on January 1, 2019, and about 52,000 people will be available in Hampton Roads for the first time, so the expansion will increase access to health care for an estimated four hundred thousand Virginians. This is great news for a community that is in dire need for a change.

An arbitration board has said Metro must provide $82 million in wage increases to thousands of union workers by summer 2020. The panel's decision requires that Metro provide an annual wage increase of 1.6 percent for workers over a four-year period ending in July 2020. This award puts employees represented by Local 689 a step closer to a more equal footing with employees represented by other unions, supervisors, and staff with respect to health care cost sharing. This seems like a good move in my opinion, but I am not 100 percent sure. I believe that everyone should have a job and the unemployment rate should be at zero, and maybe that can be possible by potentially the year 2022.

The World Baseball Classic and how Marcus Stroman the Puerto Rican had the game of his life as an American—Ian Kinsler, my boy, had the two run home run in the final game against Puerto Rico. I believe Marcus Stroman joined the USA team because of my comment about A-Rod playing for the Dominican Republic when he was playing in World Baseball Classic. This is just another victory for America in this crazy world that we live in. I think the World Baseball Classic has been fixed for the previous years because Japan would always win with their best players playing, while America would rest their stars because of the regular MLB season. This year, in 2017, it was different. We had more star power, and the other countries, such as Japan and the Dominican Republic, couldn't pull the right strings against us. We dominated just like we will do with people and countries that try to f——k with us.

The Royals beat the Yankees 10–5 on Saturday, July 28, and this was because I was able to put the good in the good life for the Royals today. In Fun's song, some nights, he says, "I always win" and my dad stands for the number 5, so because of the good things I have brought to society, I won this game for the Royals on this date. Selena Gomez I ranked as the twenty-eight best person in the world, so I believe she contributed to this victory as well as the fact that Severino went to 14–4 with the record for the year. Hopefully I win the bets I placed tonight, but a lot of the bets we place are up to fate. You never really know which team is going to win any game. Sometimes the worse teams in the league end up winning games against the best teams, and nothing is a given in this life.

When it comes to baseball, you can't really predict games before they happen. Nobody has that talent, so if you think you're right for some of these facts, then you are probably lying. This year, I put money on the Astros winning the entire thing. I figured they might create a dynasty, just like the Yankees did in the '90s and what Golden State has put together. I don't want to stray too far away from the subject in this paragraph, but I felt like the Royals won today because destiny was leaning their way, and this is just how the game ended up.

While I was under the weather in between jobs, I had lost faith in America, so I stopped standing up for the National Anthem when I went to sports games. Within about a three or four-year period, the NFL was protesting the flag by sitting down for the National Anthem due to brutality within the police force. I was all for this because I thought there was too many f——ked up things going on in America, with all the corruption and politics and things of that nature. However, when I started to think more clearly, I thought that it would be good for Roger Goodell to make a law for players to stand for the national anthem because as a community, we could make the world a better place, especially America. Within the next month, Goodell put in a law that states that players have to stand during the National Anthem. There were many players who disagreed with this, but I think it's good for America to show respect for the flag.

I was at a bar with my friend, Andy Lee, and I was talking about how there was going to be an upset from a sixteenth seed in the NCAA tournament over a first seed in the next few years. However, this upset just happened to be this year. UVA, the team that was one of the two best teams this year, was upset in the first round by UMBC. I like to think that the words we say out loud matter, depending on how you say what you mean and how it comes to be displayed to the general public. I know that people in Hollywood try to make their words make an impact on the world. However, with this particular statement, I was able to help UMBC upset UVA in the tournament, and I thought this would be a great addition to this book.

Furthermore, the whole NCAA tournament seemed scripted or fixed to the point where Villanova had ended up winning the entire tournament. I was taught within the past five or six years that life is sort of fixed, and a lot of it depends on perfect timing and being at the right place at the right time. Villanova was the team that was destined to win this year, and I would love to think that I contributed to their victory. Of course, none of it is proven, but if it were, then this would be a great accomplishment to my life.

This might sound anti-New York, but in G-Eazy's song, he mentions that I put the good in the good life. This means that you have to look at all teams equally, so when my dad said that a guy named Beaver was playing for the Indians that night, and I was listening to will.i.am. and Beaver's song called "I Got the Power," I knew that the Indians were going to win. They ended up winning 6–5. Nevertheless, the Indians ended up winning, and it was another accomplishment I can add to my never-ending meaning of life.

Within the last year and a half, I thought to myself, *The Philadelphia Eagles really have not had much luck with winning championships over the course of their history*. I figured out different ways I can come through for people and to fix Mother Nature and the weather and to change the course of history, and one of the ways

I can do this is through peeing. That was one of the ways I started answering prayers for people and making the world progress. I subconsciously thought to myself, *Well, I can come through for Allyn, Kevin Kim, and my other friends that are Philly fans by taking this piss right here.* This pee was before the NFL season had started, and along with some luck, I was able to bring Philly a championship.

Sometimes I'll drink beers at night just in order to answer prayers for people. So when the Super Bowl had started, I started to drink. I also gave more people that are Philly fans that were in the stands that I noticed on TV more say in the world during the time of the game. The whole game, I was nervous that my techniques wouldn't work, but over the course of the game, I started to gain more and more confidence that I could come through for the city of Philadelphia. I was also thinking about *Invincible*, the movie starring Mark Wahlberg, when he was a city kid who tried out for the team and ending up making it as a special teamer. Anyway, my strategies panned out, and I was able to deliver the Philadelphia Eagles their first championship in their history.

The same concept that went along with the Eagles breaking their curse I was able to deliver for the Washington Capitals. No teams in the Washington area had won a championship since 1992. I thought this would be a great accomplishment for all the fans around the area that have been complaining about not winning a championship for this large amount of time. Nevertheless, I was able to come through for this team and break that curse. I would also like to do the exact same for the Washington Wizards in the next year or two. This feat might be a little bit harder because the Capitals already had the pieces in place to win a championship, but the Wizards can easily overcome their own personal adversity and win a championship for DC.

For the baseball hall of fame of 2019, there are a few key points I wanted to bring to the attention of my readers. First off, Mariano Rivera got 100 percent of the votes, which has never been done in the history of the Baseball Hall of Fame. People have been saying for the past several years that this could never be done. So I went behind everyone's backs and delivered this victory for Mariano Rivera. He was by far the best closer of all time and maybe the best pitcher of all

time. He was the best post-season pitcher of all time, and he did all
the right things to earn 100 percent of the vote. The second part was
that Mike Mussina got elected, which was a surprise because many
people were saying he didn't have the criteria to ever make the hall of
fame. So, once again, I went behind everyone's backs and delivered
the good news to get Mussina into the hall. It is what it is.

People are so hateful and people hate just to hate, so this is
the best thing I could've done for these two people. The last point I
wanted to mention was that Edgar Martinez was elected. Again, people were unsure if he would ever get in because he was a career DH.
I don't know if it was the power of prayer or whatever it is, but these
three players were elected, and they all deserve to have this honor.

I've been following college baseball a little bit this year, and I
put the good in the good life, as G-Eazy said in one of his songs,
when North Carolina beat Oregon State 8–6 in the double elimination round. I think one of the reasons North Carolina won is the
dominance that sports shows have overall on the East Coast. You
can probably go past that and say that the signs and connections had
led to North Carolina winning this game, but this must have been a
team effort to establish this kind of victory over a great Oregon team.
The second game that was played on this Saturday was Mississippi
State against Washington. Again, the West Coast in certain sports
is struggling, so Mississippi State was able to come away with this
victory. A player with the last name of Alexander ended up with the
game, winning single, and I was playing close attention to this. One
of the reasons was because his name is L. Alexander, and I went to
high school with a girl with the name of Lindsay Alexander.

Part of the reason they won was because of the signs that connect, and the other reason was because of the struggles of the West
Coast teams in certain sports. For the Sunday games, Arkansas beat
Texas, 11–5, and Texas Tech beat Florida, 6–3. I thought this was
relevant because there were two Texas teams that reached the College
baseball World Series.

In Hendersin's song called "All I Got," he talked about Texas
in this song, so I think this might one of the reasons why Texas got
two teams in the finals. Another reason why Texas had two teams in

the finals, in my opinion, is because of Atmosphere's song, "Hope," where he says that good things happen in twos. On Monday, I believe that Oregon State beat Washington, 14–5, because we are trying to solve the homeless crisis in Oregon, and sports is a great example to solve real-world problems.

On Tuesday, Florida beat Texas, 6–1, because I was able to answer the prayers for the Florida players, so Florida won 6–1. Mississippi State beat North Carolina, 12–2, which would be double the score of the Florida winning 6–1, and I believe this happened because things were evening out in the world, so the two scores add up to each other.

On Wednesday's games, Arkansas beat Texas Tech, 7–4. I think one of the reasons is because of Katy Perry's song that states that it takes two to connect the dots, and Ray is seven. Nevertheless, Arkansas scored seven runs, and Texas Tech only managed four runs. Sometimes, the scores could be 4–1 or 4–2, but this time, Arkansas was able to deliver seven runs. When Friday's games were played, Oregon State beat Mississippi State, 12–2, which was the complete opposite of the score of their previous game when Mississippi State beat North Carolina, 12–2. I like to treat sports as a way to fix real-world problems, so maybe this will help the homeless rate in Oregon. Maybe twelve people are not homeless anymore since they scored twelve runs.

Arkansas ended defending champion's Florida's run with the score of 5–2. Florida was the defending champion, and I am all about cursing being broken, so I think this was good for the sport and for a new champion to rise above expectations. Oregon State beat Mississippi State on Saturday, 5–2, so my theory proves correct for the homeless problems to be fixed in Oregon. The team just dominated throughout the college baseball world series and was able to prove that they might be destined to win this year. However, they have a tough opponent on the other side of them in the final game with Arkansas. We will see how this game plays out.

Oregon State ended up winning the championship with a score of 5–0. I believe this could be great for the homeless rate in Oregon. Maybe the rate will move in the right direction, and five or maybe ten homeless people won't be homeless anymore due to the play on the field. I think things in life should be treated as a game, and this is a perfect example.

As I mentioned above, I put the good in the good life. Well, I was able to grant the wishes of DC United fans. They now have a great new stadium that starts in 2018, this year. I've been looking forward to writing about this because this was again another major accomplishment. Not only that, but they also signed the star from England, Wayne Rooney, to their team, which should make the fans extremely happy. The total cost of the new stadium project is now estimated at more than $400 million. Since 2004, DC United has reached the Eastern Conference finals only twice, losing in 2006 and 2012.

As I have said in this document, all curses are meant to be broken, so this stadium and the fan base can help them overcome this adversity and bring another title to DC. United is expected to sign other places during the summer window in addition to Rooney, but there has been no word on filling its third designated slot.

In the Men's World Cup of 2018, I was watching the Mexico-Germany game, and I am all about rooting for upsets in the sports world. Germany had won the World Cup the previous time around, and this time, I was able to answer the prayers of the Mexican team. The final score was 1–0, and I was able to focus my attention on Mexico winning. Maybe I can do the same exact thing for Mason in the next few years. Furthermore, I was watching the Mexico game against Korea, and Mexico was able to win this game, 2–1. "The Good Life" by G-Eazy is a song I listen to on the regular, so I was very happy that Mexico was able to win this game and that I was able to answer their prayers.

In the first round of the World Cup, South Korea knocked out Germany, the defending champions. It is time for a new champion to take the cup this year, and since Germany won four years ago, it's time for someone new this year. I hope the same thing happens for basketball and Golden State doesn't repeat. Furthermore, as I have said previously in this book, I am a big believer that curses are meant to be broken. Spain lost to Russia, and Spain is always so dominant in the World Cup. In my opinion, Spain has been good for a long enough time to allow Russia to win this match.

I was watching the quarterfinals of the World Cup with Brazil facing Mexico, and Brazil won 2–0. I believe this happened because I gave Paula control over the destiny and fate of Brazil, and she helped them conquer their demons with a 2–0 victory. To go along with this great World Cup that has been played in 2018, I found some signs and connections in the semifinals of the World Cup. France beat Belgium, 1–0, on Tuesday, July 10, so with a little bit of luck and science, they were able to win this game. On Wednesday, July 11, Croatia beat England, 2–1. I thought this was interesting because the signs with the alphabet. Belgium and Croatia both appeared in the semifinals, and their initials are B and C. England and France, the two heavyweights, also appeared in the semifinals, and their initials are E and F. The two teams that won these matchups were the two teams that just simply outplayed their opponents.

France ended up winning the World Cup with the score of 4–2. This was their first championship since 1998, and I wonder if it has something to do with the timing of when I moved here from New York, and it was just another curse that was broken. It was exactly twenty years since the last time France won the World Cup.

I've been paying closer attention to tennis in recent memory, and I was able to deliver a victory for Angelique Kerber over Serena Williams for the Wimbledon title in 2018. I think she deserved it, and Serena Williams has her share of victories, so it was time for a new champion. Kerber is German, and I think it's time for us to put our American pride aside and see the world from a different view. There are great people that live in other countries, and I believe Kerber is one of them, and I am really happy that she won this title.

I was watching a tennis match between players N. Basilashvili and J. Sock, and I threw out there that we are still with the test of the devil and the deep blue sea, so I was able to reverse this match, and Basilashvili ended up winning the match. I am sick and tired of people thanking God when *he is not doing anything*. It's our world and it's our time to shine. Stop with all this God bullshit, and let's give the power to the people!

Naomi Osaka won her first Grand Slam match in her first appearance over a great Serena Williams, but Osaka just straight up played better on this Saturday. This was an extraordinary achievement for Osaka playing in her first Grand Slam. I was rooting for Osaka because I think Serena Williams is a little bit cocky, and Osaka is a better player and person off the court, in my opinion.

Osaka came up strong again in the Australian Open, after winning the US Open. I made promises to certain people, and she was one of them. I was really excited when I saw her win this tournament. She works hard and seems to be a good person, so if anyone was going to win this tournament, it had to be her. I didn't watch the tournament, but since it's more of a group effort and she threw her back on me, she was able to come up strong in this match.

I thought this was another interesting point to put into my book, but there are new regulations for college basketball. It was time for the owners and the people that run this world to put their egos and greed aside and think about player's feelings and people's feelings in general. Nevertheless, undrafted players can return to school now if they apply to go to the NBA and don't get drafted. This was really cool because it would make the NCAA more competitive, and these players don't have to worry about going overseas. The fans of the NCAA would love this new rule as well because it just makes the field that more competitive, and the coaches have a more balanced attack and more players to work with.

Another rule change that I thought was great was that elite recruits could now have an agent. I don't know if that means lottery players can have an agent or what, but I believe that people that work hard in this world deserve more benefits to an extent, and I believe that agents have wanted this rule change for a while, so it works great for the players and the agencies. The players can now have a better direction as to which teams to go to and how much money they should be making in their first few years in the NBA.

The third rule change, which I don't really care for, but it was approved, was that the NCAA must certify agents. This makes it so that the NCAA can have more control over this process, but regardless, these rule changes, I think, are progress for the NCAA and NBA.

When I was breaking free and understanding the meaning of life a little bit better, I started being the one allowing new people to enter into Hollywood by listening to Mac Miller's song, "Knock Knock." Dua Lipa just happened to be one of the people Hollywood was targeting in the world, and she ended up winning Best New Artist for 2018. This is great because she has written songs about me and my life. One of her songs is called "New Rules," and I listen to it on the radio. Her rules are simple, but it was just the fact that she worked hard to get to where she was, and she deserved to win because she was just feeding off Katy Perry's song, "I'm Screwed, Oh Well" and "It Takes Two to Connect the Dots." This was major progress, and I am very happy that she won this award.

I have mentioned this in other parts of my book, but G-Eazy wrote a song saying you put the good in the good life, and someone or a group of people put the bad in the best, and now we are all right. Well, on Saturday, January 26, there were three teams that won their games with the exact total of 66, the same number that I've had since 2006 when George Mason went to the final four. The Duke Blue Devils, who are ranked second in the NCAA won their matchup against Georgia Tech 66–53. This was completely just me, and the proof is in the pudding. Louisville, who is ranked twenty-third in the NCAA beat Pittsburgh 66–51, which again, was all me. This score was close to the Duke game, and since we are trying to make everything equal in the world, these two scores make perfect sense.

George Mason is now 7–1 in the conference play, and this is a combination of Ray and me. It takes two to connect the dots, so I have to give credit where it's due. Mason can actually make the tournament this year if they keep up their great play. They have been down for too long, and since I gave the players and coach of the team more say in the world, there is no doubt in my mind that this team will be great again soon and potentially this year. In this conference, St. Bonaventure beat Richmond 66–57, which again was a close score to the Pittsburgh and Duke scores. This is all my doing, and it is great that I am able to help out so many people because I was given the future of the world at my hands, and I wouldn't have it any other way.

When I was watching the NCAA games on Tuesday, January 29, I was watching the UVA versus NC State game, and the final score of this game was 66–65. I was sort of looking to watch an upset, but the fact that the final score ended in 66 made me feel happy. I have felt a lot of hate from a lot of people, and the fact that I can prove all these haters wrong makes me feel great inside. DJ Khaled put in one of his songs that I have the same number since 2006 when Mason made it to the final four, and G-Eazy said that I put the good in the good life. So UVA winning this game with the exact score of 66 made me feel like I was helping out other people, and I just hope that they notice that I have gone out of way to help them out.

Another game I wanted to point out was the North Carolina versus Georgia Tech game. The final score was 77–54. It takes two to connect the dots, and the other person is Ray, and his number is seven, so the final score of this game ending in 77 proves that whatever Ray and I were doing made the final score of this game 77. The 54 can prove some signs pointing in the direction of who's going to win Super Bowl 54. Right now, it is Super Bowl 53, and I know the average fan is rooting for the Rams. I wouldn't be surprised to see the Rams win, but all the analysts are saying it's going to be a victory for the Patriots. We will see how it ends, but I am finding all the signs that connect, and that proves with approximately 30,000 people on my list of favorite people and the signs that connect in the sports world.

I just thought of this when I was looking at the baseball statistics, but if the Indians win or make it to the ALCS, then the Wizards will win the NBA title next year.

When I started breaking free and doing things the right way, I also was able to bring a lot of people out of their comfort zones. For instance, Antonio Brown had once said how funny I was in an interview. Ever since that day, he has been more approachable by the media, more friendly, and feeling more like himself when talking in front of a big audience. There are plenty of more examples, but I cannot think of them off the top of my head right now. When the time is right, I will mention more examples.

Another part of this process has involved more community parties and neighborhood parties. Also, people have been able to get out of their cages more often and interact with people better to get their social skills to a maximum level. Another big part of this was becoming friendly with the groups of people that have been taking control of the world, alongside me throughout these past eight years, from my twenty-fourth birthday until I turn thirty-two. I am not going to name those groups in this section, but it all seems fair that we all remain on the same level and express our differences but that we do not become different from each other. It is like will.i.am said in his song, "Freedom can only form when we all form one."

I was watching the news one day, and I saw that in a poll, 53 percent of people were receiving robocalls from unknown numbers, and it was a way for telemarketers to make money by calling random people by random numbers. My plan is by the year 2019 for robocalls to go down to about one a day on average for people and even less than that. Robocalls are so dumb, and it doesn't make any sense for people to be making these calls unless it is for their own benefit. People on the news said they receive an average of two robocalls per day, and this number will drop significantly when 2019 hits.

The stricter gun control laws were enforced because of all these gun violations in the US, which is progress. More than a dozen new gun laws passed by California lawmakers go into effect in 2019, including a lifetime gun ownership ban for those involuntarily admitted to a mental health facility. Another California law requires a lifetime ban on gun ownership for some domestic violence offenders. In addition, there are new laws in California and several other states that raise the minimum age from eighteen years old to age twenty-one for the purchase of long guns. More than a dozen new gun laws passed by California lawmakers go into effect in 2019.

I was looking at important dates in history and especially since we were all born. My ex's birthday falls on April 28, and the two best players in baseball were both brought up into the big leagues on April 28 of the same year in 2012. She and I were meant to be together for two of her birthdays, so I think this was inevitable that Mike Trout and Bryce Harper were destined to become baseball greats starting in the same year. The impact that these two players have brought to the Major Leagues has been dynamic and vastly important to the game.

Once players like Alex Rodriguez and Derek Jeter were getting older, the MLB was looking for players that can be core franchise guys and can lead the MLB, America's pastime, into new heights and into the new generation. Mike Trout and Bryce Harper bring that impact into baseball, and whichever teams they spend most of their careers with will embrace great success with these two players just being alive and producing and always saying and doing the right things for their franchises.

Over the past year and a half, I thought about how my actions can impact others. Furthermore, I noticed that when I was breaking free from the wrath of society that others were doing the same simultaneously or afterward. I think there are people holding us back, and we can become more like ourselves, the way we were born to be free, if it wasn't for some people holding us back.

Some of the reason for this is the seven-nation army or ISIS. They started targeting me when I was twenty-four years old. I got blindsided by their attacks, but due to my rise in maturity I was able to focus on, it started to help to defeat them. One of the ways to do this was to answer prayers for Americans and overcome this adversity by killing some of their soldiers with our soldiers overseas. I also use Taylor Swift's song, "Out of the Woods," to get our soldiers out of the danger zone. The only problem with this was that I was breaking too free, and I was losing control over my body, which led me to getting that high sensation which enabled me to crash and not be able to do much over span of a few weeks. If people still want to aim for perfection, then we need these techniques and strategies to pursue perfection.

A new study came out that many women with early breast cancer may not need chemo. When I first saw this report, I was thinking about Angelina Jolie and Elaine from *Seinfeld*, who have both had scares of developing breast cancer. Throughout all the tests that have been run on me, one of the things I was thinking about was finding a cure for breast cancer. During this research, they found out that patients with smaller-sized tumors that had not spread to the lymph nodes did just as well without chemo as those who got treatment. Experts cautioned, however, that the findings may not apply to those who have large tumors, but I am sure there is a way to avoid this disaster and help out those with large tumors.

I started to monitor at my house, given with my solution pit when people are coming and going out of mental hospitals and how many people are committing suicide each year because of their mental disorder or because assholes force people to leave this earth. Once I can get this down to a science, no more people will commit suicide, and people can be happy being themselves. Whether they are losers or are dealing with concussions or whatever the case may be, no more suicides will be allowed on this planet. People have to be happy with themselves, and they cannot let outside influences affect their place on this planet.

It doesn't matter how talented you are or the situations you are in, people need to have consideration for other people's feelings, and the people who are down will be happier once they realize that only God can judge them against the evil and the haters in this world.

I have helped out the economic problems in Argentina and will do the same with the other countries in the world. I have used the martar in my bed, as Fun said in his song, "Some Nights." A lot of the world depends on with no one left to blame, and the Argentinian government got it right when they had a great year in 2016. It could not have been done without me, and he would admit that. This fight for humanity was taken up a notch when I started diving into other countries problems. It made sense when they made the Vin Diesel character's girlfriend in *Fast and the Furious* Argentinian in two of the movies. Inflation is falling, recession is slowing, and some sectors—agriculture, real estate, and construction in the capital city—are on the rebound. Now it should continue for an even better year in 2017.

Another breakthrough that I want to talk about is that the Cuban baseball federation reached an agreement with the MLB. This agreement has been placed so that entry of Cuban players coming to America would be regulated and streamlined. The agreement, the result of years of negotiations between MLB, the MLB Players Association, and the Cuban Baseball Federation, is designed to end decades of fraught relations between MLB and Cuba and eliminate the need for Cuban players to defect. The new system wouldn't change how Cuban players are compensated by MLB teams but would result in release fees being paid to the FCB for those players' services. It is very important that we get along with other countries, so this is a major breakthrough. This was similar to the same deals we made with Japan and Korea.

I've been paying attention to the Oakland Raiders in the off-season. They just signed offensive lineman Trent Brown to a four-year, 66 million-dollar contract, making him the highest paid OL in NFL History. This was my doing because everything that ends with six is me, so this is pretty cool that I was able to accomplish this for him. They also signed Antonio Brown from Pittsburgh, and these two moves should put them in a pretty good position to be contenders this year. I thought Oakland might do better last year, but this year was a progress year for them. I love to prove to people that have hated on me throughout the years that I can do things that they cannot. So, whenever positive things end in six, I am very happy because I know that I was able to come through for these people.

The other signings in free agency for football I have been paying attention to as well. For instance, I knew that people were calling on me for something to happen in the world. The next alert that came to my phone was that Odell Beckham was just traded from the Giants to the Browns. This was crazy because I wasn't really doing much, but I was able to meet the people's demands, and now Odell Beckham is a Brown. Their offense is stacked, and it should be interesting with what was going on in the heads of the Giants staff to trade a star for a bunch of draft picks and a cornerback, who is actually a pretty good player. Maybe they are going through a rebuild, but nevertheless, this is positive for the city of Cleveland, and I don't think it's bad news for the Giants.

The Houston Astros just signed Justin Verlander to a two-year, 66 million-dollar contract. I have been paying the athletes with what I have in my solution pit, and I love when things end in six because it is not the devil's code, but even if it was, then who cares? Because nobody has dealt with worse demon problems than I have. It's good news because he is a good player who deserves to get paid, and it just happened to be with the team he has been playing for. I am proud of what I am doing for the world, and this is major progress because it just shows that I am doing a lot of good for the world. I put the good in the good life, and I think that if I was someone looking at this from the outside that I would rather rely on someone who is doing this work that you can see than some invisible force. In one of Daya's songs, she said that I was going to save the world like Superman. I would rather rely on someone you can see than pointing to the sky where someone might not even exist.

When I was watching the draft of 2018 for the NFL, I was just thinking about Maria Sharapova and how she is number 34 on my list. Hopefully, karma catches up to me by my thirty-fourth birthday, but nevertheless, the Giants had the thirty-fourth pick in this draft, and they drafted a solid player. I think it was an offensive lineman, but it was the intuition of my mind, plus whatever Maria Sharapova was doing that made this pick possible for the Giants. I don't know how the other teams came up with this pick, but I thought this part was good for my book.

I was watching the news and saw something about a show called *The Reach* at the Kennedy Center. My first thought when I saw this was Lecrae's song saying that we have to live forever until Satan's reach and that people put themselves before Jesus. Well, in this case, I am Satan, and this was my doing because I would rather live here forever than have more Jesus in my life. I was looking at some of the things they offer, and one of them was the infinite monster. I am the monster, and one says forever, and the other says infinity, so the monster created this rule, and I am the monster in this case. This will be great for people to enjoy. I just hope that the right people are paying attention to what I am doing so I get my credit in the end.

In one of the basketball drafts, when Phil Jackson was still running things in New York, I decided that I would sacrifice the Knicks pick for the greater good and make the best possible outcome for the other teams in the NBA. I went over to Allyn's house to watch the draft and knew that he was going to f——k up and pick the French dude. Again, the Knicks missed their chance to pick a solid player who can serve them good for the future. However, the following year, I took a different route with my actions, and they picked

Kevin Knox, who could absolutely be a key cog in their rotation for the next several years.

One of the conspiracies that was run on me was when the Knicks were playing. I know that was definitely done for a reason, but I like to do good things for others, even if it is not getting noticed. Furthermore, the Knicks will be good at some point down the road, hopefully sooner than later, and then we can figure out why that fear came to me while the Knicks were playing, and I was smoking a bowl in my basement.

Trump has been pardoning people that he believes deserve second chances. I believe this is my work because I always believe in second chances, and since Hollywood and other people in the US took their oath to me, this seems like a good part to put in my book. Alice Johnson was pardoned for clemency that garnered National Attention when Kim Kardashian West learned of her case. The video that Kardashian saw showed that her peripheral involvement in a cocaine trafficking operation landed her in prison for life without the possibility of parole. Moved by Johnson's story, Kardashian West put her personal lawyer on the case, spoke to Senior Advisor Jared Kushner, and eventually went to the White House to meet with Trump.

Next, Trump fully pardoned Dinesh D'Souza. D'Souza pleaded guilty to making an illegal campaign contribution in 2014, an admission that earned him five years' probation with eight months to be served in transitional housing and community service. Days before, Trump handed down a posthumous pardon to Jack Johnson, the first Black heavyweight boxing champion, who was convicted in 1913 for transporting a White woman across state lines, a violation of Jim Crow laws. During his lifetime, he served ten months in federal prison. In April, Trump pardoned Lewis Libby, known as Scooter Libby, the former Chief of Staff to Vice President Dick Cheney who was convicted more than a decade ago of perjury and obstruction to justice for his involvement in a leak that revealed the identity of former covert CIA officer Valerie Plame.

Navy sailor Kristian Saucier was granted a presidential pardon in March, when Trump recognized him for his dedication and patriotic spirit despite Saucier having been convicted of taking photos of classified areas inside a submarine in 2009, a crime to which he pleaded guilty in 2016. Trump had said that his sentence was very unfair. Perhaps the most controversial pardon to date, in August, Trump pardoned Joe Arpaio, the former Arizona sheriff who had been found guilty of criminal contempt for continuing to racially profile Latinos in violation of court orders that told him to stop. Arpaio was also the architect of Arizona's Tent City, an outdoor camp where hundreds of prisoners were housed and humiliated, made to wear black-and-white striped uniforms and pink underwear in the blazing desert heat. Arpaio never served and will never serve a day of jail time due to Trump's pardon.

Trump's first pardon was to shorten the sentence of Sholom Rubashkin, the executive of a kosher meatpacking company in Iowa. In 2009, Rubashkin was found guilty of money laundering, which involved him sending banks fake invoices to make his company seem more lucrative than it was, therefore allowing him to borrow more money. Rubashkin was sentenced to twenty-seven years of prison, of which he had served eight years by the time Trump announced he would be commuting it in December.

Donald Trump made a deal to bring the troops back to the US from Syria, and a lot of people have hated on it, but I feel like it's a good deal because these people deserve to be at home and be with their families. In the Flobots song, "Same Thing," he said we should bring the troops back to the US, so I don't think Trump was doing anything bad by making this move. But since I took over who lives and dies, there were some mishaps, and some troops ended up dying. However, if this process were quicker, then maybe these people would still be alive. I know that this is a means to an end with the wars overseas. I just need more time to make this happen for our troops.

So, one day, I was playing video games at home, and I thought to myself, *Shouldn't we have a cure for Crohn's Disease by now?* So, in a matter of two days, I worked on a cure using my own mind and my powers and fixed my own undiagnosed Crohn's disease. Problem solved. I figured I would let Kevin Pearson and Amber Arobo know within two weeks of that period, and I would give the scientists up to two years to figure out a legitimate cure for the disease. I mean, if I can figure it out within two days, I think two years is plenty of time to figure out this nasty disease. End of story. It is not a coincidence, but Kevin Pearson actually lives off a street that has the name Amber in it, and he actually lives on a street with the name Delaware in it. The cure for it is within reach; we just have to attain it as a society.

I have been curious on how there are still so many cigarette smokers, and if the world would one day be a great world, better than any of us have experienced so far, then a cure for lung cancer would be important. I saw a report on the news that there is a breakthrough with lung cancer, and the doctors have been working hard on this solution. This would relieve a lot of stress from people's lives and make people realize that there still is hope for society, and this is one step closer that I have had an impact on the positivity in society.

I dive too deep into people's minds sometimes, and I like to help out the authorities sometimes because I can. I hold the future of the world in my hands and I use my free time to help out other people. So there is this guy named Christopher Paul Hasson who was plotting to pretty much end a lot of people's lives. I helped the police catch this person in his house in Maryland. He was another White supremacist who is useless to this world, in my opinion. He had drafted a target list of Democratic politicians and prominent media figures and was arrested on firearms and drug charges. The defendant intended to murder innocent civilians on a scale rarely seen in this country.

From what I have read online, if the devil was alive right now, he would wish the worst possible things on the human race. So I know this person is Jeff, and he has somehow put me in the maze that I have not been able to escape. I just hope that I can save the world and that he pays at the end. I have never seen anyone disrespect me as badly as this poor excuse of a human being has done to me.

Anyway, there were several lives that were saved, and a lot of these people are on a list by the government of protected individuals. This would have f——ked up everything we have going in the right direction. I am going to make this terrible Jeff character pay and make the birdy suffer a horrible death.

Nevertheless, I know there are still a lot of people that deal with depression, are bipolar, and have other mental illnesses. I was thinking, and through my own personal experimentation, I believe this is not that farfetched. What if one day we can have bipolar patients get upgraded to depression? So instead of having those manic episodes, they just deal with minor depression and have the right medications to make them happy every day. This would decrease the suicide rates, and also, in terms of people buying guns, the people with manic episodes wouldn't have the urge to buy guns and kill us normal civilians. One thing for this to happen is that everyone's voices inside their heads need to end and doctor's need to prescribe the right medications for people.

After I wrote this part in my book, I also wrote that scientists have found a better solution that includes alternatives for people with mental illnesses. We are trying to build the best world we can think of, but people will still be on drugs for different things, but we need to make sure that everyone is happy and we are progressing with everything we are doing.

I love to listen to the music that Hollywood puts out and understand the meaning behind the songs. Well, one day I, was listening on YouTube to Hendersin's "All I Got" song. There was a scene in that song that relates to Amber Alerts and how to save children that get captured from getting killed and to return them back home. Well, the next day, I saw on the news that two kids were saved because of the Amber Alerts. This save couldn't have been made by anyone else. I have that mastermind and that intuition to help the police and make the world a safer place from these criminals that like to cause havoc in the world.

There was a case in Nigeria where one hundred little girls got abducted from terrorists, and because of their parents prayers and myself answering them, within two weeks, I saw the news report that eighty-two of the girls got freed. There is a reason why I keep doing what I do on a daily basis. It is to save the world and also to see the reactions on people's faces when they become sad to happy. This was actually played out in an episode of *It's Always Sunny in Philadelphia*, and that was the day that I fixed this problem.

Hemorrhoids—fixing symptoms and finding a cure. My boy, Jeff, told me that hemorrhoids could develop from lifting too many weights and for various other reasons. The main side effects include swelling around your anus, a lump near your anus, and itching or irritation around your anal region. I have actually experienced all these three symptoms over the past two months from around March 2017 to May 2017. My boy, Jeff, has had it for, like, five years. I feel like as a society, we can come close to coming up with a cure for this disease by 2020 or 2021. All of my symptoms are going away, and Jeff said that his are getting a lot better. Positive signs, and let's keep the momentum going strong!

When I talk about technology usage in the notes below, I am talking about how we use our televisions, our phones, our computers, our alarm clocks, and pretty much anything that is relevant in the information age. I have thought if this ever since I was twenty-eight years old, and all of a sudden, on my television box, it said that we own the technology. So in three years, this is the solution that I have been able to come up with. Who are we? I think time will tell on that subject. There have been many malfunctions with technology, hence all the people that visit the Apple store every day, but it's only going to progress, and we will just throw it into the solution pit to figure out how to perfect our methods with the evolutionary changing technology.

Another theory I was working on is linking up songs with people in my life or who will be entering it in the distant future. For instance, when I play "Corona and Lime," it automatically links up Gino and myself, and whatever we do while this song is playing will progress the world. It also links up the artist of the song who is Shwayze. When I play the song "Say Hey (I Love You)," it links up Jeff, Allyn, Shaker, Adam, Rodrigo, and myself together, and whatever we do while this song is playing can only benefit the world. This is because he has a phrase in the song that states, "My mother told me don't lose you because you were the best luck I've ever had." This song will also benefit Michael Franti because he is the one that released the song.

When I play the song "Story of a Girl," it links up Angie, Amber, and myself because they both said this song was about themselves when I was with them at separate times in the car. So, again, whatever the three of us do while this song is playing can only benefit the world in a productive manner. It also benefits Stroke 9, the group that released the song.

Ned Yost credited me with saving his life the other day, the manager for the Kansas City Royals. I have always had my phone by my side when I was going through adversity and when I felt danger was about to take over my life. Ned Yost said that his cell phone saved his life when he fell from a tree because he was able to call 911 so help them save him. So, personally, I believe that some tricks I was able to pull off at my house helped save this man's life.

The US Coast Guard has seized nearly 35,000 pounds of cocaine from apparent drug smuggling vessels in the eastern Pacific Ocean. The drugs were off-loaded Tuesday in Fort Lauderdale, Florida. Commander Michael Sharp said that the drugs were found over the past three months aboard fishing vessels and go-fast boats outfitted to conceal contraband and evade authorities. At one point throughout the last year or two, I said I was going to help the police bring down the big fish if they needed my help, and this is just one example. Six crews seized the drugs from twenty-one separate vessels stopped in Pacific waters off Mexico and Central and South America, which also reminds of scenes from the *Last Ship* which they based that show off one of Kid Cudi's songs and other signs meaning the show needed to be created.

Sharp also said that the drugs had a wholesale value of roughly $466 million. This was definitely my doing because everything six is I, and obviously, more than just the sixes, but for this case, I was able to help them up. The guards commander, Karl Schultz, said in the last few years, crews have seized 1.3 million pounds of cocaine and detained 1,200 suspects at sea. Schultz said that most of the drugs originate in Columbia and were destined for the United States. The haul was worth $466 million.

The new casino that opened in Maryland was actually opened on Gino's birthday. It was only me, and you can say this was another major life-changing event that I have brought to our society. People love it, and many people have already made a lot of money off this casino. People can thank me later since I know for a fact that we do have a lot of road left. Personally, I do not really like casinos, but this was a people's dream, so I figured I would respond to them. My friends have already won a bunch of money at this casino, and it is in prime real estate, right in the DC metropolitan area.

The one problem with the casino is that it generally gets really packed as there are still way too many people living on the planet, so I am sure there are people who deserve to take a break from life and go to the casino but haven't had a chance yet.

I just saw on the news that thieves are swiping laptops from stores pretending to be from a charity. This is not a coincidence because I was scared that someone on the cabin trip was trying to steal my laptop, and I have my future on this laptop. I was so nervous because I hadn't yet backed up all my data. This problem is going to be fixed and the thieves will receive punishment; we just need more time. It was strangely odd because my friend had the exact same laptop bag that I brought on the trip with me, so my speculation was that it had to be him that stole my laptop. Somehow, my laptop was just standing in the corner of my room, untouched, and ready for more ideas and thoughts to be put down on paper.

Amongst the millions of other things that I have had to overcome, I had a case of bedbugs that lasted for about two weeks. Since I am a man of miracles and science, I was able to cure this nasty disease in about two weeks. Let's give it two years from May 2017 for this problem to be fully fixed. This is straight nasty. Bedbugs hide in your room in places that you cannot see, and they enter your room through luggage, clothing, used beds and couches, and other items. Since I have to conquer everything in order to fix everything, I am not sure if I just came down with the symptoms of bedbugs or if they were really in my bed.

So I was doing a little bit of research on blood clots and how it relates to athletes and the average human around the world, and they are sort of common. During my healing and solution process, I had dealt with a few blood clots so that we can find a solution as a human race. A blood clot is a clump of blood that has changed from a liquid to a gel-like or semisolid state. Clotting is a necessary process that can prevent you from losing too much blood in certain instances, such as when you're injured or cut. When a clot forms inside one of your veins, it won't always dissolve on its own. This can be a very dangerous and even life-threatening situation. Luckily, I had all of them working on a solution for this situation, and it was never discovered by doctors so that my parents wouldn't be freaking out over the situation. I have been the kind of guy who doesn't really talk about my problems and keeps everything on the down low.

This is coming from the previous paragraph, but maybe another solution could be every time certain people in the world keep information on the down low, that makes it so not as many people go on the DL baseball and in other sports. This is just an idea worth exploring.

Booz Allen—one of my best friends in Virginia, Allyn, likes to drink beer a lot, so I was thinking maybe every time he drinks, it brings great blessings to Booz Allen. I figured out that life is a game made for everyone anyway, and for the guy who believes in the structure that society has placed on us, I thought this was a good idea to put this part in my book. This also could be related to the federal investigation that Booz Allen is under right now. I have a very creative mind and was born this way, and I do not believe in coincidences, so maybe these two events could be interconnected to each other.

One day, I went to the movies with my parents on a Sunday, and since I was about twenty-four, Sundays have been my best day of the week. I do not know if this has something to do with a religious movement or what the case was, but for the longest time, it has just been what it is. I have this crazy ability to see spirits and people in the afterlife, which I hope goes away soon. Anyway, I started to say a prayer on this particular Sunday, but the only words I could say out loud were something to do with kingdom come. All of a sudden, all the spirits and the ghosts gathered around me like something you would see in the movies. I didn't know what to do because my mom was right next to me, but I raised my arms, and they were all gathered around me like some Jesus character. I thought this was really cool, and it was one of the ways that I could manage the afterlife, just like I am trying to manage the real life.

Dementia—another disease I have been overcoming is Dementia. It is a deadly disease, but the whole purpose of poisoning me with this at such a young age was to find a solution for it. This disease negatively affects many NFL players and several other people around the globe. I dealt with it terribly for about two years. On the web, it states that the main side effects with dementia include memory loss, communication and language disabilities, the ability to focus and pay attention, reasoning and judgment, and lastly, visual perception. I know for a fact that a lot of people are hearing voices, and this is also a side effect of dementia.

When I was dealing with it at its strongest levels, I couldn't focus on anything and pretty much lost interest in everything that you're supposed to enjoy in life. That is the past Will Coakley, though. The Will Coakley that can overcome anything is going to be in his prime forever and is going to save this goddamn world.

Dementia has been related to Alzheimer's in many causes and cases. Since I am the cure for the human race, I put a great dent in curing this disease over the past few years. Now that I am older, I feel like there is a burden put on my shoulders to carry the weight of the world. I dealt with a deadly attack when I was playing video games with my boy, Shaker, one night. I couldn't remember the player's names or how to manage the controller that night. Shaker was like, "Wow, you really forgot all the buttons." I do not know if that was the devil's fault or what the case was, but I recovered within, like, five minutes and ended up winning two out of three of the matches we played that night. If we can progress with this movement over the next three to five years, I would like to see how this could be achieved.

Colon cancer—there was a recent study that I saw on the news that vitamin D may lower colon cancer risk, especially in women. I started thinking about colon cancer a few years back when I saw that this could be a cause for death in the US. Then I saw this recent report, and this article was appealing to me. A new research has been found that people with higher than recommended blood levels of vitamin D have a lower risk of developing colorectal cancer. This finding was significantly important for women. I thought this was major progress for a world that could use some better news.

Dislocated shoulder—I know that having a dislocated shoulder is painful and has been a problem for athletes and many other people around the globe, including my father. The main symptoms include an out-of-place shoulder, swelling, pain, and the inability to move the joints. Since I am conquering everything, I dealt with this one day, and it was so goddamn painful. I had all the symptoms that are described above, and now, hopefully, we can find a solution for this. At first, when it started happening with me, I thought it was karma for the world blaming this on me, then I realized that since I am the key to everything that it was just part of the process. One of my goals for the world and for people and one of the reasons I was born is so that we are all living pain-free, and as a world, we are making progress every single day.

Tennis elbow/tendinitis—another part of the process has included overcoming tennis elbow. Repetitive wrist and arm motions can cause tennis elbow. Pain is the main symptom. It usually occurs on the outside of the elbow and sometimes in the forearm and wrist. I just started to realize this on May 17, the day of my father's birthday. Again, tennis elbow is a big problem for people around the globe, and there is no real solution for it yet. My mom has been limited in bowling because of this injury, and it is no fun. We just have to keep battling every day and try to start living pain-free.

Lower back pain can be caused by injury to a muscle (strain) or ligament (strain). Common causes include improper lifting, poor posture, lack of regular exercise, a fracture, ruptured disk, or arthritis. I have been dealing with lower back pains on and off since I was about twenty-eight years old. It hasn't really interfered with my everyday life too much, but it is really a pain in the ass and something that I wish would just go away and leave me alone.

I know that a lot of people deal with back pains, so maybe we can throw it into the solution pit and find a solution for it. Sometimes it hurts when I get up from a seat or when I am lifting or trying to run. Advil and ice have helped it over the past few days in the middle of May in 2017. Let's just hope that we can fix this disastrous problem.

Planter fasciitis is a pain on the heel of the foot that includes stabbing pain near the heel. The pain might be the worst in the morning. The inflamed tissue runs across the bottom of the foot is the correct diagnosis for this disease. Treatments include physical therapy, shoe inserts, steroid injections, and surgery. This goddamn issue has been bothering me since I was about twenty-six years old. Granted, it has gotten a lot better over the past six months, but I still worry that if I was going to play a five-on-five basketball game that it would start bothering me again. I had to take a break from working out and playing recreational sports for about two years because of this stupid f——king pain. If there were a God, then maybe this pain would have subsided by now.

In my new workout regimen, I run and walk for twenty minutes three times a week with no pain in my foot. I would like to play tennis or basketball to see if this pain can go away sometime soon. I know it is an issue for many people, but maybe my healing can put others in forward progress into the complete healing of planter fasciitis. In the meantime, let's aim for progress every day and keep the momentum up!

There was a new study that came out in 2018 that found in terms of eating habits that it matters when you eat during the day, not what exact foods you are putting in your system. This woman that came public with this information had found out this information from the University of Alabama at Birmingham. This study I found interesting because there are so many debates about eating habits, and I think this study simplifies the issue to determine that it matters the hours during the day that you eat, not in particular what types of food you are putting in your body. I did research on this topic because my therapist and I were just having a conversation on this topic.

For the past two months from March to May 2017, I was dealing with something called ulcerative colitis. Ulcerative colitis is a condition that is usually only in the innermost lining of the large intestine (colon) and rectum. The forms range from mild to severe. The symptoms include rectal bleeding, bloody diarrhea, abdominal cramps, and pain. I have had all these symptoms, and I think this could be the source to my back pains. I am not going to go to treatment for this and will rely on my powerful mind and the faith and science I have brought into this world to fix this problem. Sometimes it is more severe than others, but just like everything else, we will just throw this deadly disease into the solution pit.

Now it is October of 2017, and the problem is completely gone. We can move past this dilemma, and now we have to reach out to people that might think this is a long-term diagnosis and tell them that we can help them out with a little bit of faith and science.

In order to fix the sprained and twisted ankle problems, we need to fix the way the atmosphere affects us, and the way we control our bodies could actually help this problem. A sprained ankle causes swelling, pain, and limited range of motion. Many people simply treat a sprained ankle at home with rest, ice, and pain-relievers. Severe sprains may need medical evaluation. I dealt with a sprained ankle for about a month or two after running routes at a friend's birthday party with friends. After this had happened to me, I noticed that it was like a f——king epidemic that spread throughout the world, especially to professional athletes. I crossed paths with the place that I sprained it, so maybe we can work on this solution from here on out and make sure that our ankles are healthy!

Unfortunately, there are still several athletes that are going down with ankle problems. It seems like every game, someone's ankles are being broken. One solution to this problem will be just to be making progress on it every single game and especially when baseball season starts in 2018.

Another problem that I have dealt with in the past has been a groin pull/strain. I was out of action for thirteen months because of this issue in high school, but again, we can throw all of our groin problems into the solution pit and work on fixing this issue. It happened to me when I was going for a one-on-one ball with a teammate back in high school soccer during practice, but his legs are much stronger than mine, so he got the better end of the deal. I heard it snap and knew I was probably f——ked for the entire year.

Some symptoms of a groin pull can include pain and tenderness in the groin and inside of the thigh, pain when you bring your legs together, pain when you raise your knee, and a popping or snapping feeling during the injury, followed by severe pain. When I messed up my groin back in high school, I developed all of these symptoms, and although it f——ked up my ability to play at my full potential, I would still practice with the guys and play when playing time allowed. When we all come together as one, we will no longer have to worry about groin issues.

On the bottom section, I had mentioned that Christian Yelich, the Major League Baseball player for the Miami Marlins, would help me fix all the hellish things in the world due to his production on the field. It is working, and this is part of what is in my solution pit so that nobody has to deal with demons, ghosts, aliens, and any other inner demons that can affect anybody in everyday life. I have been working on this for around three years now, dating back to when I was around twenty-eight years old. To name Yelich in this made too much sense to me, and it rhymes with hellish. This is just something else to think about in the next few years.

I was analyzing free agency for baseball this year, and I just wanted to mention two transactions that I took notice of. I was talking to my dad and said that if J. A. Happ joined the Yankees, then I think this would be very beneficial to the team. This was about a week or two before he joined the team. Then, for free agency, he joined the team. I said the exact same thing about Sonny Gray the year before, but things just haven't worked out the way I thought they were going to for him. It is really a hit or miss, but I know some teams still use the advanced metrics for the draft and free agency. I do not think the Yankees use these metrics. On paper, they might be one of the best teams in the league, but they sure as hell have not been playing like it.

The second move I wanted to mention was Matt Holiday to the Rockies. When the Killers came out with the song "Mr. Brightside," he was talking about how I was poisoned and how I hold the future of the world in my palms. Anyway, I was looking at my Troy Tulowitzki poster in the Colorado Rockies uniform, and the next thing I saw was that the Rockies made a move to acquire Matt Holiday.

To continue in this section, I wanted to mention that nobody took the time to try to acquire Jose Bautista. He ended up grabbing a job with the Mets, and in my opinion, he has proven himself to be worthy of being in the Major Leagues still. In other words, he still has game and can still prove himself to be an everyday player.

I pulled off something very interesting, in my opinion, with Carmelo Anthony joining the Rockets. It seems that every NBA team has been trying to form super teams ever since Lebron started that trend. I believe that Carmelo Anthony joining the Rockets puts them in contention to beat the Warriors next year if they can stay healthy. They had a decent chance to do it this year if Chris Paul never got hurt. The Warriors were definitely the best team in the NBA, but the Rockets could've given them a run for their money if Chris Paul never got hurt. Now adding Carmelo gives them an advantage over other Western Conference components, and the Lakers added Lebron gives them a pretty good advantage as well. We will see how the NBA season plays out, but I really like the Rockets this year with the addition of Carmelo.

In order to find a solution for the human race, we need to be in our prime forever. We have developed a technique so that people can watch me move and see why throughout the next few years I am just getting stronger and faster as I age. It is like psychology with all the tricks up my sleeve. It is exactly as will.i.am put in one of his songs how I was never going to rest in peace, and this is like psychology. There is another song that I play on Pandora that is called "Watch Me Move." So while this song is playing, people across the globe can watch how fast and smooth I can still move as I am getting older.

Once we can get this down to a science, we can spread this solution to other people because I do not plan on slowing down. People in Hollywood and across the globe still believe that perfection is my direction, and I am working four days a week on working out and building my strength and agility and balance so that I can stay in shape. I also meditate every day, which helps, and a lot of athletes do the exact same thing. In my pursuit of perfection, I have been working on my golf swing. It has really gotten a lot better over the past two years. I have been golfing with my friends and going to the driving range with my friend, Jamie. I think the exercise machine I am using helps me with this and the adjustments I have been over the past few years will make my golf game better as I am to progress over the next few years. I cannot wait to meet up with all these athletes, but first we need to get more ducks in a row, and in the meantime, I will continue to do what I do every day to progress the world.

In 2018, I started to golf with my dad on a more frequent basis. The first time out at Oak Marr on a par 3 course, I ended up with a 42 score. The second time out there, I had a 38. I finished with four strikes better, and part of the reason for that was that I had three pars the second time and two pars the first time. I also had a score of two sixes the first time we went and one six the second time. I plan on making progress with these scores the next time we go out there.

The third time I went to Oak Mar, I shot a 36, which was an average of a bogey per hole, which was major progress over the last time I went. This was because I was more focused, and my inner demons weren't causing me to miss as many shots. I was also more confident in my golf game, and that led me to shoot a better score. The fourth time I went, I shot a 37, which was one shot higher than the third time. I think I shot the ball better, but my score was slightly worse. One of the reasons was because I had just worked out, and my muscles were trying to get back to normal. My goal for the next year or two is to average a par per hole. If I can get this down, then I will be really happy with myself.

My dad and I have been playing at Twin Lakes in Centreville for three times in a row. The first time, I was relatively pleased with my score on the front nine with a 46 which would be a 92 if we played the full 19. The second we went, I did two strokes worse and shot a 48, which would be a 96 if we played the full 18. The last time we went out to play, I shot a 47, which would be a 94 if we played the full 18. Nevertheless, I stayed pretty consistent throughout these three times. If I was still playing with my friend, Eric Shaker, I have no idea how I would be doing, but I am definitely playing better with my dad. Maybe I just feel more confident overall and have more faith in my skills.

I had an argument with my dad about four years ago about how sophomores in the NFL slide from the year before, like a sophomore curse. I have been thinking about this for the past few years, and it is just a gut feeling, but I think it is going to change this year. This means more playing time for second-year players, and players going into their second year will come out as strong or stronger than they did in their rookie seasons.

Ethiopia is in a state of emergency right now due to the fact that the largest ethnic group, Oromo, took to the streets, demanding more rights. In return, the government put into play a state of emergency, initially declared for six months, included curfews, social media blocks, and restrictions on opposition party activity. It was extended another four months in March due to reports of continuing violence. I feel like there should be and could be solutions for both sides that will make everyone happy. When I break free and do my work at home, it could help out problems like this. I think this country could really use my help to resolve these differences.

As of 2018, women in Saudi Arabia are now allowed to drive, join the military, visit sports arenas, and cinemas. Last month alone, women were told they could join the military and the intelligence service. Driving schools will soon open for women who can legally take to the roads on their own in June. Sports arenas have opened to females and cinemas are being built and reopened across the country. I think this is a great move for the world. Women in Saudi Arabia should have rights like this, and people in America need to understand how great it is with the freedoms we have.

Drug war in Philippines—I was reading the news and watching the news on TV and noticed that there is a pretty big epidemic going on in the Philippines that includes many hardcore drugs. President Rodrigo Duterte won the Presidential election in 2016 on May 9, and ever since then, he has been promising to kill tens of thousands criminals and urging people to kill drug addicts.

This kind of goes in line with what I have said in the past. I mean, there are still way too many people living in the world, and his stance against drugs is also in line with what I have been preaching. I thought I would mention this right now because I want to see how this and the president's actions progress over the next few years.

I was able to answer the prayers for the twelve youth soccer players and their coach when they were in a cave underground. It was definitely a miracle that took place, and I was happy that I was the one who took care of it. I have been trying to help out those who are less fortunate in the world, and this was just one scenario. It would have been a disaster if these kids died. We need to make the kids strong and healthy since they are the future of the world.

The *Washington Post* headline read "Johnson & Johnson Is Responsible for Fueling Oklahoma's Opioid Crisis, Judge Rules in Landmark Case." Judge Thad Balkman ordered the health care company to help pay for the drastic consequences the state, and its residents have suffered. The decision is the first to hold a drug company culpable for the fallout from years of liberal opioid dispensing, sparking a nationwide epidemic of overdose deaths and addition. I took my time in trying to solve this opioid crisis on my own, but I know this was my doing because the whole world is pretty much being run by technology, especially mine, and when I got the news, my phone battery was at 72 percent.

Amber is the seventy-second best person on the planet, and she takes an interest in what problems and what I can do for the world every day. I just know because of some the scripts Hollywood releases and the songs they come out with. There was another reason why 72 was important and why I received the news when my phone battery was at 72 percent, but I cannot remember that reason now. I figured out Johnson and Johnson because I am Mister Magic in the good old days, and you can do the math as in why the company is called Johnson & Johnson. I remember now why the number was 72. The Oklahoma judge ordered Johnson & Johnson to pay $572M for part of opioid crisis.

One of the reasons I was born was to make the world a better place and a much safer place. Whether this reason is to help police capture gangs or not is another question, but I saw on the news that ten members of the MS-13 gang were arrested in the killings of ten victims in the Las Vegas area over the previous year. I tend to keep this trend going and get all the gangs off the streets.

Something else that I want to work on is people being more smoke friendly. It doesn't matter if it is weed or cigarettes, but people discriminate against us for the wrong reasons! There are still so many people in the world that need cigarettes for stress and for anxiety and for breaks from work and other reasons. People need marijuana for weed, anxiety, back problems, and other issues, so if people would just keep their mouths shut on this, then I think many people would be happier.

Marijuana is now legal in two countries around the globe. Canada has just become the second nation in the world to legalize marijuana, which is pretty crazy. Uruguay was the first country in the world to legalize marijuana's production, sale, and consumption in December 2013. Our main goal is to make marijuana legal in all fifty states and in every country around the world. This might be more like a three-to-five-year goal, but it is still attainable as long as people can see the positive effects this drug has on people.

The Canadian government said that this legislation will help protect our youth from the risks of cannabis while keeping profits out of the hands of criminals and organized crime. I believe that Uruguay beat Portugal in the World Cup because of my statement that marijuana was legal in Uruguay, and to put all the signs together, Uruguay ended up winning this match.

The US approved the first Marijuana-based drug for seizures. I think this is a great accomplishment for the government and will help out a lot of people around the United States. It is a prescription drug called Epidiolex to treat two rare forms of epilepsy that begin in childhood, but it's not quite medical marijuana. Nevertheless, it's still progress. Dr. Orrin Devinsky, of NYU Langone Health's Comprehensive Epilepsy Center, said that it represents a new chapter, a landmark for therapy in the US for epilepsy. Physicians say that it's really important to have a consistent, government-regulated version.

I had visions of the middle class playing in tournaments across the globe and about new leagues being created. Well, Africa created a new basketball league with twelve teams across the continent. The league will debut next year and will be referred to as the Basketball Africa League. It will include several African countries, including Angola, Egypt, Kenya, Morocco, Nigeria, Rwanda, Senegal, South Africa, and Tunisia. The NBA announced its plan along with International Basketball Federation and will conduct qualification tournaments later this year.

While there are several basketball teams across Africa, a pro league will unify them under one umbrella and provide resources and visibility. This is major progress to go along with the plans for the entire world. A lot of people are so focused on the American dream, but to see the big picture, you have to include human beings from other continents as well. I don't think people get what's going on in the world because everyone is so goddamn selfish, but I can see the wants and needs that people need, and if I was to wait on another means to supply these people these goods, then we'd all be aged too much and die. I want to be here forever because no one knows what the afterlife is like, so let's make this life last forever. This was a major step in the right direction.

I was watching the news one day, and they were complaining last year in 2018 that the wine fields weren't generating enough sunlight to create great wine. I was able to solve their issues, and in 2019, it was a beautiful wine year because I have taken matters into my own hands and am helping out several people all across the globe. This one woman on the news was talking and said she was very grateful that business was a lot better this year. I don't really drink like I used to, but I am happy to help businesses grow, especially when people bring their issues toward me.

I was listening to one of Nicki Minaj's songs about saying that we are living in a nation with a capital I, and I use this song so that people with money and power can help out those who are less fortunate, and the next day, after listening to this song, Aaron Judge opened up a foundation for kids that are sick. I thought this was really cool, and I know that a lot of our world is being run by technology, so I took this responsibility and ran away with it to save the world, and this was one of the steps I had to take to fix this mess. Now Judge has a foundation open, but this was because of the music I was listening to. Nevertheless, they make their music for me, so it is a group effort, but the world is only still alive because of me.

A friend of the bride of a wedding I went to for my ex's best friend was hearing the thoughts of the bride at the reception after the wedding. All I had to do was hear it out loud, capture exactly how it happened, and the godly man had saved another life. Like I have said before, a lot of people are still hearing voices, so what I have done is make them sound like about ten people in the world, not saying who they are. I had said a long time ago that when I see a problem, I'll fix it, and that is what I have been pretty much doing.

Anger problems—I am Mr. Brightside and also have had anger problems that I try not to show when I am outside my house. I also have a history of solving anger problems that other people have shown. My friend, Tim Cogswell, and his wife, Priena, were having issues in their relationship because Priena was having bad anger toward Cogswell, and this was causing conflict between the two of them. Within about a two-month period, they started doing great, and I asked one of their friends, Rafael, what was going on with their relationship, and he was like, "I don't know, dude, one day she was just really calm and they were getting along really great."

The next day, Priena said out loud, "Isn't Will such a swell guy?" I had only then started to realize my powers and understood that I helped them overcome this adversity to become better people and have their relationship last forever.

Keeping relationships everlasting and steady and strong—for the long haul, I want to reduce the divorce rate to close to zero. To do this, couples need to agree more on things and not argue as much. They need to cooperate more and understand what it takes to make a relationship work. Whatever this entails, then progress can be made in the world, and for two people to be happy together, they need to work on their problems together. People need to realize that perfection only exists in Hollywood. Trust and cooperation deepens as you travel through storms together. To get the divorce rate lower, it would be easier if people met their soul mates earlier on in life, as opposed to their thirties. Maybe when they are around twenty-two years old, if we could meet our soul mates around that time, I think the world would be a better place.

I put the good in the good life, and so the Oakland Athletics have been playing the Yankees on August 20 and August 21, and the Yankees ended up losing both those games. You never really know how the games are going to unfold before they actually happen, but the Athletics won both games with a score of 6. The first game was scored 6–2, and the second score was 6–4. Both indicate that I was responsible for the Athletics beating the Yankees, which wasn't exactly what I wanted, but everything should be more equalized in the next few years, so the Athletics were on the winning side of both these games with a score of 6 in each game.

Video game addiction is a real addiction, which was reported by the *Washington Post*. Simply playing a lot of video games does not mean that someone has a problem. The baseline of this disorder means that playing games overtakes other desires and that it escalates or continues despite negative consequences. A diagnosis would have to include evidence of this type of behavior lasting for more than twelve months. The disorder affects no more than 3 percent of gamers, according to the WHO.

I have been victimized by this gaming disorder, especially when I was in college. I would take Adderall and game from anywhere from eight to twelve hours a day, usually playing sports games. I would miss classes and exams and would not hang out with friends as much because I was so addicted to my video games. Sometimes, I would sit in my room by myself until like four or five in the morning, just playing video games instead of studying for my exams. This habit continued when I started to work in the real world.

It wasn't as serious, but when I started working at Comtek, I would come home and play video games for like five or six hours straight, smoke marijuana, put dip in my mouth, and just sit there instead of being more productive or more sociable. I have a friend, Allyn, that still suffers from this disease, and I do not want to dive into how it has hurt other aspects of his life, but I just wanted to mention in this section that this is a serious disease that still has no cure. Luckily for myself, I was able to read books and work out more often, so I stopped playing video games. I would sometimes play with my friend, Eric Shaker, but that is not really an addiction. That was just for fun. However, no bullshit, I was addicted in college.

All across the United States, I have been helping people win bets by playing MIA's song "Paper Planes." However, I wanted to talk about one of my best friends, Allyn. We have been helping each other out with sports betting for the past few years. I plugged Allyn in as the sixty-first best person in the world, so whenever his number pops up on my phone, it means that positivity is brought upon his way. When he placed money on the Cleveland Cavaliers, winning the championship, I was there to help him win that bet. Again, when he was in a rut and I encouraged him that he was going to start winning again, I helped him win that bet. Furthermore, when he placed money on the horserace when I went to our friend Kevin Pearson's house, I was there to help him win.

I do things to make people happy, and since Allyn has been there for me throughout all these years, I thought it would be great to help him out behind the scenes.

I like to see progress in the world, and this report made me pretty damn happy. The headline reads "Howard University Will Add Division 1 Golf Teams after Receiving a Sponsorship from NBA Superstar Stephen Curry." This is fabulous news, and I think people in Howard University are very happy about this. I know practically the whole world is being driven by technology and controlled by technology, so whenever I play Hollywood's songs that have an "I" in them, which they do intentionally, then it means that someone is helping out someone else in the world. Whether that person is famous or not, it still means something. Therefore, Stephen Curry went out of his way to help out this university for the next six years, and he knows things about the world that other people don't know, so I don't think he made this six-year investment by accident. He purposely made this a six-year investment so we can make sure that the world won't end because of whoever is doing Satan's work for him.

Gino and Jamie both had near-death experiences while working for the government. I don't know if the shooters of both of these disasters were victims of radiation poisoning or what, but there were shootings and closures at both of the offices that Gino and Jamie work at. I think it was also a combination of fate and the people that died because these two instances weren't supposed to live anymore. I know that sounds harsh, but because of evolution and the blossoming population, there is no room for everyone to live forever with the rest of us. Thanks to the CIA and me doing my undercover work, we were able to get by these two instances with little risk, and the people that overcame these instances came out stronger people.

After the story became big about how I went on that road trip by myself to Pennsylvania and was able to handle all those mixed signals, we have been working our asses off to protect the people that we need to have protected, and we can say goodbye to everyone else. Not everyone was going to pass the tests needed to overcome all this adversity, but in the end, the ones that are going to survive all this are the ones that deserve to live.

People's new responsibilities that have been taken over by Will Coakley

Aaron Judge—taking care of all the people who judge in the world by every home run he hits.

Cory Carlton—the Black god.

Adam Seaman—a guy from the Bible; so many things he does have an impact on the world. I know exactly who he was from the book in the past, but I will add that in this section when the time is right.

Allyn Scott—Moses; every time the word *awesome* is said, something great or good happens (Mac in *It's Always Sunny in Philadelphia*).

Steph Bortz—helped me get through my fear of the sun (Dee in *It's Always Sunny*).

Sandra Correa—sun problems in the world and Spain.

Jonathan Shmuel and Jeff Veltri—the two guys that have helped me make this happen.

Jeff Veltri—Joey (character from *Friends*).

Amber Arobo—my soul sister and my avatar sister.

Romy Kadir and Ray Zayas—business minds, making sure we progress with business each day, week, month, and year and that others learn from us.

Darren Bahn—dictionary.

David Shmuel—dictionary.

Gino Marin—technology usage is starting to help us out everywhere with anything related to the word *gym*, and he is also George from *Seinfeld* (his personality is perfect). Also, all the signs led me to the fact that his first name starts with G, and so does *gym* and *George*.

Chris Zayas—Kramer.

Will Coakley—Chandler; Jerry (he uses his first name just like half the world knows my first name); Charlie in *It's Always Sunny*.

Rodrigo—Ross (the *Friends* character)

Meghan—minds; Monica (the character from *Friends*)

Rodrigo (sister's husband)—can help me monitor the roads, less casualties, etc. I have already been using him for this, and I think the roads are cleaner now. If it does not appear that way to people now, then wait for two or three more years.

Rebecca—Rachel (character from *Friends*) and also Elaine from *Seinfeld* (Rebecca Elsie); the white storm.

Lauren Copp—Lisa Kudrow (Phoebe from *Friends*).

Francisco—Facebook.

Eric Shaker—stars; *Star Wars*; battle between the sinners and saints. Every single star in the universe is instrumental to this, and with Eric Shakers' technology usage, this will put the good guys ahead by a long shot. Dennis in *Its Always Sunny*.

Dad—the character Denbo from *The Blacklist*.

Uncle John—acting as God in England.

Frieda—freedom for America.

Marcus Walker—change of seasons.

Tim Cogswell—time.

Trevor Story—all of our stories, by his production on the field, especially since he is coming back from a rookie year when he was derailed by an injury.

Christian Yelich—get rid of all the hellish things in our society.

Dustin Pedroia—he is going to help me control the periods so that so many people aren't having kids.

Denard Span—he is going to help me get rid of all the spam in the world.

Brett Donnelly—stock market.

Silvia Fowles (WNBA player)—help me get the foul situation corrected in sports.

Ryan Eggold (*The Blacklist*)—helping me keeping relationships intact with girlfriends and boyfriends/husbands and wives and keeping them together for the long haul.

Christian Press—helping me organize the press a little better and so the athletes actually benefit from press conferences instead of feeling hate and disrespect.

Megan Koster—fix all the foster problems in the world.

Jackie Cook—the problems in Japan.

Kim Le—the problems in North Korea.

Jaime Hoang—the problems in South Korea.

Mike Fiers—get rid of everything that makes us live in fear in the world.

Lagarette Blount—help me with the legalizing of marijuana in the US by his production on the field.

This is so we have all the teams covered for the cities in the United States, by their technology usage

Allyn Scott—Philadelphia; everything except Phillies and Eagles.

Bradley Cooper—Philadelphia Eagles.

Kevin Hart—Philly.

Kevin Kim—Philadelphia Phillies.

Jeff Veltri—everything Washington except Wizards.

Andy Lee—Washington Wizards; joint effort.

Chris Lewis—Washington Wizards; joint effort.

Heather Fitchel—West Virginia.

Olaide Olabanji—Canada; joint effort.

Fefe Dobson—Canada; joint effort.

Drake—Toronto.

Jon Doveala—Ohio.

Romy Kadir—half of Florida teams.

Frank Dinello—half of Florida teams.

Adam Seaman—New York Rangers.

Jonathan Shmuel—New York Jets, Mets.

Bill Coakley—New York Yankees.

Chris Zayas—New York Giants.

Mike Coppinger—New York Knicks.
Will Coakley—everything else New York.
Paul xxx—upstate NY; joint effort.
George Gavagan—upstate NY; joint effort.
Adam Burdell—everything Pittsburgh except Penguins.
Reid Derco—Pittsburgh Penguins.
Jennifer Lawrence—Kentucky.
Angie Bell—New England except sports.
Spose the rapper—New England except sports.
Eric Shaker—New England except Red Sox.
John Goodman—Boston Red Sox.
Carli Lloyd—New Jersey.
Eminem—Detroit.
Kevin Pearson—Tennessee.
Sandra Bullock—Mississippi.
Selena Gomez—Texas.
Don Dixon—Arkansas.
Eric Slesinger—Missouri.
Chris Lewis—South Carolina.
Ryan Bullock—North Carolina, VCU.
Amy (Dr. Goldsteins)—Arizona.
Lauren Copp—Illinois (Chicago).
Sarah Wayne Callies (*Prison Break*)—Chicago—joint effort.
Ryan Austin Owens—Dallas.
Kara Killmer (Chicago Fire)—everything else Texas, except Dallas Cowboys.
Brett Cameron—UCLA.
Tracy Purdue—Purdue University.
Amber Arobo—Baltimore.
Michelle Beadle—San Antonio.
Ronda Rousey—Vegas.
Rachel (Meg's friend)—San Francisco; joint effort.
Matt McKulsky—San Francisco; joint effort.
Lela Loren (Power)—Sacramento and its surrounding areas.
G-Eazy (rapper)—Oakland.
Lewis Boore—San Diego.

Jacob Lattimore (*Collateral Beauty*)—Milwaukee, Wisconsin.
Atmosphere, the rapper—Minnesota; joint effort.
Adam Young (Owl City)—Minnesota; joint effort.
Omari Hardwick (Power)—Georgia.
Dyme Def (Rapper)—Washington; joint effort.
Ray Zayas—Washington; joint effort.
Jenn Jiron—Hawaii.
Tinie Tempah (rapper)—United Kingdom.
Dominic Purcell (*Prison Break*)—United Kingdom.
Lily James (*Baby Driver*)—United Kingdom.
Kate Moss (Model)—United Kingdom.
Jesse Spencer (*Chicago Fire*)—Australia.
Miranda Kerr (Model)—Australia.
Amaury Nolasco (*Prison Break*)—Puerto Rico; joint effort.
Rico Plumb—Puerto Rico; joint effort.
Joan Smalls (Model)—Puerto Rico; joint effort.
Priena—Portugal.
Sandra Correa—Spain.
Rodrigo—Spain.
Shakira—Spain.
Barbara Palvin (Model)—Hungary.
Jackie Cook—Columbia and Ecuador.
Alessandra Ambrosio (Model)—Brazil; joint effort.
Paola—Shakers girl—Brazil; joint effort.
Natalia Vodianova (Model); Russia.
Lara Stone (Model)—Netherlands.
Liu Wen (Model)—China.
Rose Bertrand (Model)—Belgium.
Cardi B—Twins.

About the Author

My name is Will Coakley, and I am originally from Long Island, New York, but have been living in Northern Virginia since I was twelve years old. I am a big sports fan and also love to watch movies and TV shows. I love to play sports outside and hang out with friends and family as much as possible. I have two great parents and two perfect sisters, whom I have been close to my entire life. My friends have always played a big role in my life, and I am thankful for the fact that I still have oxygen. I have been known to have a big heart and always being nice to people. I believe that you should treat others as they treat you and always look at the bright side of life.

This book is about my life and how we are all affected by the events that are taking place in our society right now. I have a sports section, which shows how I view certain sports events and my view on the evolution on sports. There is also a section where I talk about neighbors and community and how certain people play big roles in our society has grown into a beautiful place, with examples such as intuition and how it is also good to have positive momentum and a positive attitude about life.

I also talk about things I have learned from other people, such as why the weather is nice some days and why Mother Nature is affecting us negatively. I also talk about the problems I have solved in this world, such as back problems and diseases that have affected many people.

There are many signs and symbols that I pick up on in our everyday lives, and I provided my definitions based on my knowledge of the world. In my book, I talk about how Hollywood has affected my life and how I feel the words in their movies and songs speak to me. The songs and movies that Hollywood produces have a lot of messages that speak to me, so I wanted to tell people how they benefit me and the entire world.

Ingram Content Group UK Ltd.
Milton Keynes UK
UKHW010948200323
418838UK00001B/64